5.95

THE APOSTOLIC FATHERS

THE APOSTOLIC FATHERS

BY

J. B. LIGHTFOOT

Edited and Completed by

J. R. Harmer

BAKER BOOK HOUSE

Grand Rapids, Michigan

Library of Congress Catalog Card Number: 56-11603

ISBN: 0-8010-5514-8

First Printing, July 1956
Second Printing, March 1962
Third Printing, June 1965
Fourth Printing, September 1967
Fifth Printing, February 1970
Sixth Printing, October 1971
Seventh Printing, August 1973
Eighth Printing, November 1974
Ninth Printing, June 1976
Tenth printing, June 1978

This English translation of The Apostolic
Fathers is reprinted from the edition published in 1891 by Macmillan and Company. London.

PHOTOLITHOPRINTED BY CUSHING - MALLOY, INC.
ANN ARBOR, MICHIGAN, UNITED STATES OF AMERICA
1978

INTRODUCTORY NOTE

THE introductions throughout (with the exceptions of those which deal with the text, and the short prefatory note to the Fragments of Papias) were either written by Dr Lightfoot for this work, or are derived from his larger work *The Apostolic Fathers, Part I. S. Clement of Rome* (2 vols., Macmillan & Co., 1890); *Part II. S. Ignatius, S. Polycarp* (2nd edition, 3 vols., Macmillan & Co., 1889).

The translations of the Epistles of Clement, Ignatius, and Polycarp and of the Martyrdom of Polycarp are reprinted from the larger edition. The rest of the translations are based upon rough notes found among his papers, but in the case of the Reliques of the Elders Keble's translation of Irenæus in the *Library of Fathers of the Holy Catholic Church* (Parker & Co., 1872) has been adopted with a few verbal alterations.

TABLE OF CONTENTS

THE EPISTLES

OF

S. CLEMENT OF ROME

I. *GENUINE EPISTLE TO THE CORINTHIANS.*

II. *ANCIENT HOMILY, COMMONLY CALLED THE SECOND EPISTLE.*

S. CLEMENT OF ROME

1

THE EPISTLE was. written in the name of the Roman Church to the Christian brotherhood at Corinth. The author was Clement, the Bishop of the Roman Christians, but he does not write in his own name. Hence it is mentioned by early Christian writers, sometimes as the work of the Roman Church, sometimes as written by or sent by the hand of Clement. Its date was nearly simultaneous with the close of Diocletian's persecution, when the emperor's cousin, Flavius Clemens, the namesake of the writer, perished during or immediately after the year of his consulate (A.D. 95), and his wife Domitilla, Domitian's own niece, was driven into banishment on charges apparently connected with Christianity.

A feud had broken out in the Church of Corinth. Presbyters appointed by Apostles, or their immediate successors, had been unlawfully deposed. A spirit of insubordination was rife. The letter of Clement was written to rebuke these irregularities. Allusion is made in it to the persecution at Rome, as an apology for the delay in attending to the matter. Some information is thus given incidentally respecting the character of the persecution in the course of the letter. But more precise and definite facts are contained elsewhere respecting the earlier and more severe assault on the Christians in the latter years of the reign of Nero, where reference is made especially to the martyrdoms of S. Peter and S. Paul.

2

Besides the patristic quotations more especially those in Clement of Alexandria, and in some later fathers, the text is mainly due to three sources.

(1) The famous Alexandrian uncial MS of the New Testament [A] in the British Museum, belonging to the fifth century, to which it is

added as a sort of appendix together with the spurious so-called Second Epistle of Clement to the Corinthians. This MS is mutilated at the close of both Epistles besides being torn or illegible in many passages of the first. From this was published the *Editio princeps* of Patricius Junius (1633).

(2) The Constantinopolitan or Hierosolymitan MS [C] belonging to the library of the Greek Patriarch of Jerusalem, whose chief residence is at Constantinople. From this the two Epistles of Clement (the Genuine and the Spurious) were first printed in full (1875) by Bryennios, then Metropolitan of Serræ, but now Patriarch of Nicomedia. This MS is dated A.D. 1056.

(3) The Syriac translation discovered a few years ago and now in the possession of the Cambridge University Library. This is not yet published, but all the various readings were given in Lightfoot's *S. Clement of Rome* Appendix, London, 1877. This Syriac Version bears a date corresponding to A.D. 1170.

The relations of these authorities are fully discussed in the larger edition of Clement. Here it is sufficient to say that A, as being the most ancient, is likewise far the best authority; but owing to the lacunae in it and other reasons the two other authorities are of the highest value in different ways.

The square brackets [ ] throughout the book denote that a word so included is of doubtful authority and ought perhaps to be neglected; corruptions in the text are indicated by daggers † † placed on each side of the corrupt passage. Brackets of this form ( ) include words in the English translation which have been supplied to help the sense of the passage, and are not represented in the Greek or Latin original.

THE EPISTLE OF S. CLEMENT

TO

THE CORINTHIANS

THE Church of God which sojourneth in Rome to the Church of God which sojourneth in Corinth, to them which are called and sanctified by the will of God through our Lord Jesus Christ. Grace to you and peace from Almighty God through Jesus Christ be multiplied.

1. By reason of the sudden and repeated calamities and reverses which are befalling us, brethren, we consider that we have been somewhat tardy in giving heed to the matters of dispute that have arisen among you, dearly beloved, and to the detestable and unholy sedition, so alien and strange to the elect of God, which a few headstrong and self-willed persons have kindled to such a pitch of madness that your name, once revered and renowned and lovely in the sight of all men, hath been greatly reviled. For who that had sojourned among you did not approve your most virtuous and stedfast faith? Who did not admire your sober and forbearing piety in Christ? Who did not publish abroad your magnificent disposition of hospitality? Who did not congratulate you on your perfect and sound knowledge? For ye did all things without respect of persons, and ye walked after the ordinances of God, submitting yourselves to your rulers and rendering to the older men among you the honour which is their due. On the young too ye enjoined modest and seemly thoughts: and the women ye charged to perform all their duties in a blameless and seemly and pure conscience, cherishing their own husbands, as is meet; and ye taught them to keep in the rule of obedience, and to manage the affairs of their household in seemliness, with all discretion.

2. And ye were all lowly in mind and free from arrogance, yielding rather than claiming submission, *more glad to give than to receive*, and content with the provisions which God supplieth. And giving heed unto His words, ye laid them up diligently in your hearts, and His sufferings were before your eyes. Thus a profound and rich peace was given to all, and an insatiable desire of doing good. An abundant out-pouring also of the Holy Spirit fell upon all; and, being full of holy counsel, in excellent zeal and with a pious confidence ye stretched out your hands to Almighty God, supplicating Him to be propitious, if unwillingly ye had committed any sin. Ye had conflict day and night for all the brotherhood, that the number of His elect might be saved with fearfulness and intentness of mind. Ye were sincere and simple and free from malice one towards another. Every sedition and every schism was abominable to you. Ye mourned over the transgressions of your neighbours: ye judged their shortcomings to be your own. Ye repented not of any well-doing, but were *ready unto every good work*. Being adorned with a most virtuous and honourable life, ye performed all your duties in the fear of Him. The commandments and the ordinances of the Lord were *written on the tables of your hearts*.

3. All glory and enlargement was given unto you, and that was fulfilled which is written; *My beloved ate and drank and was enlarged and waxed fat and kicked*. Hence come jealousy and envy, strife and sedition, persecution and tumult, war and captivity. So men were stirred up, *the mean against the honourable*, the ill-reputed against the highly-reputed, the foolish against the wise, *the young against the elder*. For this cause *righteousness* and peace *stand aloof*, while each man hath forsaken the fear of the Lord and become purblind in the faith of Him, neither walketh in the ordinances of His commandments nor liveth according to that which becometh Christ, but each goeth after the lusts of his evil heart, seeing that they have conceived an unrighteous and ungodly jealousy, through which also *death entered into the world*.

4. For so it is written, *And it came to pass after certain days that Cain brought of the fruits of the earth a sacrifice unto God, and Abel he also brought of the firstlings of the sheep and of their fatness. And God looked upon Abel and upon his gifts, but unto Cain and unto his sacrifices He gave no heed. And Cain sorrowed exceedingly, and his countenance fell. And God said unto Cain, Wherefore art thou very sorrowful? and wherefore did thy countenance fall? If thou hast offered aright and hast not divided aright, didst thou not sin? Hold thy peace. Unto thee shall*

he turn, and thou shalt rule over him. And Cain said unto Abel his
brother, Let us go over unto the plain. And it came to pass, while they
were in the plain, that Cain rose up against Abel his brother and slew
him. Ye see, brethren, jealousy and envy wrought a brother's murder.
By reason of jealousy our father Jacob ran away from the face of Esau
his brother. Jealousy caused Joseph to be persecuted even unto death,
and to come even unto bondage. Jealousy compelled Moses to flee
from the face of Pharaoh king of Egypt while it was said to him by his
own countryman, *Who made thee a judge or a decider over us? Wouldest*
thou slay me, even as yesterday thou slewest the Egyptian? By reason of
jealousy Aaron and Miriam were lodged outside the camp. Jealousy
brought Dathan and Abiram down alive to hades, because they made
sedition against Moses the servant of God. By reason of jealousy
David was envied not only by the Philistines, but was persecuted also
by Saul[king of Israel].

5. But, to pass from the examples of ancient days, let us come to
those champions who lived nearest to our time. Let us set before us
the noble examples which belong to our generation. By reason of
jealousy and envy the greatest and most righteous pillars of the Church
were persecuted, and contended even unto death. Let us set before
our eyes the good Apostles. There was Peter who by reason of
unrighteous jealousy endured not one nor two but many labours, and
thus having borne his testimony went to his appointed place of glory.
By reason of jealousy and strife Paul by his example pointed out the
prize of patient endurance. After that he had been seven times in
bonds, had been driven into exile, had been stoned, had preached in
the East and in the West, he won the noble renown which was the
reward of his faith, having taught righteousness unto the whole world
and having reached the farthest bounds of the West; and when he had
borne his testimony before the rulers, so he departed from the world and
went unto the holy place, having been found a notable pattern of
patient endurance.

6. Unto these men of holy lives was gathered a vast multitude of
the elect, who through many indignities and tortures, being the victims
of jealousy, set a brave example among ourselves. By reason of
jealousy women being persecuted, after that they had suffered cruel
and unholy insults †as Danaids and Dircæ†, safely reached the goal
in the race of faith, and received a noble reward, feeble though they
were in body. Jealousy hath estranged wives from their husbands and

changed the saying of our father Adam, *This now is bone of my bones and flesh of my flesh.* Jealousy and strife have overthrown great cities and uprooted great nations.

7.   These things, dearly beloved, we write, not only as admonishing you, but also as putting ourselves in remembrance.   For we are in the same lists, and the same contest awaiteth us.   Wherefore let us forsake idle and vain thoughts; and let us conform to the glorious and venerable rule which hath been handed down to us; and let us see what is good and what is pleasant and what is acceptable in the sight of Him that made us.   Let us fix our eyes on the blood of Christ and understand how precious it is unto His Father, because being shed for our salvation it won for the whole world the grace of repentance.   Let us review all the generations in turn, and learn how from generation to generation the Master hath given a place for repentance unto them that desire to turn to Him.   Noah preached repentance, and they that obeyed were saved.   Jonah preached destruction unto the men of Nineveh; but they, repenting of their sins, obtained pardon of God by their supplications and received salvation, albeit they were aliens from God.

8.   The ministers of the grace of God through the Holy Spirit spake concerning repentance.   Yea and the Master of the universe Himself spake concerning repentance with an oath; *For, as I live, saith the Lord, I desire not the death of the sinner, so much as his repentance;* and He added also a merciful judgment: *Repent ye, O house of Israel, of your iniquity; say unto the sons of My people, Though your sins reach from the earth even unto the heaven, and though they be redder than scarlet and blacker than sackcloth, and ye turn unto Me with your whole heart and say Father, I will give ear unto you as unto a holy people.* And in another place He saith on this wise, *Wash, be ye clean. Put away your iniquities from your souls out of My sight. Cease from your iniquities; learn to do good; seek out judgment; defend him that is wronged: give judgment for the orphan, and execute righteousness for the widow; and come and let us reason together, saith He; and though your sins be as crimson, I will make them white as snow; and though they be as scarlet, I will make them white as wool. And if ye be willing and will hearken unto Me, ye shall eat the good things of the earth; but if ye be not willing, neither hearken unto Me, a sword shall devour you; for the mouth of the Lord hath spoken these things.* Seeing then that He desireth all His beloved to be partakers of repentance, He confirmed it by an act of His almighty will.

9. Wherefore let us be obedient unto His excellent and glorious will; and presenting ourselves as suppliants of His mercy and goodness, let us fall down before Him and betake ourselves unto His compassions, forsaking the vain toil and the strife and the jealousy which leadeth unto death. Let us fix our eyes on them that ministered perfectly unto His excellent glory. Let us set before us Enoch, who being found righteous in obedience was translated, and his death was not found. Noah, being found faithful, by his ministration preached regeneration unto the world, and through him the Master saved the living creatures that entered into the ark in concord.

10. Abraham, who was called the 'friend,' was found faithful in that he rendered obedience unto the words of God. He through obedience went forth from his land and from his kindred and from his father's house, that leaving a scanty land and a feeble kindred and a mean house he might inherit the promises of God. For He saith unto him; *Go forth from thy land and from thy kindred and from thy father's house unto the land which I shall show thee, and I will make thee into a great nation, and I will bless thee and will magnify thy name, and thou shalt be blessed. And I will bless them that bless thee, and I will curse them that curse thee; and in thee shall all the tribes of the earth be blessed.* And again, when he was parted from Lot, God said unto him; *Look up with thine eyes, and behold from the place where thou now art, unto the north and the south and the sunrise and the sea; for all the land which thou seest, I will give it unto thee and to thy seed for ever; and I will make thy seed as the dust of the earth. If any man can count the dust of the earth, then shall thy seed also be counted.* And again He saith; *God led Abraham forth and said unto him, Look up unto the heaven and count the stars, and see whether thou canst number them. So shall thy seed be. And Abraham believed God, and it was reckoned unto him for righteousness.* For his faith and hospitality a son was given unto him in old age, and by obedience he offered him a sacrifice unto God on one of the mountains which He showed him.

11. For his hospitality and godliness Lot was saved from Sodom, when all the country round about was judged by fire and brimstone; the Master having thus foreshown that He forsaketh not them which set their hope on Him, but appointeth unto punishment and torment them which swerve aside. For when his wife had gone forth with him, being otherwise-minded and not in accord, she was appointed for a sign hereunto, so that she became a pillar of salt unto this day, that it might be

known unto all men that they which are double-minded and they which doubt concerning the power of God are set for a judgment and for a token unto all the generations.

12. For her faith and hospitality Rahab the harlot was saved. For when the spies were sent forth unto Jericho by Joshua the son of Nun, the king of the land perceived that they were come to spy out his country, and sent forth men to seize them, that being seized they might be put to death. So the hospitable Rahab received them and hid them in the upper chamber under the flax-stalks. And when the messengers of the king came near and said, *The spies of our land entered in unto thee: bring them forth, for the king so ordereth:* then she answered, *The men truly, whom ye seek, entered in unto me, but they departed forthwith and are journeying on the way;* and she pointed out to them the opposite road. And she said unto the men, *Of a surety I perceive that the Lord your God delivereth this city unto you; for the fear and the dread of you is fallen upon the inhabitants thereof. When therefore it shall come to pass that ye take it, save me and the house of my father.* And they said unto her, *It shall be even so as thou hast spoken unto us. Whensoever therefore thou perceivest that we are coming, thou shalt gather all thy folk beneath thy roof, and they shall be saved; for as many as shall be found without the house shall perish.* And moreover they gave her a sign, that she should hang out from her house a scarlet thread, thereby showing beforehand that through the blood of the Lord there shall be redemption unto all them that believe and hope on God. Ye see, dearly beloved, not only faith, but prophecy, is found in the woman.

13. Let us therefore be lowly-minded, brethren, laying aside all arrogance and conceit and folly and anger, and let us do that which is written. For the Holy Ghost saith, *Let not the wise man boast in his wisdom, nor the strong in his strength, neither the rich in his riches; but he that boasteth let him boast in the Lord, that he may seek Him out, and do judgment and righteousness;* most of all remembering the words of the Lord Jesus which He spake, teaching forbearance and long-suffering: for thus He spake; *Have mercy, that ye may receive mercy: forgive, that it may be forgiven to you. As ye do, so shall it be done to you. As ye give, so shall it be given unto you. As ye judge, so shall ye be judged. As ye show kindness, so shall kindness be showed unto you. With what measure ye mete, it shall be measured withal to you.* With this commandment and these precepts let us confirm ourselves, that we may walk in obedience to His hallowed words, with lowliness of mind. For

the holy word saith, *Upon whom shall I look, save upon him that is gentle and quiet and feareth Mine oracles ?*

14. Therefore it is right and proper, brethren, that we should be obedient unto God, rather than follow those who in arrogance and unruliness have set themselves up as leaders in abominable jealousy. For we shall bring upon us no common harm, but rather great peril, if we surrender ourselves recklessly to the purposes of men who launch out into strife and seditions, so as to estrange us from that which is right. Let us be good one towards another according to the compassion and sweetness of Him that made us. For it is written : *The good shall be dwellers in the land, and the innocent shall be left on it; but they that transgress shall be destroyed utterly from it.* And again He saith; *I saw the ungodly lifted up on high and exalted as the cedars of Lebanon. And I passed by, and behold he was not ; and I sought out his place, and I found it not. Keep innocence and behold uprightness; for there is a remnant for the peaceful man.*

15. Therefore let us cleave unto them that practise peace with godliness, and not unto them that desire peace with dissimulation. For He saith in a certain place; *This people honoureth Me with their lips, but their heart is far from Me ;* and again, *They blessed with their mouth, but they cursed with their heart.* And again He saith, *They loved Him with their mouth, and with their tongue they lied unto Him ; and their heart was not upright with Him, neither were they stedfast in His covenant. For this cause let the deceitful lips be made dumb which speak iniquity against the righteous.* And again ; *May the Lord utterly destroy all the deceitful lips, the tongue that speaketh proud things, even them that say, Let us magnify our tongue ; our lips are our own; who is lord over us ? For the misery of the needy and for the groaning of the poor I will now arise, saith the Lord. I will set him in safety ; I will deal boldly by him.*

16. For Christ is with them that are lowly of mind, not with them that exalt themselves over the flock. The sceptre [of the majesty] of God, even our Lord Jesus Christ, came not in the pomp of arrogance or of pride, though He might have done so, but in lowliness of mind, according as the Holy Spirit spake concerning Him. For He saith ; *Lord, who believed our report? and to whom was the arm of the Lord revealed? We announced Him in His presence. As a child was He, as a root in a thirsty ground. There is no form in Him, neither glory. And we beheld Him, and He had no form nor comeliness, but His form was*

mean, lacking more than the form of men. He was a man of stripes and of toil, and knowing how to bear infirmity: for His face is turned away. He was dishonoured and held of no account. He beareth our sins and suffereth pain for our sakes: and we accounted Him to be in toil and in stripes and in affliction. And He was wounded for our sins and hath been afflicted for our iniquities. The chastisement of our peace is upon Him. With His bruises we were healed. We all went astray like sheep, each man went astray in his own path: and the Lord delivered Him over for our sins. And He openeth not His mouth, because He is afflicted. As a sheep He was led to slaughter; and as a lamb before his shearer is dumb, so openeth He not His mouth. In His humiliation His judgment was taken away. His generation who shall declare? For His life is taken away from the earth. For the iniquities of my people He is come to death. And I will give the wicked for His burial, and the rich for His death; for He wrought no iniquity, neither was guile found in His mouth. And the Lord desireth to cleanse Him from His stripes. If ye offer for sin, your soul shall see a long-lived seed. And the Lord desireth to take away from the toil of His soul, to show Him light and to mould Him with understanding, to justify a Just One that is a good servant unto many. And He shall bear their sins. Therefore He shall inherit many, and shall divide the spoils of the strong; because His soul was delivered unto death, and He was reckoned unto the transgressors; and He bare the sins of many, and for their sins was He delivered up. And again He Himself saith; *But I am a worm and no man, a reproach of men and an outcast of the people. All they that beheld me mocked at me; they spake with their lips; they wagged their heads, saying, He hoped on the Lord; let Him deliver him, or let Him save him, for He desireth him.* Ye see, dearly beloved, what is the pattern that hath been given unto us; for, if the Lord was thus lowly of mind, what should we do, who through Him have been brought under the yoke of His grace?

17. Let us be imitators also of them which went about in goatskins and sheepskins, preaching the coming of Christ. We mean Elijah and Elisha and likewise Ezekiel, the prophets, and besides them those men also that obtained a good report. Abraham obtained an exceeding good report and was called the friend of God; and looking stedfastly on the glory of God, he saith in lowliness of mind, *But I am dust and ashes.* Moreover concerning Job also it is thus written; *And Job was righteous and unblameable, one that was true and honoured God and abstained from all evil.* Yet he himself accuseth himself saying, *No*

man is clean from filth; no, not though his life be but for a day. Moses
was called *faithful in all His house,* and through his ministration God
judged Egypt with the plagues and the torments which befel them.
Howbeit he also, though greatly glorified, yet spake no proud words,
but said, when an oracle was given to him at the bush, *Who am I,
that Thou sendest me? Nay, I am feeble of speech and slow of tongue.*
And again he saith, *But I am smoke from the pot.*

18. But what must we say of David that obtained a good report?
of whom God said, *I have found a man after My heart, David the son of
Jesse: with eternal mercy have I anointed him.* Yet he too saith unto
God; *Have mercy upon me, O God, according to Thy great mercy; and
according to the multitude of Thy compassions, blot out mine iniquity.
Wash me yet more from mine iniquity, and cleanse me from my sin. For
I acknowledge mine iniquity, and my sin is ever before me. Against Thee
only did I sin, and I wrought evil in Thy sight; that Thou mayest be
justified in Thy words, and mayest conquer in Thy pleading. For behold,
in iniquities was I conceived, and in sins did my mother bear me. For
behold Thou hast loved truth: the dark and hidden things of Thy wisdom
hast Thou showed unto me. Thou shalt sprinkle me with hyssop, and I
shall be made clean. Thou shalt wash me, and I shall become whiter than
snow. Thou shalt make me to hear of joy and gladness. The bones
which have been humbled shall rejoice. Turn away Thy face from my
sins, and blot out all mine iniquities. Make a clean heart within me, O
God, and renew a right spirit in mine inmost parts. Cast me not away
from Thy presence, and take not Thy Holy Spirit from me. Restore unto
me the joy of Thy salvation, and strengthen me with a princely spirit. I
will teach sinners Thy ways, and godless men shall be converted unto Thee.
Deliver me from bloodguiltiness, O God, the God of my salvation. My
tongue shall rejoice in Thy righteousness. Lord, Thou shalt open my
mouth, and my lips shall declare Thy praise. For, if Thou hadst desired
sacrifice, I would have given it: in whole burnt offerings Thou wilt have
no pleasure. A sacrifice unto God is a contrite spirit; a contrite and
humbled heart God will not despise.*

19. The humility therefore and the submissiveness of so many and
so great men, who have thus obtained a good report, hath through
obedience made better not only us but also the generations which were
before us, even them that received His oracles in fear and truth. Seeing
then that we have been partakers of many great and glorious doings,
let us hasten to return unto the goal of peace which hath been handed

down to us from the beginning, and let us look stedfastly unto the Father and Maker of the whole world, and cleave unto His splendid and excellent gifts of peace and benefits. Let us behold Him in our mind, and let us look with the eyes of our soul unto His long-suffering will. Let us note how free from anger He is towards all His creatures.

20. The heavens are moved by His direction and obey Him in peace. Day and night accomplish the course assigned to them by Him, without hindrance one to another. The sun and the moon and the dancing stars according to His appointment circle in harmony within the bounds assigned to them, without any swerving aside. The earth, bearing fruit in fulfilment of His will at her proper seasons, putteth forth the food that supplieth abundantly both men and beasts and all living things which are thereupon, making no dissension, neither altering anything which He hath decreed. Moreover, the inscrutable depths of the abysses and the unutterable †statutes† of the nether regions are constrained by the same ordinances. The basin of the boundless sea, gathered together by His workmanship *into its reservoirs*, passeth not the barriers wherewith it is surrounded; but even as He ordered it, so it doeth. For He said, *So far shalt thou come, and thy waves shall be broken within thee.* The ocean which is impassable for men, and the worlds beyond it, are directed by the same ordinances of the Master. The seasons of spring and summer and autumn and winter give way in succession one to another in peace. The winds in their several quarters at their proper season fulfil their ministry without disturbance; and the everflowing fountains, created for enjoyment and health, without fail give their breasts which sustain the life for men. Yea, the smallest of living things come together in concord and peace. All these things the great Creator and Master of the universe ordered to be in peace and concord, doing good unto all things, but far beyond the rest unto us who have taken refuge in His compassionate mercies through our Lord Jesus Christ, to whom be the glory and the majesty for ever and ever. Amen.

21. Look ye, brethren, lest His benefits, which are many, turn unto judgment to all of us, if we walk not worthily of Him, and do those things which are good and well-pleasing in His sight with concord. For He saith in a certain place, *The Spirit of the Lord is a lamp searching the closets of the belly.* Let us see how near He is, and how that nothing escapeth Him of our thoughts or our devices which we make. It is right therefore that we should not be deserters from

His will.   Let us rather give offence to foolish and senseless men who
exalt themselves and boast in the arrogance of their words, than to God.
Let us fear the Lord Jesus[Christ],whose blood was given for us.   Let
us reverence our rulers; let us honour our elders; let us instruct our
young men in the lesson of the fear of God.   Let us guide our women
toward that which is good : let them show forth their lovely disposition
of purity ; let them prove their sincere affection of gentleness ; let them
make manifest the moderation of their tongue through their silence ;
let them show their love, not in factious preferences but without
partiality towards all them that fear God, in holiness.   Let our children
be partakers of the instruction which is in Christ : let them learn how
lowliness of mind prevaileth with God, what power chaste love hath
with God, how the fear of Him is good and great and saveth all them
that walk therein in a pure mind with holiness.   For He is the searcher
out of the intents and desires ; whose breath is in us, and when He
listeth, He shall take it away.

22.   Now all these things the faith which is in Christ confirmeth :
for He Himself through the Holy Spirit thus inviteth us : *Come, my
children, hearken unto Me, I will teach you the fear of the Lord.   What
man is he that desireth life and loveth to see good days?   Make thy
tongue to cease from evil, and thy lips that they speak no guile.   Turn
aside from evil and do good.   Seek peace and ensue it.   The eyes of the
Lord are over the righteous, and His ears are turned to their prayers.
But the face of the Lord is upon them that do evil, to destroy their
memorial from the earth.   The righteous cried out, and the Lord heard
him, and delivered him from all his troubles.   Many are the troubles of
the righteous, and the Lord shall deliver him from them all.*   And again;
*Many are the stripes of the sinner, but them that set their hope on the
Lord mercy shall compass about.*

23.   The Father, who is pitiful in all things, and ready to do good,
hath compassion on them that fear Him, and kindly and lovingly
bestoweth His favours on them that draw nigh unto Him with a
single mind.   Wherefore let us not be double-minded, neither let our
soul indulge in idle humours respecting His exceeding and glorious
gifts.   Let this scripture be far from us where He saith; *Wretched are
the double-minded, which doubt in their soul and say, These things we did
hear in the days of our fathers also, and behold we have grown old, and
none of these things hath befallen us.   Ye fools, compare yourselves unto a
tree; take a vine.   First it sheddeth its leaves, then a shoot cometh, then a*

leaf, then a flower, and after these a sour berry, then a full ripe grape.
Ye see that in a little time the fruit of the tree attaineth unto mellow-
ness.   Of a truth quickly and suddenly shall His will be accomplished,
the scripture also bearing witness to it, saying; *He shall come quickly
and shall not tarry; and the Lord shall come suddenly into His temple,
even the Holy One, whom ye expect.*

24.   Let us understand, dearly beloved, how the Master continually
showeth unto us the resurrection that shall be hereafter; whereof He
made the Lord Jesus Christ the firstfruit, when He raised Him from the
dead.   Let us behold, dearly beloved, the resurrection which happeneth
at its proper season.   Day and night show unto us the resurrection.
The night falleth asleep, and day ariseth; the day departeth, and
night cometh on.   Let us mark the fruits, how and in what manner the
sowing taketh place.   *The sower goeth forth* and casteth into the earth
each of the seeds; and these falling into the earth dry and bare decay:
then out of their decay the mightiness of the Master's providence raiseth
them up, and from being one they increase manifold and bear fruit.

25.   Let us consider the marvellous sign which is seen in the
regions of the east, that is, in the parts about Arabia.   There is a bird,
which is named the phœnix.   This, being the only one of its kind,
liveth for five hundred years; and when it hath now reached the time of
its dissolution that it should die, it maketh for itself a coffin of frankincense and myrrh and the other spices, into the which in the fulness of
time it entereth, and so it dieth.   But, as the flesh rotteth, a certain
worm is engendered, which is nurtured from the moisture of the dead
creature and putteth forth wings.   Then, when it is grown lusty,
it taketh up that coffin where are the bones of its parent, and carrying
them journeyeth from the country of Arabia even unto Egypt, to the
place called the City of the Sun; and in the day time in the sight of all,
flying to the altar of the Sun, it layeth them thereupon; and this done,
it setteth forth to return.   So the priests examine the registers of the
times, and they find that it hath come when the five hundredth year is
completed.

26.   Do we then think it to be a great and marvellous thing, if the
Creator of the universe shall bring about the resurrection of them that
have served Him with holiness in the assurance of a good faith, seeing
that He showeth to us even by a bird the magnificence of His promise?
For He saith in a certain place; *And Thou shalt raise me up, and I will
praise Thee;* and; *I went to rest and slept, I was awaked, for Thou art*

with me. And again Job saith; *And Thou shalt raise this my flesh which hath endured all these things.*

27. With this hope therefore let our souls be bound unto Him that is faithful in His promises and that is righteous in His judgments. He that commanded not to lie, much more shall He Himself not lie: for nothing is impossible with God save to lie. Therefore let our faith in Him be kindled within us, and let us understand that all things are nigh unto Him. By a word of His majesty He compacted the universe; and by a word He can destroy it. *Who shall say unto Him, What hast thou done? or who shall resist the might of His strength?* When He listeth, and as He listeth, He will do all things; and nothing shall pass away of those things that He hath decreed. All things are in His sight, and nothing escapeth His counsel, seeing that *The heavens declare the glory of God, and the firmament proclaimeth His handiwork. Day uttereth word unto day, and night proclaimeth knowledge unto night; and there are neither words nor speeches, whose voices are not heard.*

28. Since therefore all things are seen and heard, let us fear Him and forsake the abominable lusts of evil works, that we may be shielded by His mercy from the coming judgments. For where can any of us escape from His strong hand? And what world will receive any of them that desert from His service? For the holy writing saith in a certain place; *Where shall I go, and where shall I be hidden from Thy face? If I ascend into the heaven, Thou art there; if I depart into the farthest parts of the earth, there is Thy right hand; if I make my bed in the depths, there is Thy Spirit.* Whither then shall one depart, or where shall one flee, from Him that embraceth the universe?

29. Let us therefore approach Him in holiness of soul, lifting up pure and undefiled hands unto Him, with love towards our gentle and compassionate Father who made us an elect portion unto Himself. For thus it is written: *When the Most High divided the nations, when He dispersed the sons of Adam, He fixed the boundaries of the nations according to the number of the angels of God. His people Jacob became the portion of the Lord, and Israel the measurement of His inheritance.* And in another place He saith; *Behold, the Lord taketh for Himself a nation out of the midst of the nations, as a man taketh the firstfruits of his threshing floor; and the holy of holies shall come forth from that nation.*

30. Seeing then that we are the special portion of a Holy God, let us do all things that pertain unto holiness, forsaking evil-speakings, abominable and impure embraces, drunkennesses and tumults and

hateful lusts, abominable adultery, hateful pride ; *For God*, He saith, *resisteth the proud, but giveth grace to the lowly.* Let us therefore cleave unto those to whom grace is given from God. Let us clothe ourselves in concord, being lowly-minded and temperate, holding ourselves aloof from all backbiting and evil speaking, being justified by works and not by words. For He saith ; *He that saith much shall hear also again. Doth the ready talker think to be righteous ? Blessed is the offspring of a woman that liveth but a short time. Be not thou abundant in words.* Let our praise be with God, and not of ourselves : for God hateth them that praise themselves. Let the testimony to our well-doing be given by others, as it was given unto our fathers who were righteous. Boldness and arrogance and daring are for them that are accursed of God ; but forbearance and humility and gentleness are with them that are blessed of God.

31. Let us therefore cleave unto His blessing, and let us see what are the ways of blessing. Let us study the records of the things that have happened from the beginning. Wherefore was our father Abraham blessed ? Was it not because he wrought righteousness and truth through faith ? Isaac with confidence, as knowing the future, was led a willing sacrifice. Jacob with humility departed from his land because of his brother, and went unto Laban and served ; and the twelve tribes of Israel were given unto him.

32. If any man will consider them one by one in sincerity, he shall understand the magnificence of the gifts that are given by Him. For of Jacob are all the priests and levites who minister unto the altar of God ; of him is the Lord Jesus as concerning the flesh ; of him are kings and rulers and governors in the line of Judah ; yea and the rest of his tribes are held in no small honour, seeing that God promised saying, *Thy seed shall be as the stars of heaven.* They all therefore were glorified and magnified, not through themselves or their own works or the righteous doing which they wrought, but through His will. And so we, having been called through His will in Christ Jesus, are not justified through ourselves or through our own wisdom or understanding or piety or works which we wrought in holiness of heart, but through faith, whereby the Almighty God justified all men that have been from the beginning ; to whom be the glory for ever and ever. Amen.

33. What then must we do, brethren ? Must we idly abstain from doing good, and forsake love? May the Master never allow this to befal us at least ; but let us hasten with instancy and zeal to accomplish

every good work. For the Creator and Master of the universe Himself rejoiceth in His works. For by His exceeding great might He established the heavens, and in His incomprehensible wisdom He set them in order. And the earth He separated from the water that surroundeth it, and He set it firm on the sure foundation of His own will; and the living creatures which walk upon it He commanded to exist by His ordinance. Having before created the sea and the living creatures therein, He enclosed it by His own power. Above all, as the most excellent and exceeding great work of His intelligence, with His sacred and faultless hands He formed man in the impress of His own image. For thus saith God; *Let us make man after our image and after our likeness. And God made man; male and female made He them.* So having finished all these things, He praised them and blessed them and said, *Increase and multiply.* We have seen that all the righteous were adorned in good works. Yea, and the Lord Himself having adorned Himself with works rejoiced. Seeing then that we have this pattern, let us conform ourselves with all diligence to His will; let us with all our strength work the work of righteousness.

34. The good workman receiveth the bread of his work with boldness, but the slothful and careless dareth not look his employer in the face. It is therefore needful that we should be zealous unto well-doing, for of Him are all things: since He forewarneth us saying, *Behold, the Lord, and His reward is before His face, to recompense each man according to his work.* He exhorteth us therefore to believe on Him with our whole heart, and to be not idle nor careless unto every good work. Let our boast and our confidence be in Him: let us submit ourselves to His will; let us mark the whole host of His angels, how they stand by and minister unto His will. For the scripture saith; *Ten thousands of ten thousands stood by Him, and thousands of thousands ministered unto Him: and they cried aloud, Holy, holy, holy is the Lord of Sabaoth; all creation is full of His glory.* Yea, and let us ourselves then, being gathered together in concord with intentness of heart, cry unto Him as from one mouth earnestly that we may be made partakers of His great and glorious promises. For He saith, *Eye hath not seen and ear hath not heard, and it hath not entered into the heart of man what great things He hath prepared for them that patiently await Him.*

35. How blessed and marvellous are the gifts of God, dearly beloved! Life in immortality, splendour in righteousness, truth in boldness, faith in confidence, temperance in sanctification! And all

these things fall under our apprehension. What then, think ye, are the things preparing for them that patiently await Him? The Creator and Father of the ages, the All-holy One Himself knoweth their number and their beauty. Let us therefore contend, that we may be found in the number of those that patiently await Him, to the end that we may be partakers of His promised gifts. But how shall this be, dearly beloved? If our mind be fixed through faith towards God; if we seek out those things which are well pleasing and acceptable unto Him; if we accomplish such things as beseem His faultless will, and follow the way of truth, casting off from ourselves all unrighteousness and iniquity, covetousness, strifes, malignities and deceits, whisperings and back-bitings, hatred of God, pride and arrogance, vainglory and inhospitality. For they that do these things are hateful to God; and not only they that do them, but they also that consent unto them. For the scripture saith; *But unto the sinner said God, Wherefore dost thou declare Mine ordinances, and takest My covenant upon thy lips? Yet thou didst hate instruction and didst cast away My words behind thee. If thou sawest a thief, thou didst keep company with him, and with the adulterers thou didst set thy portion. Thy mouth multiplied wickedness, and thy tongue wove deceit. Thou sattest and spakest against thy brother, and against the son of thy mother thou didst lay a stumbling-block. These things thou hast done, and I kept silence. Thou thoughtest, unrighteous man, that I should be like unto thee. I will convict thee and will set thee face to face with thyself. Now understand ye these things, ye that forget God, lest at any time He seize you as a lion, and there be none to deliver. The sacrifice of praise shall glorify Me, and there is the way wherein I will show him the salvation of God.*

36. This is the way, dearly-beloved, wherein we found our salvation, even Jesus Christ the High-priest of our offerings, the Guardian and Helper of our weakness. Through Him let us look stedfastly unto the heights of the heavens; through Him we behold as in a mirror His faultless and most excellent visage; through Him the eyes of our hearts were opened; through Him our foolish and darkened mind springeth up unto the light; through Him the Master willed that we should taste of the immortal knowledge; *Who being the brightness of His majesty is so much greater than angels, as He hath inherited a more excellent name.* For so it is written; *Who maketh His angels spirits and His ministers a flame of fire;* but of His Son the Master said thus; *Thou art My Son, I this day have begotten Thee. Ask of Me,*

and I will give Thee the Gentiles for Thine inheritance, and the ends of the earth for Thy possession. And again He saith unto Him ; *Sit Thou on My right hand, until I make Thine enemies a footstool for Thy feet.* Who then are these enemies? They that are wicked and resist His will.

37. Let us therefore enlist ourselves, brethren, with all earnestness in His faultless ordinances. Let us mark the soldiers that are enlisted under our rulers, how exactly, how readily, how submissively, they execute the orders given them. All are not prefects, nor rulers of thousands, nor rulers of hundreds, nor rulers of fifties, and so forth ; but each man in his own rank executeth the orders given by the king and the governors. The great without the small cannot exist, neither the small without the great. There is a certain mixture in all things, and therein is utility. Let us take our body as an example. The head without the feet is nothing ; so likewise the feet without the head are nothing : even the smallest limbs of our body are necessary and useful for the whole body : but all the members conspire and unite in subjection, that the whole body may be saved.

38. So in our case let the whole body be saved in Christ Jesus, and let each man be subject unto his neighbour, according as also he was appointed with his special grace. Let not the strong neglect the weak ; and let the weak respect the strong. Let the rich minister aid to the poor ; and let the poor give thanks to God, because He hath given him one through whom his wants may be supplied. Let the wise display his wisdom, not in words, but in good works. He that is lowly in mind, let him not bear testimony to himself, but leave testimony to be borne to him by his neighbour. He that is pure in the flesh, let him be so, and not boast, knowing that it is Another who bestoweth his continence upon him. Let us consider, brethren, of what matter we were made ; who and what manner of beings we were, when we came into the world ; from what a sepulchre and what darkness He that moulded and created us brought us into His world, having prepared His benefits aforehand ere ever we were born. Seeing therefore that we have all these things from Him, we ought in all things to give thanks to Him, to whom be the glory for ever and ever. Amen.

39. Senseless and stupid and foolish and ignorant men jeer and mock at us, desiring that they themselves should be exalted in their imaginations. For what power hath a mortal? or what strength hath a child of earth? For it is written ; *There was no form before mine eyes ; only I heard a breath and a voice.* *What then? Shall a mortal be clean*

*in the sight of the Lord ; or shall a man be unblameable for his works ?
seeing that He is distrustful against His servants and noteth some perversity
against His angels. Nay, the heaven is not clean in His sight. Away
then, ye that dwell in houses of clay, whereof, even of the same clay, we
ourselves are made. He smote them like a moth, and from morn to even
they are no more. Because they could not succour themselves, they
perished. He breathed upon them and they died, because they had no
wisdom. But call thou, if perchance one shall obey thee, or if thou shalt
see one of the holy angels. For wrath killeth the foolish man, and envy
slayeth him that is gone astray. And I have seen fools throwing out roots,
but forthwith their habitation was eaten up. Far be their sons from
safety. May they be mocked at the gates of inferiors, and there shall be
none to deliver them. For the things which are prepared for them, the
righteous shall eat ; but they themselves shall not be delivered from evils.*

40. Forasmuch then as these things are manifest beforehand, and
we have searched into the depths of the Divine knowledge, we ought
to do all things in order, as many as the Master hath commanded us to
perform at their appointed seasons. Now the offerings and ministrations
He commanded to be performed with care, and not to be done rashly
or in disorder, but at fixed times and seasons. And where and by
whom He would have them performed, He Himself fixed by His
supreme will : that all things being done with piety according to His
good pleasure might be acceptable to His will. They therefore that
make their offerings at the appointed seasons are acceptable and
blessed : for while they follow the institutions of the Master they cannot
go wrong. For unto the high-priest his proper services have been
assigned, and to the priests their proper office is appointed, and upon
the levites their proper ministrations are laid. The layman is bound
by the layman's ordinances.

41. Let each of you, brethren, in his own order give thanks unto
God, maintaining a good conscience and not transgressing the appointed
rule of his service, but acting with all seemliness. Not in every place,
brethren, are the continual daily sacrifices offered, or the freewill
offerings, or the sin offerings and the trespass offerings, but in Jerusalem
alone. And even there the offering is not made in every place, but
before the sanctuary in the court of the altar ; and this too through the
high-priest and the aforesaid ministers, after that the victim to be
offered hath been inspected for blemishes. They therefore who do any
thing contrary to the seemly ordinance of His will receive death as the

penalty. Ye see, brethren, in proportion as greater knowledge hath been vouchsafed unto us, so much the more are we exposed to danger.

42. The Apostles received the Gospel for us from the Lord Jesus Christ; Jesus Christ was sent forth from God. So then Christ is from God, and the Apostles are from Christ. Both therefore came of the will of God in the appointed order. Having therefore received a charge, and having been fully assured through the resurrection of our Lord Jesus Christ and confirmed in the word of God with full assurance of the Holy Ghost, they went forth with the glad tidings that the kingdom of God should come. So preaching everywhere in country and town, they appointed their first-fruits, when they had proved them by the Spirit, to be bishops and deacons unto them that should believe. And this they did in no new fashion; for indeed it had been written concerning bishops and deacons from very ancient times; for thus saith the scripture in a certain place, *I will appoint their bishops in righteousness and their deacons in faith.*

43. And what marvel, if they which were entrusted in Christ with such a work by God appointed the aforesaid persons? seeing that even the blessed Moses who was *a faithful servant in all His house* recorded for a sign in the sacred books all things that were enjoined upon him. And him also the rest of the prophets followed, bearing witness with him unto the laws that were ordained by him. For he, when jealousy arose concerning the priesthood, and there was dissension among the tribes which of them was adorned with the glorious name, commanded the twelve chiefs of the tribes to bring to him rods inscribed with the name of each tribe. And he took them and tied them and sealed them with the signet rings of the chiefs of the tribes, and put them away in the tabernacle of the testimony on the table of God. And having shut the tabernacle he sealed the keys and likewise also the doors. And he said unto them, Brethren, the tribe whose rod shall bud, this hath God chosen to be priests and ministers unto Him. Now when morning came, he called together all Israel, even the six hundred thousand men, and showed the seals to the chiefs of the tribes and opened the tabernacle of the testimony and drew forth the rods. And the rod of Aaron was found not only with buds, but also bearing fruit. What think ye, dearly beloved? Did not Moses know beforehand that this would come to pass? Assuredly he knew it. But that disorder might not arise in Israel, he did thus, to the end that the Name of the true and only God might be glorified: to whom be the glory for ever and ever. Amen.

44. And our Apostles knew through our Lord Jesus Christ that there would be strife over the name of the bishop's office. For this cause therefore, having received complete foreknowledge, they appointed the aforesaid persons, and afterwards they provided a continuance, that if these should fall asleep, other approved men should succeed to their ministration. Those therefore who were appointed by them, or afterward by other men of repute with the consent of the whole Church, and have ministered unblameably to the flock of Christ in lowliness of mind, peacefully and with all modesty, and for long time have borne a good report with all—these men we consider to be unjustly thrust out from their ministration. For it will be no light sin for us, if we thrust out those who have offered the gifts of the bishop's office unblameably and holily. Blessed are those presbyters who have gone before, seeing that their departure was fruitful and ripe : for they have no fear lest any one should remove them from their appointed place. For we see that ye have displaced certain persons, though they were living honourably, from the ministration which †had been respected by them† blamelessly.

45. Be ye contentious, brethren, and jealous about the things that pertain unto salvation. Ye have searched the scriptures, which are true, which were given through the Holy Ghost ; and ye know that nothing unrighteous or counterfeit is written in them. Ye will not find that righteous persons have been thrust out by holy men. Righteous men were persecuted, but it was by the lawless ; they were imprisoned, but it was by the unholy. They were stoned by transgressors : they were slain by those who had conceived a detestable and unrighteous jealousy. Suffering these things, they endured nobly. For what must we say, brethren? Was Daniel cast into the lions' den by them that feared God? Or were Ananias and Azarias and Misael shut up in the furnace of fire by them that professed the excellent and glorious worship of the Most High? Far be this from our thoughts. Who then were they that did these things? Abominable men and full of all wickedness were stirred up to such a pitch of wrath, as to bring cruel suffering upon them that served God in a holy and blameless purpose, not knowing that the Most High is the champion and protector of them that in a pure conscience serve His excellent Name : unto whom be the glory for ever and ever. Amen. But they that endured patiently in confidence inherited glory and honour ; they were exalted, and had their names recorded by God in their memorial for ever and ever. Amen.

46. To such examples as these therefore, brethren, we also ought to cleave. For it is written; *Cleave unto the saints, for they that cleave unto them shall be sanctified.* And again He saith in another place; *With the guiltless man thou shalt be guiltless, and with the elect thou shalt be elect, and with the crooked thou shalt deal crookedly* Let us therefore cleave to the guiltless and righteous: and these are the elect of God. Wherefore are there strifes and wraths and factions and divisions and war among you? Have we not one God and one Christ and one Spirit of grace that was shed upon us? And is there not one calling in Christ? Wherefore do we tear and rend asunder the members of Christ, and stir up factions against our own body, and reach such a pitch of folly, as to forget that we are members one of another? Remember the words of Jesus our Lord: for He said, *Woe unto that man; it were good for him if he had not been born, rather than that he should offend one of Mine elect. It were better for him that a mill-stone were hanged about him, and he cast into the sea, than that he should pervert one of Mine elect.* Your division hath perverted many; it hath brought many to despair, many to doubting, and all of us to sorrow. And your sedition still continueth.

47. Take up the epistle of the blessed Paul the Apostle. What wrote he first unto you in the beginning of the Gospel? Of a truth he charged you in the Spirit concerning himself and Cephas and Apollos, because that even then ye had made parties. Yet that making of parties brought less sin upon you; for ye were partisans of Apostles that were highly reputed, and of a man approved in their sight. But now mark ye, who they are that have perverted you and diminished the glory of your renowned love for the brotherhood. It is shameful, dearly beloved, yes, utterly shameful and unworthy of your conduct in Christ, that it should be reported that the very stedfast and ancient Church of the Corinthians, for the sake of one or two persons, maketh sedition against its presbyters. And this report hath reached not only us, but them also which differ from us, so that ye even heap blasphemies on the Name of the Lord by reason of your folly, and moreover create peril for yourselves.

48. Let us therefore root this out quickly, and let us fall down before the Master and entreat Him with tears, that He may show Himself propitious and be reconciled unto us, and may restore us to the seemly and pure conduct which belongeth to our love of the brethren. For this is a gate of righteousness opened unto life, as it is written;

*Open me the gates of righteousness, that I may enter in thereby and praise
the Lord. This is the gate of the Lord; the righteous shall enter in
thereby.* Seeing then that many gates are opened, this is that gate
which is in righteousness, even that which is in Christ, whereby all are
blessed that have entered in and direct their path in holiness and
righteousness, performing all things without confusion. Let a man be
faithful, let him be able to expound a deep saying, let him be wise in
the discernment of words, let him be strenuous in deeds, let him be
pure; for so much the more ought he to be lowly in mind, in proportion as he seemeth to be the greater; and he ought to seek the
common advantage of all, and not his own.

49. Let him that hath love in Christ fulfil the commandments of
Christ. Who can declare the bond of the love of God? Who is
sufficient to tell the majesty of its beauty? The height, whereunto love
exalteth, is unspeakable. Love joineth us unto God; *love covereth a
multitude of sins;* love endureth all things, is long-suffering in all things.
There is nothing coarse, nothing arrogant in love. Love hath no divisions, love maketh no seditions, love doeth all things in concord. In
love were all the elect of God made perfect; without love nothing is
well-pleasing to God: in love the Master took us unto Himself; for the
love which He had toward us, Jesus Christ our Lord hath given His
blood for us by the will of God, and His flesh for our flesh and His life
for our lives.

50. Ye see, dearly beloved, how great and marvellous a thing is
love, and there is no declaring its perfection. Who is sufficient to be
found therein, save those to whom God shall vouchsafe it? Let us
therefore entreat and ask of His mercy, that we may be found blameless
in love, standing apart from the factiousness of men. All the generations from Adam unto this day have passed away: but they that by
God's grace were perfected in love dwell in the abode of the pious; and
they shall be made manifest in the visitation of the Kingdom of God.
For it is written; *Enter into the closet for a very little while, until Mine
anger and My wrath shall pass away, and I will remember a good day
and will raise you from your tombs.* Blessed were we, dearly beloved,
if we should be doing the commandments of God in concord of love, to
the end that our sins may through love be forgiven us. For it is
written; *Blessed are they whose iniquities are forgiven, and whose sins are
covered. Blessed is the man to whom the Lord shall impute no sin, neither
is guile in his mouth.* This declaration of blessedness was pronounced

upon them that have been elected by God through Jesus Christ our Lord, to whom be the glory for ever and ever. Amen.

51. For all our transgressions which we have committed through any of the wiles of the adversary, let us entreat that we may obtain forgiveness. Yea and they also, who set themselves up as leaders of faction and division, ought to look to the common ground of hope. For such as walk in fear and love desire that they themselves should fall into suffering rather than their neighbours; and they pronounce condemnation against themselves rather than against the harmony which hath been handed down to us nobly and righteously. For it is good for a man to make confession of his trespasses rather than to harden his heart, as the heart of those was hardened who made sedition against Moses the servant of God; whose condemnation was clearly manifest, for they went down to hades alive, and *Death shall be their shepherd.* Pharaoh and his host and all the rulers of Egypt, *their chariots and their horsemen,* were overwhelmed in the depths of the Red Sea, and perished for none other reason but because their foolish hearts were hardened after that the signs and the wonders had been wrought in the land of Egypt by the hand of Moses the servant of God.

52. The Master, brethren, hath need of nothing at all. He desireth not anything of any man, save to confess unto Him. For the elect David saith; *I will confess unto the Lord, and it shall please Him more than a young calf that groweth horns and hoofs. Let the poor see it, and rejoice.* And again He saith; *Sacrifice to God a sacrifice of praise, and pay thy vows to the Most High: and call upon Me in the day of thine affliction, and I will deliver thee, and thou shalt glorify Me. For a sacrifice unto God is a broken spirit.*

53. For ye know, and know well, the sacred scriptures, dearly beloved, and ye have searched into the oracles of God. We write these things therefore to put you in remembrance. When Moses went up into the mountain and had spent forty days and forty nights in fasting and humiliation, God said unto him; *Moses, Moses, come down quickly hence, for My people whom thou leddest forth from the land of Egypt have wrought iniquity: they have transgressed quickly out of the way which thou didst command unto them: they have made for themselves molten images. And the Lord said unto him; I have spoken unto thee once and twice, saying, I have seen this people, and behold it is stiff-necked. Let Me destroy them utterly, and I will blot out their name from under heaven, and I will make of thee a nation great and wonderful and numerous more*

than this. And Moses said; *Nay, not so, Lord. Forgive this people their sin, or blot me also out of the book of the living.* O mighty love! O unsurpassable perfection! The servant is bold with his Master; he asketh forgiveness for the multitude, or he demandeth that himself also be blotted out with them.

54.   Who therefore is noble among you? Who is compassionate? Who is fulfilled with love? Let him say; If by reason of me there be faction and strife and divisions, I retire, I depart, whither ye will, and I do that which is ordered by the people: only let the flock of Christ be at peace with its duly appointed presbyters. He that shall have done this, shall win for himself great renown in Christ, and every place will receive him: for *the earth is the Lord's and the fulness thereof.* Thus have they done and will do, that live as citizens of that kingdom of God which bringeth no regrets.

55.   But, to bring forward examples of Gentiles also; many kings and rulers, when some season of pestilence pressed upon them, being taught by oracles have delivered themselves over to death, that they might rescue their fellow citizens through their own blood. Many have retired from their own cities, that they might have no more seditions. We know that many among ourselves have delivered themselves to bondage, that they might ransom others. Many have sold themselves to slavery, and receiving the price paid for themselves have fed others. Many women being strengthened through the grace of God have performed many manly deeds. The blessed Judith, when the city was beleaguered, asked of the elders that she might be suffered to go forth into the camp of the aliens. So she exposed herself to peril and went forth for love of her country and of her people which were beleaguered; and the Lord delivered Holophernes into the hand of a woman. To no less peril did Esther also, who was perfect in faith, expose herself, that she might deliver the twelve tribes of Israel, when they were on the point to perish. For through her fasting and her humiliation she entreated the all-seeing Master, the God of the ages; and He, seeing the humility of her soul, delivered the people for whose sake she encountered the peril.

56.   Therefore let us also make intercession for them that are in any transgression, that forbearance and humility may be given them, to the end that they may yield not unto us, but unto the will of God. For so shall the compassionate remembrance of them with God and the saints be fruitful unto them, and perfect. Let us accept chastisement,

whereat no man ought to be vexed, dearly beloved. The admonition which we give one to another is good and exceeding useful; for it joineth us unto the will of God. For thus saith the holy word; *The Lord hath indeed chastened me, and hath not delivered me over unto death. For whom the Lord loveth He chasteneth, and scourgeth every son whom He receiveth. For the righteous,* it is said, *shall chasten me in mercy and shall reprove me, but let not the †mercy† of sinners anoint my head.* And again He saith; *Blessed is the man whom the Lord hath reproved, and refuse not thou the admonition of the Almighty. For He causeth pain, and He restoreth again: He hath smitten, and His hands have healed. Six times shall He rescue thee from afflictions: and at the seventh no evil shall touch thee. In famine He shall deliver thee from death, and in war He shall release thee from the arm of the sword. And from the scourge of the tongue shall He hide thee, and thou shalt not be afraid when evils approach. Thou shalt laugh at the unrighteous and wicked, and of the wild beasts thou shalt not be afraid. For wild beasts shall be at peace with thee. Then shalt thou know that thy house shall be at peace: and the abode of thy tabernacle shall not go wrong, and thou shalt know that thy seed is many, and thy children as the plenteous herbage of the field. And thou shalt come to the grave as ripe corn reaped in due season, or as the heap of the threshing floor gathered together at the right time.* Ye see, dearly beloved, how great protection there is for them that are chastened by the Master: for being a kind father He chasteneth us to the end that we may obtain mercy through His holy chastisement.

57. Ye therefore that laid the foundation of the sedition, submit yourselves unto the presbyters and receive chastisement unto repentance, bending the knees of your heart. Learn to submit yourselves, laying aside the arrogant and proud stubbornness of your tongue. For it is better for you to be found little in the flock of Christ and to have your name on God's roll, than to be had in exceeding honour and yet be cast out from the hope of Him. For thus saith the All-virtuous Wisdom; *Behold I will pour out for you a saying of My breath, and I will teach you My word. Because I called and ye obeyed not, and I held out words and ye heeded not, but made My counsels of none effect, and were disobedient unto My reproofs; therefore I also will laugh at your destruction, and will rejoice over you when ruin cometh upon you, and when confusion overtaketh you suddenly, and your overthrow is at hand like a whirlwind, or when anguish and beleaguerment come upon you. For it shall be, when ye call upon Me, yet will I not hear you. Evil men*

shall seek Me and shall not find Me: for they hated wisdom, and chose not the fear of the Lord, neither would they give heed unto My counsels, but mocked at My reproofs. Therefore they shall eat the fruits of their own way, and shall be filled with their own ungodliness. For because they wronged babes, they shall be slain, and inquisition shall destroy the ungodly. But he that heareth Me shall dwell safely trusting in hope, and shall be quiet from fear of all evil.

58. Let us therefore be obedient unto His most holy and glorious Name, thereby escaping the threatenings which were spoken of old by the mouth of Wisdom against them which disobey, that we may dwell safely, trusting in the most holy Name of His majesty. Receive our counsel, and ye shall have no occasion of regret. For as God liveth, and the Lord Jesus Christ liveth, and the Holy Spirit, who are the faith and the hope of the elect, so surely shall he, who with lowliness of mind and instant in gentleness hath without regretfulness performed the ordinances and commandments that are given by God, be enrolled and have a name among the number of them that are saved through Jesus Christ, through whom is the glory unto Him for ever and ever. Amen.

59. But if certain persons should be disobedient unto the words spoken by Him through us, let them understand that they will entangle themselves in no slight transgression and danger; but we shall be guiltless of this sin. And we will ask, with instancy of prayer and supplication, that the Creator of the universe may guard intact unto the end the number that hath been numbered of His elect throughout the whole world, through His beloved Son Jesus Christ, through whom He called us from darkness to light, from ignorance to the full know-ledge of the glory of His Name.

[Grant unto us, Lord,] that we may set our hope on Thy Name which is the primal source of all creation, and open the eyes of our hearts, that we may know Thee, who alone *abidest Highest in the lofty, Holy in the holy;* who *layest low the insolence of the proud,* who *scatterest the imaginings of nations;* who *settest the lowly on high,* and *bringest the lofty low;* who *makest rich and makest poor;* who *killest and makest alive;* who alone art the Benefactor of spirits and the God of all flesh; who *lookest into the abysses,* who scannest the works of man; the Succour of them that are in peril, the *Saviour of them that are in despair;* the Creator and Overseer of every spirit; who multipliest the nations upon earth, and hast chosen out from all men those that love Thee through Jesus Christ, Thy beloved Son, through whom Thou didst instruct us, didst sanctify us, didst honour us. We beseech Thee, Lord and Master, to be *our help and succour.* Save those among us who are in tribulation; have mercy on the lowly; lift up the fallen; show Thyself unto the needy; heal the ungodly; convert the wanderers of Thy people; feed the hungry; release our prisoners; raise up the weak; comfort the faint-hearted. *Let* all *the Gentiles know that Thou art God alone,* and Jesus Christ is Thy Son, and *we are Thy people and the sheep of Thy pasture.*

60. Thou through Thine operations didst make manifest the everlasting fabric of the world. Thou, Lord, didst create the earth. Thou that art faithful throughout all generations, righteous in Thy judgments, marvellous in strength and excellence, Thou that art wise in creating and prudent in establishing that which Thou hast made, that art good in the things which are seen and faithful with them that trust on Thee, *pitiful and compassionate,* forgive us our iniquities and our unrighteousnesses and our transgressions and shortcomings. Lay not to our account every sin of Thy servants and Thine handmaids, but cleanse us with the cleansing of Thy truth, and *guide our steps to walk in holiness* and righteousness and singleness *of heart* and *to do such things as are good and well-pleasing in Thy sight* and in the sight of our rulers. Yea, Lord, *make Thy face to shine upon us* in peace for our good, that we may be sheltered *by Thy mighty hand and* delivered from every sin *by Thine uplifted arm.* And deliver us from them that hate us wrongfully. Give concord and peace to us and to all that dwell on the earth, as Thou gavest to our fathers, *when they called on* Thee *in faith and truth* with holiness, [that we may be saved,] while we render obedience to Thine almighty and most excellent Name, and to our rulers and governors upon the earth.

61. Thou, Lord and Master, hast given them the power of sovereignty through Thine excellent and unspeakable might, that we knowing the glory and honour which Thou hast given them may submit ourselves unto them, in nothing resisting Thy will. Grant unto them therefore, O Lord, health, peace, concord, stability, that they may administer the government which Thou hast given them without failure. For Thou, O heavenly Master, King of the ages, givest to the sons of men glory and honour and power over all things that are upon the earth. Do Thou, Lord, direct their counsel according to that which is good and well-pleasing in Thy sight, that, administering in peace and gentleness with godliness the power which Thou hast given them, they may obtain Thy

favour. O Thou, who alone art able to do these things and things far
more exceeding good than these for us, we praise Thee through the
High-priest and Guardian of our souls, Jesus Christ, through whom
be the glory and the majesty unto Thee both now and for all generations and for ever and ever. Amen.

62. As touching those things which befit our religion and are most
useful for a virtuous life to such as would guide [their steps] in holiness
and righteousness, we have written fully unto you, brethren. For concerning faith and repentance and genuine love and temperance and
sobriety and patience we have handled every argument, putting you in
remembrance, that ye ought to please Almighty God in righteousness
and truth and long-suffering with holiness, laying aside malice and pursuing concord in love and peace, being instant in gentleness ; even as
our fathers, of whom we spake before, pleased Him, being lowly-
minded towards their Father and God and Creator and towards all
men. And we have put you in mind of these things the more gladly,
since we knew well that we were writing to men who are faithful and
highly accounted and have diligently searched into the oracles of the
teaching of God.

63. Therefore it is right for us to give heed to so great and so
many examples and to submit the neck and occupying the place of
obedience to take our side with them that are the leaders of our souls,
that ceasing from this foolish dissension we may attain unto the goal
which lieth before us in truthfulness, keeping aloof from every fault.
For ye will give us great joy and gladness, if ye render obedience unto
the things written by us through the Holy Spirit, and root out the unrighteous anger of your jealousy, according to the entreaty which we
have made for peace and concord in this letter. And we have also
sent faithful and prudent men that have walked among us from youth
unto old age unblameably, who shall also be witnesses between you
and us. And this we have done that ye might know that we have
had, and still have, every solicitude that ye should be speedily at
peace.

64. Finally may the All-seeing God and Master of spirits and Lord
of all flesh, who chose the Lord Jesus Christ, and us through Him for a
peculiar people, grant unto every soul that is called after His excellent
and holy Name faith, fear, peace, patience, long-suffering, temperance,
chastity and soberness, that they may be well-pleasing unto His Name
through our High-priest and Guardian Jesus Christ, through whom

unto Him be glory and majesty, might and honour, both now and for ever and ever. Amen.

65. Now send ye back speedily unto us our messengers Claudius Ephebus and Valerius Bito, together with Fortunatus also, in peace and with joy, to the end that they may the more quickly report the peace and concord which is prayed for and earnestly desired by us, that we also may the more speedily rejoice over your good order.

The grace of our Lord Jesus Christ be with you and with all men in all places. who have been called by God and through Him, through whom be glory and honour, power and greatness and eternal dominion, unto Him, from the ages past and for ever and ever. Amen.

AN ANCIENT HOMILY

BY AN

UNKNOWN AUTHOR

THE so-called Second Epistle of S. Clement to the Corinthians follows immediately upon the first in all the three MS authorities, and is apparently ascribed to S. Clement by them. It has however no claim to this designation; for, although it was known to the Fathers of the fourth century and later, it is not quoted by early writers as being the work of S. Clement, and the internal evidence both of style and doctrine, so far as it goes, is distinctly against this conclusion. There are some indications (§ 7) that it was indeed written or spoken in the first instance to the Corinthians, but its language and character point to its being a homily rather than a letter. This view has been confirmed by the recent discovery of the latter half of the Epistle. The speaker addresses his hearers more than once towards the close as 'Brothers and sisters' (§§ 19, 20). Elsewhere he appeals to them in language which is quite explicit on the point at issue. 'Let us not think', he says, 'to give heed and believe now only, while we are being admonished by the presbyters; but likewise when we have departed home, let us remember the commandments of the Lord, etc.' (§ 17). We may therefore now definitely regard it as the earliest Christian homily extant. As a literary production it has no value, but it is at least interesting for the high moral tone and unswerving faith which it displays throughout. Its date may with some confidence be assigned to the first half of the second century, probably c. A.D. 120—140.

AN ANCIENT HOMILY

BRETHREN, we ought so to think of Jesus Christ, as of God, as of the Judge of quick and dead. And we ought not to think mean things of our Salvation : for when we think mean things of Him, we expect also to receive mean things. And they that listen as concerning mean things do wrong; and we ourselves do wrong, not knowing whence and by whom and unto what place we were called, and how many things Jesus Christ endured to suffer for our sakes. What recompense then shall we give unto Him? or what fruit worthy of His own gift to us? And how many mercies do we owe to Him! For He bestowed the light upon us; He spake to us, as a father to his sons; He saved us, when we were perishing. What praise then shall we give to Him? or what payment of recompense for those things which we received? we who were maimed in our understanding, and worshipped stocks and stones and gold and silver and bronze, the works of men; and our whole life was nothing else but death. While then we were thus wrapped in darkness and oppressed with this thick mist in our vision, we recovered our sight, putting off by His will the cloud wherein we were wrapped. For He had mercy on us, and in His compassion saved us, having beheld in us much error and perdition, even when we had no hope of salvation, save that which came from Him. For He called us, when we were not, and from not being He willed us to be.

2. *Rejoice, thou barren that bearest not. Break out and cry, thou that travailest not; for more are the children of the desolate than of her that hath the husband.* In that He said *Rejoice, thou barren that bearest not,* He spake of us: for our Church was barren, before that children were given unto her. And in that He said, *Cry aloud, thou that travailest not,* He meaneth this; Let us not, like women in travail, grow weary of offering up our prayers with simplicity to God. Again, in that He said, *For the children of the desolate are more than of her that hath the*

44

husband, He so spake, because our people seemed desolate and forsaken of God, whereas now, having believed, we have become more than those who seemed to have God. Again another scripture saith, *I came not to call the righteous, but sinners.* He meaneth this; that it is right to save them that are perishing. For this indeed is a great and marvellous work, to establish, not those things which stand, but those which are falling. So also Christ willed to save the things which were perishing. And He saved many, coming and calling us when we were even now perishing.

3. Seeing then that He bestowed so great mercy on us; first of all, that we, who are living, do not sacrifice to these dead gods, neither worship them, but through Him have known the Father of truth. What else is this knowledge to Himward, but not to deny Him through whom we have known Him? Yea, He Himself saith, *Whoso confesseth Me, Him will I confess before the Father.* This then is our reward, if verily we shall confess Him through whom we were saved. But wherein do we confess Him? When we do that which He saith and are not disobedient unto His commandments, and not only *honour Him with our lips*, but *with our whole heart and with our whole mind.* Now He saith also in Isaiah, *This people honoureth Me with their lips, but their heart is far from Me.*

4. Let us therefore not only call Him Lord, for this will not save us: for He saith, *Not every one that saith unto Me, Lord, Lord, shall be saved, but he that doeth righteousness.* So then, brethren, let us confess Him in our works, by loving one another, by not committing adultery nor speaking evil one against another nor envying, but being temperate, merciful, kindly. And we ought to have fellow-feeling one with another and not to be covetous. By these works let us confess Him, and not by the contrary. And we ought not rather to fear men but God. For this cause, if yo do these things, the Lord said, *Though ye be gathered together with Me in My bosom, and do not My commandments, I will cast you away and will say unto you, Depart from Me, I know you not whence ye are, ye workers of iniquity.*

5. Wherefore, brethren, let us forsake our sojourn in this world and do the will of Him that called us, and let us not be afraid to depart out of this world. For the Lord saith, *Ye shall be as lambs in the midst of wolves.* But Peter answered and said unto Him, *What then, if the wolves should tear the lambs?* Jesus said unto Peter, *Let not the lambs fear the wolves after they are dead; and ye also, fear ye not them that kill*

you and are not able to do anything to you; but fear Him that after ye are dead hath power over soul and body, to cast them into the gehenna of fire. And ye know, brethren, that the sojourn of this flesh in this world is mean and for a short time, but the promise of Christ is great and marvellous, even the rest of the kingdom that shall be and of life eternal. What then can we do to obtain them, but walk in holiness and righteousness, and consider these worldly things as alien to us, and not desire them? For when we desire to obtain these things we fall away from the righteous path.

6. But the Lord saith, *No servant can serve two masters.* If we desire to serve both God and mammon, it is unprofitable for us : *For what advantage is it, if a man gain the whole world and forfeit his soul?* Now this age and the future are two enemies. The one speaketh of adultery and defilement and avarice and deceit, but the other biddeth farewell to these. We cannot therefore be friends of the two, but must bid farewell to the one and hold companionship with the other. Let us consider that it is better to hate the things which are here, because they are mean and for a short time and perishable, and to love the things which are there, for they are good and imperishable. For, if we do the will of Christ, we shall find rest; but if otherwise, then nothing shall deliver us from eternal punishment, if we should disobey His commandments. And the scripture also saith in Ezekiel, *Though Noah and Job and Daniel should rise up, they shall not deliver their children* in the captivity. But if even such righteous men as these cannot by their righteous deeds deliver their children, with what confidence shall we, if we keep not our baptism pure and undefiled, enter into the kingdom of God? Or who shall be our advocate, unless we be found having holy and righteous works?

7. So then, my brethren, let us contend, knowing that the contest is nigh at hand, and that, while many resort to the corruptible contests, yet not all are crowned, but only they that have toiled hard and contended bravely. Let us then contend that we all may be crowned. Wherefore let us run in the straight course, the incorruptible contest. And let us resort to it in throngs and contend, that we may also be crowned. And if we cannot all be crowned, let us at least come near to the crown. We ought to know that he which contendeth in the corruptible contest, if he be found dealing corruptly with it, is first flogged, and then removed and driven out of the race-course. What think ye? What shall be done to him that hath dealt corruptly with the contest of

incorruption? For as concerning them that have not kept the seal, He saith, *Their worm shall not die, and their fire shall not be quenched, and they shall be for a spectacle unto all flesh.*

8. While we are on earth then, let us repent: for we are clay under the craftsman's hand. For in like manner as the potter, if he be making a vessel, and it get twisted or crushed in his hands, reshapeth it again; but if he have once put it into the fiery oven, he shall no longer mend it: so also let us, while we are in this world, repent with our whole heart of the evil things which we have done in the flesh, that we may be saved by the Lord, while we have yet time for repentance. For after that we have departed out of the world, we can no more make confession there, or repent any more. Wherefore, brethren, if we shall have done the will of the Father and kept the flesh pure and guarded the commandments of the Lord, we shall receive life eternal. For the Lord saith in the Gospel, *If ye kept not that which is little, who shall give unto you that which is great? For I say unto you that he which is faithful in the least, is faithful also in much.* So then He meaneth this, Keep the flesh pure and the seal unstained, to the end that we may receive life.

9. And let not any one of you say that this flesh is not judged neither riseth again. Understand ye. In what were ye saved? In what did ye recover your sight? if ye were not in this flesh. We ought therefore to guard the flesh as a temple of God: for in like manner as ye were called in the flesh, ye shall come also in the flesh. If Christ the Lord who saved us, being first spirit, then became flesh, and so called us, in like manner also shall we in this flesh receive our reward. Let us therefore love one another, that we all may come unto the kingdom of God. While we have time to be healed, let us place ourselves in the hands of God the physician, giving Him a recompense. What recompense? Repentance from a sincere heart. For He discerneth all things beforehand and knoweth what is in our heart. Let us therefore give unto Him eternal praise, not from our lips only, but also from our heart, that He may receive us as sons. For the Lord also said, *These are My brethren, which do the will of My Father.*

10. Wherefore, my brethren, let us do the will of the Father which called us, that we may live; and let us the rather pursue virtue, but forsake vice as the forerunner of our sins, and let us flee from ungodliness, lest evils overtake us. For if we be diligent in doing good, peace will pursue us. For for this cause is a man unable to †attain happiness†,

seeing that they call in the fears of men, preferring rather the enjoyment which is here than the promise which is to come. For they know not how great torment the enjoyment which is here bringeth, and what delight the promise which is to come bringeth. And if verily they were doing these things by themselves alone, it had been tolerable : but now they continue teaching evil to innocent souls, not knowing that they shall have their condemnation doubled, both themselves and their hearers.

11. Let us therefore serve God in a pure heart, and we shall be righteous; but if we serve Him not, because we believe not the promise of God, we shall be wretched. For the word of prophecy also saith : *Wretched are the double-minded, that doubt in their heart and say, These things we heard of old in the days of our fathers also, yet we have waited day after day and have seen none of them. Ye fools! compare yourselves unto a tree ; take a vine. First it sheddeth its leaves, then a shoot cometh, after this a sour berry, then a full ripe grape. So likewise My people had tumults and afflictions: but afterward they shall receive good things.* Wherefore, my brethren, let us not be double-minded but endure patiently in hope, that we may also obtain our reward. *For faithful is He that promised* to pay to each man the recompense of his works. If therefore we shall have wrought righteousness in the sight of God, we shall enter into His kingdom and shall receive the promises which *ear hath not heard nor eye seen, neither hath it entered into the heart of man.*

12. Let us therefore await the kingdom of God betimes in love and righteousness, since we know not the day of God's appearing. For the Lord Himself, being asked by a certain person when His kingdom would come, said, *When the two shall be one, and the outside as the inside, and the male with the female, neither male nor female.* Now *the two* are *one*, when we speak truth among ourselves, and in two bodies there shall be one soul without dissimulation. And by *the outside as the inside* He meaneth this : by the inside He meaneth the soul and by the outside the body. Therefore in like manner as thy body appeareth, so also let thy soul be manifest in its good works. And by *the male with the female, neither male nor female,* He meaneth this ; that a brother seeing a sister should have no thought of her as of a female, and that a sister seeing a brother should not have any thought of him as of a male. These things if ye do, saith He, the kingdom of my Father shall come.

13. Therefore, brethren, let us repent forthwith. Let us be sober unto that which is good: for we are full of much folly and wickedness. Let us wipe away from us our former sins, and let us repent with our whole soul and be saved. And let us not be found men-pleasers. Neither let us desire to please one another only, but also those men that are without, by our righteousness, that the Name be not blasphemed by reason of us. For the Lord saith, *Every way My Name is blasphemed among all the Gentiles;* and again, *Woe unto him by reason of whom My Name is blasphemed.* Wherein is it blasphemed? In that ye do not the things which I desire. For the Gentiles, when they hear from our mouth the oracles of God, marvel at them for their beauty and greatness; then, when they discover that our works are not worthy of the words which we speak, forthwith they betake themselves to blasphemy, saying that it is an idle story and a delusion. For when they hear from us that God saith, *It is no thank unto you, if ye love them that love you, but this is thank unto you, if ye love your enemies and them that hate you;* when they hear these things, I say, they marvel at their exceeding goodness; but when they see that we not only do not love them that hate us, but not even them that love us, they laugh us to scorn, and the Name is blasphemed.

14. Wherefore, brethren, if we do the will of God our Father, we shall be of the first Church, which is spiritual, which was created before the sun and moon; but if we do not the will of the Lord, we shall be of the scripture that saith, *My house was made a den of robbers.* So therefore let us choose rather to be of the Church of life, that we may be saved. And I do not suppose ye are ignorant that the living Church is *the body of Christ:* for the scripture saith, *God made man, male and female.* The male is Christ and the female is the Church. And the Books and the Apostles plainly declare that the Church existeth not now for the first time, but hath been from the beginning: for she was spiritual, as our Jesus also was spiritual, but was manifested in the last days that He might save us. Now the Church, being spiritual, was manifested in the flesh of Christ, thereby showing us that, if any of us guard her in the flesh and defile her not, he shall receive her again in the Holy Spirit: for this flesh is the counterpart and copy of the spirit. No man therefore, when he hath defiled the copy, shall receive the original for his portion. This therefore is what He meaneth, brethren; Guard ye the flesh, that ye may partake of the spirit. But if we say that the flesh is the Church and the spirit is Christ, then he that hath

dealt wantonly with the flesh hath dealt wantonly with the Church. Such an one therefore shall not partake of the spirit, which is Christ. So excellent is the life and immortality which this flesh can receive as its portion, if the Holy Spirit be joined to it.   No man can declare or tell *those things which the Lord hath prepared* for His elect.

15.   Now I do not think that I have given any mean counsel respecting continence, and whosoever performeth it shall not repent thereof, but shall save both himself and me his counsellor.   For it is no mean reward to convert a wandering and perishing soul, that it may be saved.   For this is the recompense which we are able to pay to God who created us, if he that speaketh and heareth both speak and hear with faith and love.   Let us therefore abide in the things which we believed, in righteousness and holiness, that we may with boldness ask of God who saith, *Whiles thou art still speaking I will say, Behold, I am here*.   For this word is the token of a great promise : for the Lord saith of Himself that He is more ready to give than he that asketh to ask. Seeing then that we are partakers of so great kindness, let us not grudge ourselves the obtaining of so many good things.   For in proportion as the pleasure is great which these words bring to them that have performed them, so also is the condemnation great which they bring to them that have been disobedient.

16.   Therefore, brethren, since we have found no small opportunity for repentance, seeing that we have time, let us turn again unto God that called us, while we have still One that receiveth us.   For if we bid farewell to these enjoyments and conquer our soul in refusing to fulfil its evil lusts, we shall be partakers of the mercy of Jesus.   But ye know that the day of judgment cometh even now *as a burning oven, and the powers of the heavens shall melt*, and all the earth as lead melting on the fire, and then shall appear the secret and open works of men.   Almsgiving therefore is a good thing, even as repentance from sin.   Fasting is better than prayer, but almsgiving than both.   And *love covereth a multitude of sins*, but prayer out of a good conscience delivereth from death.   Blessed is every man that is found full of these.   For almsgiving lifteth off the burden of sin.

17.   Let us therefore repent with our whole heart, lest any of us perish by the way.   For if we have received commands, that we should make this also our business, to tear men away from idols and to instruct them, how much more is it wrong that a soul which knoweth God already should perish !   Therefore let us assist one another, that

we may also lead the weak upward as touching that which is good, to the end that we all may be saved: and let us convert and admonish one another. And let us not think to give heed and believe now only, while we are admonished by the presbyters; but likewise when we have departed home, let us remember the commandments of the Lord, and not suffer ourselves to be dragged off the other way by our worldly lusts; but coming hither more frequently, let us strive to go forward in the commands of the Lord, that we all having the same mind may be gathered together unto life. For the Lord said, *I come to gather together all the nations, tribes, and languages.* Herein He speaketh of the day of His appearing, when He shall come and redeem us, each man according to his works. *And* the unbelievers *shall see His glory* and His might: and they shall be amazed when they see the kingdom of the world given to Jesus, saying, Woe unto us, for Thou wast, and we knew it not, and believed not; and we obeyed not the presbyters when they told us of our salvation. And *Their worm shall not die, and their fire shall not be quenched, and they shall be for a spectacle unto all flesh.* He speaketh of that day of judgment, when men shall see those among us that lived ungodly lives and dealt falsely with the commandments of Jesus Christ. But the righteous, having done good and endured torments and hated the pleasures of the soul, when they shall behold them that have done amiss and denied Jesus by their words or by their deeds, how that they are punished with grievous torments in unquenchable fire, shall give glory to God, saying, There will be hope for him that hath served God with his whole heart.

18. Therefore let us also be found among those that give thanks, among those that have served God, and not among the ungodly that are judged. For I myself too, being an utter sinner and not yet escaped from temptation, but being still amidst the engines of the devil, do my diligence to follow after righteousness, that I may prevail so far at least as to come near unto it, while I fear the judgment to come.

19. Therefore, brothers and sisters, after the God of truth hath been heard, I read to you an exhortation to the end that ye may give heed to the things which are written, so that ye may save both yourselves and him that readeth in the midst of you. For I ask of you as a reward that ye repent with your whole heart, and give salvation and life to yourselves. For doing this we shall set a goal for all the young who desire to toil in the study of piety and of the goodness of

God.　And let us not be displeased and vexed, fools that we are, whensoever any one admonisheth us and turneth us aside from unrighteousness unto righteousness.　For sometimes while we do evil things, we perceive it not by reason of the double-mindedness and unbelief which is in our breasts, and *we are darkened in our understanding* by our vain lusts.　Let us therefore practise righteousness that we may be saved unto the end.　Blessed are they that obey these ordinances.　Though they may endure affliction for a short time in the world, they will gather the immortal fruit of the resurrection.　Therefore let not the godly be grieved, if he be miserable in the times that now are: a blessed time awaiteth him.　He shall live again in heaven with the fathers, and shall have rejoicing throughout a sorrowless eternity.

20.　Neither suffer ye this again to trouble your mind, that we see the unrighteous possessing wealth, and the servants of God straitened. Let us then have faith, brothers and sisters.　We are contending in the lists of a living God; and we are trained by the present life, that we may be crowned with the future.　No righteous man hath reaped fruit quickly, but waiteth for it.　For if God had paid the recompense of the righteous speedily, then straightway we should have been training ourselves in merchandise, and not in godliness; for we should seem to be righteous, though we were pursuing not that which is godly, but that which is gainful.　And for this cause Divine judgment overtaketh a spirit that is not just, and loadeth it with chains.

To the only God invisible, the Father of truth, who sent forth unto us the Saviour and Prince of immortality, through whom also He made manifest unto us the truth and the heavenly life, to Him be the glory for ever and ever.　Amen.

THE EPISTLES

OF

S. IGNATIUS

A MAP TO ILLUSTRATE THE EPISTLES OF S. IGNATIUS.

Scale of English Miles.

Route (or alternative routes) of S. Ignatius

Route of the Messengers & Delegates

THE EPISTLES OF S. IGNATIUS

I

THESE seven epistles were written in the early years of the second century, when the writer was on his way from Antioch to Rome, having been condemned to death and expecting to be thrown to the wild beasts in the amphitheatre on his arrival. They fall into two groups, written at two different halting-places on his way. The letters to the Ephesians, Magnesians, Trallians, and Romans, were sent from *Smyrna*, while Ignatius was staying there and was in personal communication with Polycarp the bishop. The three remaining letters, to the Philadelphians, to the Smyrnæans, and to Polycarp, were written at a subsequent stage in his journey, at *Alexandria Troas*, where again he halted for a time, before crossing the sea for Europe. The place of writing in every case is determined from notices in the epistles themselves.

The order in which they are printed here is the order given by Eusebius (*H. E.* iii. 36). Whether he found them in this order in his manuscript, or whether he determined the places of writing (as we might determine them) from internal evidence and arranged the epistles accordingly, may be questioned. So arranged, they fall into two groups, according to the place of writing. The letters themselves however contain no indication of their chronological order in their respective groups; and, unless Eusebius simply followed his manuscript, he must have exercised his judgment in the sequence adopted in each group, e.g. Ephesians, Magnesians, Trallians, and Romans.

The two groups, besides having been written at different places, are separated from each other by another distinctive feature. All the epistles written from Smyrna are addressed to churches which he had not visited in person but knew only through their delegates. On the

55

other hand all the epistles written from Troas are addressed to those, whether churches (as in the case of the Philadelphians and Smyrnæans) or individuals (as in the case of Polycarp), with whom he had already held personal communication at some previous stage in his journey.

At some point in his journey (probably Laodicea on the Lycus), where there was a choice of roads, his guards selected the northern road through Philadelphia and Sardis to Smyrna[1]. If they had taken the southern route instead, they would have passed in succession through Tralles, Magnesia, and Ephesus, before they reached their goal. It is probable that, at the point where the roads diverged, the Christian brethren sent messengers to the churches lying on the southern road, apprising them of the martyr's destination; so that these churches would despatch their respective delegates without delay, and thus they would arrive at Smyrna as soon as, or even before, Ignatius himself.

The first group then consists of letters to these three churches, whose delegates had thus met him at Smyrna, together with a fourth to the Roman Christians apprising them of his speedy arrival among them—this last probably having been called forth by some opportunity (such as was likely to occur at Smyrna) of communicating with the metropolis. The three are arranged in a topographical order (Ephesus, Magnesia, Tralles) according to the distances of these cities from Smyrna, which is taken as the starting-point.

The second group consists of a letter to the Philadelphians whom he had visited on his way to Smyrna, and another to the Smyrnæans with whom he had stayed before going to Troas, together with a third to his friend Polycarp closing the series.

The order however in the Greek MS and in the versions (so far as it can be traced) is quite different, and disregards the places of writing. In these documents they stand in the following order:

1.	Smyrnæans	5.	Philadelphians
2.	Polycarp	6.	Trallians
3.	Ephesians	7.	Romans.
4.	Magnesians		

This sequence is consistent with the supposition that we have here the collection of the martyr's letters made at the time by Polycarp, who writing to the Philippians says 'The Epistles of Ignatius which were sent to us by him, and others as many as we had with us, we send

[1] See the map facing p. 55

to you, even as ye directed : they are subjoined to this letter' (§ 13). But though this order, which is given in the documents, has high claims for consideration as representing the earliest form of the collected epistles, I have substituted the chronological arrangement of Eusebius as more instructive for purposes of continuous reading.

2

Our documents are as follows.

1. The *Manuscript of the Greek Original* (G), the famous Medicean MS at Florence, from which Voss published the *editio princeps* in 1646. It is incomplete at the end, and does not contain the Epistle to the Romans. If this MS had been, as Turrianus described it, 'emendatissimus', we should have had no further trouble about the text. But since this is far from being the case, the secondary authorities are of the highest moment in settling the readings.

2. Among these the *Latin Version* (L) holds the first place, as being an extremely literal rendering of the original. The history of this version is especially interesting to Englishmen. It was discovered by Ussher in English libraries in two MSS, one of which has been since lost, and was given to the world by him in 1644. It was certainly translated in England, probably by Robert Grosseteste, Bishop of Lincoln (c. A.D. 1250), or his immediate circle. It exhibits a much purer form of the text, being free from several corruptions and a few interpolations and omissions which disfigure the Greek. At the same time however it is clear, both from the contents of the collection and from other indications, that this version was translated from a Greek MS of the same type as the extant Greek MS; and therefore its value, as a check upon the readings of this MS, is limited. Whenever GL coincide, they must be regarded as one witness, not as two.

3. The *Syriac Version* (S) would therefore have been invaluable as an independent check, if we had possessed it entire, since it cannot have been made later than the fourth or fifth century, and would have exhibited the text much nearer to the fountain-head than either the Greek or the Latin. Unfortunately however only a few fragments (S_1, S_2, S_3, S_4) belonging to this version are preserved. But this defect is made up to a considerable extent in two ways. *First.* We have a rough *Abridgment* or *Collection of Excerpts* (Σ) from this Syriac Version

for three epistles (Ephesians, Romans, Polycarp) together with a fragment of a fourth (Trallians), preserving whole sentences and even
paragraphs in their original form or with only slight changes. *Secondly*.
There is extant also an *Armenian Version* (A) of the whole, made from
the Syriac (S). This last however has passed through so many vicissi-
tudes, that it is often difficult to discern the original Greek reading
underlying its tertiary text. It will thus be seen that AΣ have no independent authority, where S is otherwise known, and that SAΣ must be
regarded as one witness, not as three.

4.   There is likewise extant a fragment of a *Coptic Version* (C), in
the Sahidic (Thebaic) dialect of the Egyptian language, comprising the
first six chapters of the Epistle to the Smyrnæans, besides the end of the
spurious Epistle to Hero.   The date of this version is uncertain, though
probably early; but the text appears to be quite independent of our
other authorities, and it is therefore much to be regretted that so little
is preserved.

5.   Another and quite independent witness is the *Greek Text of
the Long Recension* (g) of the Ignatian Epistles.   This Long Recension
consists of the seven genuine Epistles but interpolated throughout,
together with six additional Epistles (Mary to Ignatius, Ignatius to Mary,
to the Tarsians, to the Philippians, to the Antiochenes and to Hero).
The *Latin Version* (l) of the Long Recension has no independent
value, and is only important as assisting in determining the original
form of this recension.   The practice of treating it as an independent
authority is altogether confusing.   The text of the Long Recension,
once launched into the world, had its own history, which should be kept
quite distinct from that of the genuine Epistles of Ignatius.   For the
purpose of determining the text of the latter, we are only concerned with
its original form.

The Long Recension was constructed by some unknown author,
probably in the latter half of the fourth century, from the genuine
Ignatian Epistles by interpolation, alteration, and omission.   If therefore we can ascertain in any given passage the Greek text of the genuine
epistles which this author had before him, we have traced the reading
back to an earlier point in the stream than the direct Greek and Latin
authorities, probably even than the Syriac Version.   This however it is
not always easy to do, by reason of the freedom and capriciousness of
the changes.   No rule of universal application can be laid down.   But
the interpolator is obviously much more given to change at some times

than at others; and, where the fit is upon him, no stress can be laid on minor variations. On the other hand, where he adheres pretty closely to the text of the genuine Ignatius, as for instance through great parts of the Epistles to Polycarp and to the Romans, the readings of this recension deserve every consideration.

Thus it will be seen that though this witness is highly important, because it cannot be suspected of collusion with other witnesses, yet it must be subject to careful cross-examination, before the truth underlying its statements can be ascertained.

6. Besides manuscripts and versions, we have a fair number of *Quotations*, of which the value will vary according to their age and independence.

From the above statement it will be seen that, though each authority separately may be regarded as more or less unsatisfactory, yet, as they are very various in kind, they act as checks one upon another, the one frequently supplying just that element of certainty which is lacking to the other, so that the result is fairly adequate. Thus A will often give what g withholds, and conversely. Moreover it will appear from what has been said that a combination of the secondary and capricious authorities must often decide a reading against the direct and primary. For instance, the combination Ag is, as a rule, decisive in favour of a reading, as against the more direct witnesses GL, notwithstanding that A singly, or g singly, is liable to any amount of aberration, though in different directions.

The foregoing account applies to six out of the seven letters. The text of the *Epistle to the Romans* has had a distinct history and is represented by separate authorities of its own. This epistle was at an early date incorporated into the Antiochene Acts of Martyrdom of Ignatius, and thus dissociated from the other six. In its new connexion, it was disseminated and translated separately. It so happens that the Greek MSS which contain this epistle (the Colbertine, 18 *S. Sab.*, and 519 *Sin.*) are even less satisfactory than the Greek MS of the other six (the Medicean); but on the other hand we have more than compensation for this inferiority in the fact that the Acts of Martyrdom (with the incorporated epistle) were translated independently both into Syriac (S_m) and into Armenian (A_m); and these two versions, which are extant, furnish two additional authorities for the text. Moreover the Metaphrast, who compiled his Acts of Ignatius from this and another

Martyrology, has retained the Epistle to the Romans in his text, though in an abridged and altered form.

From this account it will be seen that the authorities for the Epistle to the Romans fall into three classes.

(1) Those authorities, which contain the epistle as part of the Martyrology. These are the Greek (G), the Latin (L), the Syriac (S$_m$), and the Armenian (A$_m$), besides the Metaphrast (M). These authorities however are of different values. When the epistle was first incorporated in the Acts of Martyrdom, it still preserved a comparatively pure form. When it has arrived at the stage in which it appears in the extant Greek MS (G), it is very corrupt. In this last form, among other corruptions, it exhibits interpolations and alterations which have been introduced from the Long Recension (g). The MS used by the Metaphrast exhibited a text essentially the same as that of G.

(2) The independent *Syriac Version* (S) of which only a few fragments remain, but which is represented, as before, by the *Syriac Abridgment* (Σ) and the *Armenian Version* (A).

(3) The *Long Recension* (g), which in great parts of this epistle keeps close to the text of the original Ignatius.

3

Though the principles on which a text of the Seven Epistles should be constructed are sufficiently obvious, they have been strangely overlooked.

The first period in the history of the text of the genuine Ignatius commences with the publication of the Latin Version by Ussher (1644), and of the Greek original by Isaac Voss (1646). The Greek of the Epistle to the Romans was first published by Ruinart (1689). The text of Voss was a very incorrect transcript of the Medicean MS, and in this respect subsequent collations have greatly improved on his *editio princeps*. But beyond this next to nothing was done to emend the Greek text. Though some very obvious corrections are suggested by the Latin Version, these were either neglected altogether by succeeding editors or were merely indicated by them in their notes without being introduced into the text. There was the same neglect also of the aid which might have been derived from the Long Recension. Moreover the practice of treating the several MSS and the Latin Version of the Long Recension independently of one another and recording them co-ordinately with the Greek and Latin of the genuine Ignatius (instead of using them apart to ascertain the original form of the Long Recension, and then employing the text of this Recension, when thus ascertained, as a single authority) threw the criticism of the text into great confusion. Nor was any attention paid to the quotations, which in several instances have the highest value. Hence it happened that during this period which extended over two centuries from Voss to Hefele (ed. 1, 1839; ed. 3, 1847) and Jacobson (ed. 1, 1838; ed. 3, 1847) inclusive, nothing or next to nothing (beyond the more accurate collation of the Medicean MS) was done for the Greek text.

The second period dates from the publication of the Oriental versions—the Syriac Abridgment with the Syriac Fragments by Cureton (1845, 1849), and the Armenian Version by Petermann (1849)[1]. New materials of the highest value were thus placed in the hands of critics; but, notwithstanding the interest which the Ignatian question excited, nearly thirty years elapsed before any proper use was made of them. In some cases the failure was due, at least in part, to a false solution of the Ignatian question. The text of Bunsen (1847), Cureton (1849), and Lipsius (1859), which started from the assumption that the Syriac Abridgment represented the genuine Ignatius, must necessarily have foundered on this rock, even if the principles adopted had been sound in other respects. Petermann and Dressel (1857) however maintained the priority of the Seven Epistles of the Vossian text to the Three of the Curetonian; and so far they built upon the true basis. But Petermann contented himself with a casual emendation of the text here and there from the versions; while Dressel neglected them altogether. Jacobson (ed. 4, 1863) and Hefele (ed. 4, 1855) also, in their more recent editions which have appeared since the Oriental versions were rendered accessible, have been satisfied with recording some of the phenomena of these versions in their notes without applying them to the correction of the text, though they also were unhampered by the false theory which maintained the priority of the Curetonian Abridgment. It was reserved for the most recent editors, Zahn (1876), and Funk (1878), to make use of all the available materials

---

[1] The editio princeps of the Armenian was published at Constantinople in 1783; but this version was practically unknown to scholars until Petermann's edition appeared.

and to reconstruct the text for the first time on sound and intelligible principles.

The text which I have given was constructed independently of both these editions, and before I had seen them, but the main principles are the same. Indeed these principles must be sufficiently obvious to those who have investigated the materials with any care. In the details however my views frequently differ from theirs, as must necessarily be the case with independent editors; and in some respects I have had the advantage of more complete or more accurate materials than were accessible to them.

EPISTLES OF S. IGNATIUS

TO THE EPHESIANS

IGNATIUS, who is also Theophorus, unto her which hath been blessed in greatness through the plenitude of God the Father; which hath been foreordained before the ages to be for ever unto abiding and unchangeable glory, united and elect in a true passion, by the will of the Father and of Jesus Christ our God; even unto the church which is in Ephesus [of Asia], worthy of all felicitation : abundant greeting in Christ Jesus and in blameless joy.

1. While I welcomed in God [your] well-beloved name which ye bear by natural right, [in an upright and virtuous mind], by faith and love in Christ Jesus our Saviour—being imitators of God, and having your hearts kindled in the blood of God, ye have perfectly fulfilled your congenial work—for when ye heard that I was on my way from Syria, in bonds for the sake of the common Name and hope, and was hoping through your prayers to succeed in fighting with wild beasts in Rome, that by so succeeding I might have power to be a disciple, ye were eager to visit me :—seeing then that in God's name I have received your whole multitude in the person of Onesimus, whose love passeth utterance and who is moreover your bishop [in the flesh]—and I pray that ye may love him according to Jesus Christ and that ye all may be like him; for blessed is He that granted unto you according to your deserving to have such a bishop :—

2. But as touching my fellow-servant Burrhus, who by the will of God is your deacon blessed in all things, I pray that he may remain with me to the honour of yourselves and of your bishop. Yea, and Crocus also, who is worthy of God and of you, whom I received as an ensample of the love which ye bear me, hath relieved me in all ways—

even so may the Father of Jesus Christ refresh him—together with Onesimus and Burrhus and Euplus and Fronto; in whom I saw you all with the eyes of love. May I have joy of you always, if so be I am worthy of it. It is therefore meet for you in every way to glorify Jesus Christ who glorified you; that being perfectly joined together in one submission, submitting yourselves to your bishop and presbytery, ye may be sanctified in all things.

3. I do not command you, as though I were somewhat. For even though I am in bonds for the Name's sake, I am not yet perfected in Jesus Christ. [For] now am I beginning to be a disciple; and I speak to you as to my school-fellows. For I ought to be trained by you for the contest in faith, in admonition, in endurance, in long-suffering. But, since love doth not suffer me to be silent concerning you, therefore was I forward to exhort you, that ye run in harmony with the mind of God: for Jesus Christ also, our inseparable life, is the mind of the Father, even as the bishops that are settled in the farthest parts of the earth are in the mind of Jesus Christ.

4. So then it becometh you to run in harmony with the mind of the bishop; which thing also ye do. For your honourable presbytery, which is worthy of God, is attuned to the bishop, even as its strings to a lyre. Therefore in your concord and harmonious love Jesus Christ is sung. And do ye, each and all, form yourselves into a chorus, that being harmonious in concord and taking the key note of God ye may in unison sing with one voice through Jesus Christ unto the Father, that He may both hear you and acknowledge you by your good deeds to be members of His Son. It is therefore profitable for you to be in blameless unity, that ye may also be partakers of God always.

5. For if I in a short time had such converse with your bishop, which was not after the manner of men but in the Spirit, how much more do I congratulate you who are closely joined with him as the Church is with Jesus Christ and as Jesus Christ is with the Father, that all things may be harmonious in unity. Let no man be deceived. If any one be not within the precinct of the altar, he lacketh the bread [of God]. For, if the prayer of one and another hath so great force, how much more that of the bishop and of the whole Church. Whosoever therefore cometh not to the congregation, he doth thereby show his pride and hath separated himself; for it is written, *God resisteth the proud.* Let us therefore be careful not to resist the bishop, that by our submission we may give ourselves to God.

6. And in proportion as a man seeth that his bishop is silent, let him fear him the more. For every one whom the Master of the household sendeth to be steward over His own house, we ought so to receive as Him that sent him. Plainly therefore we ought to regard the bishop as the Lord Himself. Now Onesimus of his own accord highly praiseth your orderly conduct in God, for that ye all live according to truth, and that no heresy hath a home among you : nay, ye do not so much as listen to any one, if he speak of aught else save concerning Jesus Christ in truth.

7. For some are wont of malicious guile to hawk about the Name, while they do certain other things unworthy of God. These men ye ought to shun, as wild-beasts; for they are mad dogs, biting by stealth; against whom ye ought to be on your guard, for they are hard to heal. There is one only physician, of flesh and of spirit, generate and in-generate, God in man, true Life in death, Son of Mary and Son of God, first passible and then impassible, Jesus Christ our Lord.

8. Let no one therefore deceive you, as indeed ye are not de-ceived, seeing that ye belong wholly to God. For when no lust is established in you, which hath power to torment you, then truly ye live after God. I devote myself for you, and I dedicate myself as an offering for the church of you Ephesians which is famous unto all the ages. They that are of the flesh cannot do the things of the Spirit, neither can they that are of the Spirit do the things of the flesh; even as faith cannot do the things of unfaithfulness, neither unfaithfulness the things of faith. Nay, even those things which ye do after the flesh are spiritual; for ye do all things in Jesus Christ.

9. But I have learned that certain persons passed through you from yonder, bringing evil doctrine; whom ye suffered not to sow seed in you, for ye stopped your ears, so that ye might not receive the seed sown by them; forasmuch as ye are stones of a temple, which were prepared beforehand for a building of God the Father, being hoisted up to the heights through the engine of Jesus Christ, which is the Cross, and using for a rope the Holy Spirit; while your faith is your windlass, and love is the way that leadeth up to God. So then ye are all com-panions in the way, carrying your God and your shrine, your Christ and your holy things, being arrayed from head to foot in the commandments of Jesus Christ. And I too, taking part in the festivity, am permitted by letter to bear you company and to rejoice with you, that ye set not your love on anything after the common life of men, but only on God.

10.   And pray ye also without ceasing for the rest of mankind (for there is in them a hope of repentance), that they may find God. Therefore permit them to take lessons at least from your works. Against their outbursts of wrath be ye meek; against their proud words be ye humble; against their railings set ye your prayers; against their errors be ye *stedfast in the faith;* against their fierceness be ye gentle. And be not zealous to imitate them by requital.   Let us show ourselves their brothers by our forbearance; but let us be zealous to be imitators of the Lord, vying with each other who shall suffer the greater wrong, who shall be defrauded, who shall be set at nought; that no herb of the devil be found in you: but in all purity and temperance abide ye in Christ Jesus, with your flesh and with your spirit.

11.   These are the last times.   Henceforth let us have reverence; let us fear the long-suffering of God, lest it turn into a judgment against us.   For either let us fear the wrath which is to come or let us love the grace which now is—the one or the other; provided only that we be found in Christ Jesus unto true life.   Let nothing glitter in your eyes apart from Him, in whom I carry about my bonds, my spiritual pearls in which I would fain rise again through your prayer, whereof may it be my lot to be always a partaker, that I may be found in the company of those Christians of Ephesus who moreover were ever of one mind with the Apostles in the power of Jesus Christ.

12.   I know who I am and to whom I write.   I am a convict, ye have received mercy: I am in peril, ye are established.   Ye are the high-road of those that are on their way to die unto God.   Ye are associates in the mysteries with Paul, who was sanctified, who obtained a good report, who is worthy of all felicitation; in whose foot-steps I would fain be found treading, when I shall attain unto God; who in every letter maketh mention of you in Christ Jesus.

13.   Do your diligence therefore to meet together more frequently for thanksgiving to God and for His glory.   For when ye meet together frequently, the powers of Satan are cast down; and his mischief cometh to nought in the concord of your faith.   There is nothing better than peace, in which all warfare of things in heaven and things on earth is abolished.

14.   None of these things is hidden from you, if ye be perfect in your faith and love toward Jesus Christ, for these are the beginning and end of life—faith is the beginning and love is the end—and the two being found in unity are God, while all things else follow in their train

unto true nobility. No man professing faith sinneth, and no man possessing love hateth. *The tree is manifest from its fruit;* so they that profess to be Christ's shall be seen through their actions. For the Work is not a thing of profession now, but is seen then when one is found in the power of faith unto the end.

15. It is better to keep silence and to be, than to talk and not to be. It is a fine thing to teach, if the speaker practise. Now there is one teacher, who *spake and it came to pass*: yea and even the things which He hath done in silence are worthy of the Father. He that truly possesseth the word of Jesus is able also to hearken unto His silence, that he may be perfect; that through his speech he may act and through his silence he may be known. Nothing is hidden from the Lord, but even our secrets are nigh unto Him. Let us therefore do all things as knowing that He dwelleth in us, to the end that we may be His temples and He Himself may be in us as our God. This is so, and it will also be made clear in our sight from the love which we rightly bear towards Him.

16. Be not deceived, my brethren. Corrupters of houses *shall not inherit the kingdom of God.* If then they which do these things after the flesh are put to death, how much more if a man through evil doctrine corrupt the faith of God for which Jesus Christ was crucified. Such a man, having defiled himself, shall go into the unquenchable fire ; and in like manner also shall he that hearkeneth unto him.

17. For this cause the Lord received ointment on His head, that He might breathe incorruption upon the Church. Be not anointed with the ill odour of the teaching of the prince of this world, lest he lead you captive and rob you of the life which is set before you. And wherefore do we not all walk prudently, receiving the knowledge of God, which is Jesus Christ? Why perish we in our folly, not knowing the gift of grace which the Lord hath truly sent?

18. My spirit is made an offscouring for the Cross, which is a stumbling-block to them that are unbelievers, but to us salvation and life eternal. *Where is the wise? Where is the disputer?* Where is the boasting of them that are called prudent? For our God, Jesus the Christ, was conceived in the womb by Mary according to a dispensation, of the seed of David but also of the Holy Ghost; and He was born and was baptized that by His passion He might cleanse water.

19. And hidden from the prince of this world were the virginity of Mary and her child-bearing and likewise also the death of the Lord—

three mysteries to be cried aloud—the which were wrought in the silence of God. How then were they made manifest to the ages? A star shone forth in the heaven above all the stars; and its light was unutterable, and its strangeness caused amazement; and all the rest of the constellations with the sun and moon formed themselves into a chorus about the star; but the star itself far outshone them all; and there was perplexity to know whence came this strange appearance which was so unlike them. From that time forward every sorcery and every spell was dissolved, the ignorance of wickedness vanished away, the ancient kingdom was pulled down, when God appeared in the likeness of man unto *newness of* everlasting *life;* and that which had been perfected in the counsels of God began to take effect. Thence all things were perturbed, because the abolishing of death was taken in hand.

20. If Jesus Christ should count me worthy through your prayer, and it should be the Divine will, in my second tract, which I intend to write to you, I will further set before you the dispensation whereof I have begun to speak, relating to the new man Jesus Christ, which consisteth in faith towards Him and in love towards Him, in His passion and resurrection, especially if the Lord should reveal aught to me. Assemble yourselves together in common, every one of you severally, man by man, in grace, in one faith and one Jesus Christ, who after the flesh was of David's race, who is Son of Man and Son of God, to the end that ye may obey the bishop and the presbytery without distraction of mind; breaking one bread, which is the medicine of immortality and the antidote that we should not die but live for ever in Jesus Christ.

21. I am devoted to you and to those whom for the honour of God ye sent to Smyrna; whence also I write unto you with thanksgiving to the Lord, having love for Polycarp as I have for you also. Remember me, even as I would that Jesus Christ may also remember you. Pray for the church which is in Syria, whence I am led a prisoner to Rome— I who am the very last of the faithful there; according as I was counted worthy to be found unto the honour of God. Fare ye well in God the Father and in Jesus Christ our common hope.

2.

TO THE MAGNESIANS

IGNATIUS, who is also Theophorus, unto her which hath been blessed through the grace of God the Father in Christ Jesus our Saviour, in whom I salute the church which is in Magnesia on the Mæander, and I wish her abundant greeting in God the Father and in Jesus Christ.

1. When I learned the exceeding good order of your love in the ways of God, I was gladdened and I determined to address you in the faith of Jesus Christ. For being counted worthy to bear a most godly name, in these bonds, which I carry about, I sing the praise of the churches; and I pray that there may be in them union of the flesh and of the spirit which are Jesus Christ's, our never-failing life—an union of faith and of love which is preferred before all things, and—what is more than all—an union with Jesus and with the Father; in whom if we endure patiently all the despite of the prince of this world and escape therefrom, we shall attain unto God.

2. Forasmuch then as I was permitted to see you in the person of Damas your godly bishop and your worthy presbyters Bassus and Apollonius and my fellow-servant the deacon Zotion, of whom I would fain have joy, for that he is subject to the bishop as unto the grace of God and to the presbytery as unto the law of Jesus Christ:—

3. Yea, and it becometh you also not to presume upon the youth of your bishop, but according to the power of God the Father to render unto him all reverence, even as I have learned that the holy presbyters also have not taken advantage of his outwardly youthful estate, but give place to him as to one prudent in God; yet not to him, but to the Father of Jesus Christ, even to the Bishop of all. For the honour therefore of Him that desired you, it is meet that ye should be obedient without dissimulation. For a man doth not so much deceive this bishop who is seen, as cheat that other who is invisible; and in such a case he must reckon not with flesh but with God who knoweth the hidden things.

4. It is therefore meet that we not only be called Christians, but also be such; even as some persons have the bishop's name on their

lips, but in everything act apart from him. Such men appear to me not
to keep a good conscience, forasmuch as they do not assemble themselves together lawfully according to commandment.

5. Seeing then that all things have an end, and these two—life
and death—are set before us together, and each man shall go *to his own
place;* for just as there are two coinages, the one of God and the other
of the world, and each of them hath its proper stamp impressed upon it,
the unbelievers the stamp of this world, but the faithful in love the
stamp of God the Father through Jesus Christ, through whom unless
of our own free choice we accept to die unto His passion, His life is
not in us :—

6. Seeing then that in the aforementioned persons I beheld your
whole people in faith and embraced them, I advise you, be ye zealous
to do all things in godly concord, the bishop presiding after the likeness
of God and the presbyters after the likeness of the council of the
Apostles, with the deacons also who are most dear to me, having been
entrusted with the diaconate of Jesus Christ, who was with the Father
before the worlds and appeared at the end of time. Therefore do ye all
study conformity to God and pay reverence one to another ; and let no
man regard his neighbour after the flesh, but love ye one another in
Jesus Christ always. Let there be nothing among you which shall have
power to divide you, but be ye united with the bishop and with them
that preside over you as an ensample and a lesson of incorruptibility.

7. Therefore as the Lord did nothing without the Father, [being
united with Him], either by Himself or by the Apostles, so neither do
ye anything without the bishop and the presbyters. And attempt not
to think anything right for yourselves apart from others : but let there
be one prayer in common, one supplication, one mind, one hope, in
love and in joy unblameable, which is Jesus Christ, than whom there
is nothing better. Hasten to come together all of you, as to one temple,
even God ; as to one altar, even to one Jesus Christ, who came forth
from One Father and is with One and departed unto One.

8. Be not seduced by strange doctrines nor by antiquated fables,
which are profitless. For if even unto this day we live after the manner
of Judaism, we avow that we have not received grace : for the divine
prophets lived after Christ Jesus. For this cause also they were persecuted, being inspired by His grace to the end that they which are
disobedient might be fully persuaded that there is one God who manifested Himself through Jesus Christ His Son, who is His Word that

proceeded from silence, who in all things was well-pleasing unto Him that sent Him.

9. If then those who had walked in ancient practices attained unto newness of hope, no longer observing sabbaths but fashioning their lives after the Lord's day, on which our life also arose through Him and through His death which some men deny—a mystery whereby we attained unto belief, and for this cause we endure patiently, that we may be found disciples of Jesus Christ our only teacher—if this be so, how shall we be able to live apart from Him? seeing that even the prophets, being His disciples, were expecting Him as their teacher through the Spirit. And for this cause He whom they rightly awaited, when He came, raised them from the dead.

10. Therefore let us not be insensible to His goodness. For if He should imitate us according to our deeds, we are lost. For this cause, seeing that we are become His disciples, let us learn to live as beseemeth Christianity. For whoso is called by another name besides this, is not of God. Therefore put away the vile leaven which hath waxed stale and sour, and betake yourselves to the new leaven, which is Jesus Christ. Be ye salted in Him, that none among you grow putrid, seeing that by your savour ye shall be proved. It is monstrous to talk of Jesus Christ and to practise Judaism. For Christianity did not believe in Judaism, but Judaism in Christianity, wherein *every tongue* believed and *was gathered together* unto God.

11. Now these things I say, my dearly beloved, not because I have learned that any of you are so minded; but as being less than any of you, I would have you be on your guard betimes, that ye fall not into the snares of vain doctrine; but be ye fully persuaded concerning the birth and the passion and the resurrection, which took place in the time of the governorship of Pontius Pilate; for these things were truly and certainly done by Jesus Christ our hope; from which hope may it not befal any of you to be turned aside.

12. Let me have joy of you in all things, if I be worthy. For even though I am in bonds, yet am I not comparable to one of you who are at liberty. I know that ye are not puffed up; for ye have Jesus Christ in yourselves. And, when I praise you, I know that ye only feel the more shame; as it is written *The righteous man is a self-accuser.*

13. Do your diligence therefore that ye be confirmed in the ordinances of the Lord and of the Apostles, that ye may *prosper in all*

things whatsoever ye do in flesh and spirit, by faith and by love, in the Son and Father and in the Spirit, in the beginning and in the end, with your revered bishop, and with the fitly wreathed spiritual circlet of your presbytery, and with the deacons who walk after God. Be obedient to the bishop and to one another, as Jesus Christ was to the Father [according to the flesh], and as the Apostles were to Christ and to the Father, that there may be union both of flesh and of spirit.

14. Knowing that ye are full of God, I have exhorted you briefly. Remember me in your prayers, that I may attain unto God; and remember also the church which is in Syria, whereof I am not worthy to be called a member. For I have need of your united prayer and love in God, that it may be granted to the church which is in Syria to be refreshed by the dew of your fervent supplication.

15. The Ephesians from Smyrna salute you, from whence also I write to you. They are here with me for the glory of God, as also are ye; and they have comforted me in all things, together with Polycarp bishop of the Smyrnæans. Yea, and all the other churches salute you in the honour of Jesus Christ. Fare ye well in godly concord, and possess ye a stedfast spirit, which is Jesus Christ.

3.

TO THE TRALLIANS

IGNATIUS, who is also Theophorus, unto her that is beloved by God the Father of Jesus Christ; to the holy church which is in Tralles of Asia, elect and worthy of God, having peace in flesh and spirit through the passion of Jesus Christ, who is our hope through our resurrection unto Him; which church also I salute in the Divine plenitude after the apostolic fashion, and I wish her abundant greeting.

1. I have learned that ye have a mind unblameable and stedfast in patience, not from habit, but by nature, according as Polybius your bishop informed me, who by the will of God and of Jesus Christ visited me in Smyrna; and so greatly did he rejoice with me in my bonds in Christ Jesus, that in him I beheld the whole multitude of you. Having therefore received your godly benevolence at his hands, I gave glory,

forasmuch as I had found you to be imitators of God, even as I had learned.

2. For when ye are obedient to the bishop as to Jesus Christ, it is evident to me that ye are living not after men but after Jesus Christ, who died for us, that believing on His death ye might escape death. It is therefore necessary, even as your wont is, that ye should do nothing without the bishop; but be ye obedient also to the presbytery, as to the Apostles of Jesus Christ our hope; for if we live in Him, we shall also be found in Him. And those likewise who are deacons of the mysteries of Jesus Christ must please all men in all ways. For they are not deacons of meats and drinks but servants of the Church of God. It is right therefore that they should beware of blame as of fire.

3. In like manner let all men respect the deacons as Jesus Christ, even as they should respect the bishop as being a type of the Father and the presbyters as the council of God and as the college of Apostles. Apart from these there is not even the name of a church. And I am persuaded that ye are so minded as touching these matters: for I received the ensample of your love, and I have it with me, in the person of your bishop, whose very demeanour is a great lesson, while his gentleness is power—a man to whom I think even the godless pay reverence. Seeing that I love you I thus spare you, though I might write more sharply on his behalf: but I did not think myself competent for this, that being a convict I should order you as though I were an Apostle.

4. I have many deep thoughts in God: but I take the measure of myself, lest I perish in my boasting. For now I ought to be the more afraid and not to give heed to those that would puff me up: for they that say these things to me are a scourge to me. For though I desire to suffer, yet I know not whether I am worthy: for the envy of the devil is unseen indeed by many, but against me it wages the fiercer war. So then I crave gentleness, whereby the prince of this world is brought to nought.

5. Am I not able to write to you of heavenly things? But I fear lest I should cause you harm being babes. So bear with me, lest not being able to take them in, ye should be choked. For I myself also, albeit I am in bonds and can comprehend heavenly things and the arrays of the angels and the musterings of the principalities, things visible and things invisible—I myself am not yet by reason of this a disciple. For we lack many things, that God may not be lacking to us.

6. I exhort you therefore—yet not I, but the love of Jesus Christ—take ye only Christian food, and abstain from strange herbage, which is heresy: for these men do even mingle poison with Jesus Christ, imposing upon others by a show of honesty, like persons administering a deadly drug with honied wine, so that one who knoweth it not, fearing nothing, drinketh in death with a baneful delight.

7. Be ye therefore on your guard against such men. And this will surely be, if ye be not puffed up and if ye be inseparable from [God] Jesus Christ and from the bishop and from the ordinances of the Apostles. He that is within the sanctuary is clean; but he that is without the sanctuary is not clean, that is, he that doeth aught without the bishop and presbytery and deacons, this man is not clean in his conscience.

8. Not indeed that I have known of any such thing among you, but I keep watch over you betimes, as my beloved, for I foresee the snares of the devil. Do ye therefore arm yourselves with gentleness and recover yourselves in faith which is the flesh of the Lord, and in love which is the blood of Jesus Christ. Let none of you bear a grudge against his neighbour. Give no occasion to the Gentiles, lest by reason of a few foolish men the godly multitude be blasphemed: for *Woe unto him through whom My name is vainly blasphemed before some.*

9. Be ye deaf therefore, when any man speaketh to you apart from Jesus Christ, who was of the race of David, who was the Son of Mary, who was truly born and ate and drank, was truly persecuted under Pontius Pilate, was truly crucified and died in the sight of those in heaven and those on earth and those under the earth; who moreover was truly raised from the dead, His Father having raised Him, who in the like fashion will so raise us also who believe on Him—His Father, I say, will raise us—in Christ Jesus, apart from whom we have not true life.

10. But if it were as certain persons who are godless, that is unbelievers, say, that He suffered only in semblance, being themselves mere semblance, why am I in bonds? And why also do I desire to fight with wild beasts? So I die in vain. Truly then I lie against the Lord.

11. Shun ye therefore those vile offshoots that gender a deadly fruit, whereof if a man taste, forthwith he dieth. For these men are not the Father's planting: for if they had been, they would have been

seen to be branches of the Cross, and their fruit imperishable—the Cross whereby He through His passion inviteth us, being His members. Now it cannot be that a head should be found without members, seeing that God promiseth union, and this union is Himself.

12. I salute you from Smyrna, together with the churches of God that are present with me ; men who refreshed me in all ways both in flesh and in spirit. My bonds exhort you, which for Jesus Christ's sake I bear about, entreating that I may attain unto God ; abide ye in your concord and in prayer one with another. For it becometh you severally, and more especially the presbyters, to cheer the soul of your bishop unto the honour of the Father [and to the honour] of Jesus Christ and of the Apostles. I pray that ye may hearken unto me in love, lest I be for a testimony against you by having so written. And pray ye also for me who have need of your love in the mercy of God, that I may be vouchsafed the lot which I am eager to attain, to the end that I be not found reprobate.

13. The love of the Smyrnæans and Ephesians saluteth you. Remember in your prayers the church which is in Syria ; whereof [also] I am not worthy to be called a member, being the very last of them. Fare ye well in Jesus Christ, submitting yourselves to the bishop as to the commandment, and likewise also to the presbytery ; and each of you severally love one another with undivided heart. My spirit is offered up for you, not only now, but also when I shall attain unto God. For I am still in peril ; but the Father is faithful in Jesus Christ to fulfil my petition and yours. May we be found unblameable in Him.

4.

TO THE ROMANS

IGNATIUS, who is also Theophorus, unto her that hath found mercy in the bountifulness of the Father Most High and of Jesus Christ His only Son ; to the church that is beloved and enlightened through the will of Him who willed all things that are, by faith and love towards Jesus Christ our God ; even unto her that hath the presidency in the country of the region of the Romans, being worthy of God, worthy of honour, worthy of felicitation, worthy of praise, worthy of success, worthy in purity, and having the presidency of love, walking in the law of Christ and bearing the Father's name; which church also I salute in the name of Jesus Christ the Son of the Father; unto them that in flesh and spirit are united unto His every commandment, being filled with the grace of God without wavering, and filtered clear from every foreign stain; abundant greeting in Jesus Christ our God in blamelessness.

1. Forasmuch as in answer to my prayer to God it hath been granted me to see your godly countenances, so that I have obtained even more than I asked; for wearing bonds in Christ Jesus I hope to salute you, if it be the Divine will that I should be counted worthy to reach unto the end; for the beginning verily is well ordered, if so be I shall attain unto the goal, that I may receive mine inheritance without hindrance. For I dread your very love, lest it do me an injury; for it is easy for you to do what ye will, but for me it is difficult to attain unto God, unless ye shall spare me.

2. For I would not have you to be men-pleasers but to please God, as indeed ye do please Him. For neither shall I myself ever find an opportunity such as this to attain unto God, nor can ye, if ye be silent, win the credit of any nobler work. For, if ye be silent and leave me alone, I am a word of God; but if ye desire my flesh, then shall I be again a mere cry. [Nay] grant me nothing more than that I be poured out a libation to God, while there is still an altar ready; that forming yourselves into a chorus in love ye may sing to the Father in Jesus Christ, for that God hath vouchsafed that the bishop from Syria should be found in the West, having summoned him from the East. It is good to set from the world unto God, that I may rise unto Him.

3. Ye never grudged any one; ye were the instructors of others. And my desire is that those lessons shall hold good which as teachers ye enjoin. Only pray that I may have power within and without, so that I may not only say it but also desire it; that I may not only be called a Christian, but also be found one. For if I shall be found so, then can I also be called one, and be faithful then, when I am no more visible to the world. Nothing visible is good. For our God Jesus Christ, being in the Father, is the more plainly visible. The Work is not of persuasiveness, but Christianity is a thing of might, whensoever it is hated by the world.

4. I write to all the churches, and I bid all men know, that of my own free will I die for God, unless ye should hinder me. I exhort

you, be ye not an unseasonable kindness to me. Let me be given to the wild beasts, for through them I can attain unto God. I am God's wheat, and I am ground by the teeth of wild beasts that I may be found pure bread [of Christ]. Rather entice the wild beasts, that they may become my sepulchre and may leave no part of my body behind, so that I may not, when I am fallen asleep, be burdensome to any one. Then shall I be truly a disciple of Jesus Christ, when the world shall not so much as see my body. Supplicate the Lord for me, that through these instruments I may be found a sacrifice to God. I do not enjoin you, as Peter and Paul did. They were Apostles, I am a convict; they were free, but I am a slave to this very hour. Yet if I shall suffer, then am I a freed-man of Jesus Christ, and I shall rise free in Him. Now I am learning in my bonds to put away every desire.

5. From Syria even unto Rome I fight with wild beasts, by land and sea, by night and by day, being bound amidst ten leopards, even a company of soldiers, who only wax worse when they are kindly treated. Howbeit through their wrong doings I become more completely a disciple; *yet am I not hereby justified.* May I have joy of the beasts that have been prepared for me; and I pray that I may find them prompt; nay I will entice them that they may devour me promptly, not as they have done to some, refusing to touch them through fear. Yea though of themselves they should not be willing while I am ready, I myself will force them to it. Bear with me. I know what is expedient for me. Now am I beginning to be a disciple. May naught of things visible and things invisible envy me; that I may attain unto Jesus Christ. Come fire and cross and grapplings with wild beasts, [cuttings and manglings,] wrenching of bones, hacking of limbs, crushings of my whole body, come cruel tortures of the devil to assail me. Only be it mine to attain unto Jesus Christ.

6 The farthest bounds of the universe shall profit me nothing, neither the kingdoms of this world. It is good for me to die for Jesus Christ rather than to reign over the farthest bounds of the earth. Him I seek, who died on our behalf; Him I desire, who rose again [for our sake]. The pangs of a new birth are upon me. Bear with me, brethren. Do not hinder me from living; do not desire my death. Bestow not on the world one who desireth to be God's, neither allure him with material things. Suffer me to receive the pure light. When I am come thither, then shall I be a man. Permit me to be an imitator of the passion of my God. If any man hath Him within himself,

let him understand what I desire, and let him have fellow-feeling with me, for he knoweth the things which straiten me.

7. The prince of this world would fain tear me in pieces and corrupt my mind to Godward. Let not any of you therefore who are near abet him. Rather stand ye on my side, that is on God's side. Speak not of Jesus Christ and withal desire the world. Let not envy have a home in you. Even though I myself, when I am with you, should beseech you, obey me not; but rather give credence to these things which I write to you. [For] I write to you in the midst of life, yet lusting after death. My lust hath been crucified, and there is no fire of material longing in me, but only water living †and speaking† in me, saying within me, Come to the Father. I have no delight in the food of corruption or in the delights of this life. I desire the bread of God, which is the flesh of Christ who was of the seed of David; and for a draught I desire His blood, which is love incorruptible.

8. I desire no longer to live after the manner of men; and this shall be, if ye desire it. Desire ye, that ye yourselves also may be desired. In a brief letter I beseech you; believe me. And Jesus Christ shall make manifest unto you these things, that I speak the truth—Jesus Christ, the unerring mouth in whom the Father hath spoken [truly]. Entreat ye for me, that I may attain [through the Holy Spirit]. I write not unto you after the flesh, but after the mind of God. If I shall suffer, it was your desire; if I shall be rejected, it was your hatred.

9. Remember in your prayers the church which is in Syria, which hath God for its shepherd in my stead. Jesus Christ alone shall be its bishop—He and your love. But for myself I am ashamed to be called one of them; for neither am I worthy, being the very last of them and an untimely birth: but I have found mercy that I should be some one, if so be I shall attain unto God. My spirit saluteth you, and the love of the churches which received me in the name of Jesus Christ, not as a mere wayfarer: for even those churches which did not lie on my route after the flesh went before me from city to city.

10. Now I write these things to you from Smyrna by the hand of the Ephesians who are worthy of all felicitation. And Crocus also, a name very dear to me, is with me, with many others besides.

As touching those who went before me from Syria to Rome unto the glory of God, I believe that ye have received instructions; whom also apprise that I am near; for they all are worthy of God and of you, and it becometh you to refresh them in all things. These things I write to you on the 9th before the Kalends of September. Fare ye well unto the end in the patient waiting for Jesus Christ.

5.

TO THE PHILADELPHIANS

IGNATIUS, who is also Theophorus, to the church of God the Father and of Jesus Christ, which is in Philadelphia of Asia, which hath found mercy and is firmly established in the concord of God and rejoiceth in the passion of our Lord and in His resurrection without wavering, being fully assured in all mercy; which church I salute in the blood of Jesus Christ, that is eternal and abiding joy; more especially if they be at one with the bishop and the presbyters who are with him, and with the deacons that have been appointed according to the mind of Jesus Christ, whom after His own will He confirmed and established by His Holy Spirit.

1. This your bishop I have found to hold the ministry which pertaineth to the common weal, not of himself or through men, nor yet for vain glory, but in the love of God the Father and the Lord Jesus Christ. And I am amazed at his forbearance; whose silence is more powerful than others' speech. For he is attuned in harmony with the commandments, as a lyre with its strings. Wherefore my soul blesseth his godly mind, for I have found that it is virtuous and perfect —even the imperturbable and calm temper which he hath, while living in all godly forbearance.

2. As children therefore [of the light] of the truth, shun division and wrong doctrines; and where the shepherd is, there follow ye as sheep. For many specious wolves with baneful delights lead captive the runners in God's race; but, where ye are at one, they will find no place.

3. Abstain from noxious herbs, which are not the husbandry of Jesus Christ, because they are not the planting of the Father. Not that I have found division among you, but filtering. For as many as are of God and of Jesus Christ, they are with the bishop; and as many as shall repent and enter into the unity of the Church, these also

shall be of God, that they may be living after Jesus Christ. Be not deceived, my brethren. If any man followeth one that maketh a schism, *he doth not inherit the kingdom of God.* If any man walketh in strange doctrine, he hath no fellowship with the passion.

4. Be ye careful therefore to observe one eucharist (for there is one flesh of our Lord Jesus Christ and one cup unto union in His blood; there is one altar, as there is one bishop, together with the presbytery and the deacons my fellow-servants), that whatsoever ye do, ye may do it after God.

5. My brethren, my heart overfloweth altogether in love towards you; and rejoicing above measure I watch over your safety; yet not I, but Jesus Christ, wearing whose bonds I am the more afraid, because I am not yet perfected. But your prayer will make me perfect [unto God], that I may attain unto the inheritance wherein I have found mercy, taking refuge in the Gospel as the flesh of Jesus and in the Apostles as the presbytery of the Church. Yea, and we love the prophets also, because they too pointed to the Gospel in their preaching and set their hope on Him and awaited Him; in whom also having faith they were saved in the unity of Jesus Christ, being worthy of all love and admiration as holy men, approved of Jesus Christ and numbered together in the Gospel of our common hope.

6. But if any one propound Judaism unto you, hear him not: for it is better to hear Christianity from a man who is circumcised than Judaism from one uncircumcised. But if either the one or the other speak not concerning Jesus Christ, I look on them as tombstones and graves of the dead, whereon are inscribed only the names of men. Shun ye therefore the wicked arts and plottings of the prince of this world, lest haply ye be crushed by his devices, and wax weak in your love. But assemble yourselves all together with undivided heart. And I give thanks to my God, that I have a good conscience in my dealings with you, and no man can boast either in secret or openly, that I was burdensome to any one in small things or in great. Yea and for all among whom I spoke, it is my prayer that they may not turn it into a testimony against themselves.

7. For even though certain persons desired to deceive me after the flesh, yet the spirit is not deceived, being from God; for *it knoweth whence it cometh and where it goeth,* and it searcheth out the hidden things. I cried out, when I was among you; I spake with a loud voice, with God's own voice, Give ye heed to the bishop and the

presbytery and deacons. Howbeit there were those who suspected me of saying this, because I knew beforehand of the division of certain persons. But He in whom I am bound is my witness that I learned it not from flesh of man; it was the preaching of the Spirit who spake on this wise; Do nothing without the bishop; keep your flesh as a temple of God; cherish union; shun divisions; be imitators of Jesus Christ, as He Himself also was of His Father.

8. I therefore did my own part, as a man composed unto union. But where there is division and anger, there God abideth not. Now the Lord forgiveth all men when they repent, if repenting they return to the unity of God and to the council of the bishop. I have faith in the grace of Jesus Christ, who shall strike off every fetter from you; and I entreat you, Do ye nothing in a spirit of factiousness but after the teaching of Christ. For I heard certain persons saying, If I find it not in the charters, I believe it not in the Gospel. And when I said to them, It is written, they answered me That is the question. But as for me, my charter is Jesus Christ, the inviolable charter is His cross and His death and His resurrection, and faith through Him; wherein I desire to be justified through your prayers.

9. The priests likewise were good, but better is the High-priest to whom is committed the holy of holies; for to Him alone are committed the hidden things of God; He Himself being the door of the Father, through which Abraham and Isaac and Jacob enter in, and the Prophets and the Apostles and the whole Church; all these things combine in the unity of God. But the Gospel hath a singular preeminence in the advent of the Saviour, even our Lord Jesus Christ, and His passion and resurrection. For the beloved Prophets in their preaching pointed to Him; but the Gospel is the completion of immortality. All things together are good, if ye believe through love.

10. Seeing that in answer to your prayer and to the tender sympathy which ye have in Christ Jesus, it hath been reported to me that the church which is in Antioch of Syria hath peace, it is becoming for you, as a church of God, to appoint a deacon to go thither as God's ambassador, that he may congratulate them when they are assembled together, and may glorify the Name. Blessed in Jesus Christ is he that shall be counted worthy of such a ministration; and ye yourselves shall be glorified. Now if ye desire it, it is not impossible for you to do this for the name of God; even as the churches which are nearest have sent bishops, and others presbyters and deacons.

11. But as touching Philo the deacon from Cilicia, a man of good report, who now also ministereth to me in the word of God, together with Rhaius Agathopus, an elect one who followeth me from Syria, having bidden farewell to this present life; the same who also bear witness to you—and I myself thank God on your behalf, because ye received them, as I trust the Lord will receive you. But may those who treated them with dishonour be redeemed through the grace of Jesus Christ. The love of the brethren which are in Troas saluteth you; from whence also I write to you by the hand of Burrhus, who was sent with me by the Ephesians and Smyrnæans as a mark of honour. The Lord shall honour them, even Jesus Christ, on whom their hope is set in flesh and soul and spirit, by faith, by love, by concord. Fare ye well in Christ Jesus our common hope.

6.

TO THE SMYRNÆANS

IGNATIUS, who is also Theophorus, to the church of God the Father and of Jesus Christ the Beloved, which hath been mercifully endowed with every grace, being filled with faith and love and lacking in no grace, most reverend and bearing holy treasures; to the church which is in Smyrna of Asia, in a blameless spirit and in the word of God abundant greeting.

1. I give glory to Jesus Christ the God who bestowed such wisdom upon you; for I have perceived that ye are established in faith immovable, being as it were nailed on the cross of the Lord Jesus Christ, in flesh and in spirit, and firmly grounded in love in the blood of Christ, fully persuaded as touching our Lord that He is truly of the race of David according to the flesh, but Son of God by the Divine will and power, truly born of a virgin and baptized by John that *all righteousness might be fulfilled* by Him, truly nailed up in the flesh for our sakes under Pontius Pilate and Herod the tetrarch (of which fruit are we—that is, of His most blessed passion); that *He might set up an ensign* unto all the ages through His resurrection, for His saints and faithful people, whether among Jews or among Gentiles, in one body of His Church.

2. For He suffered all these things for our sakes [that we might be saved]; and He suffered truly, as also He raised Himself truly ; not as

certain unbelievers say, that He suffered in semblance, being themselves mere semblance. And according as their opinions are, so shall it happen to them, for they are without body and demon-like.

3. For I know and believe that He was in the flesh even after the resurrection; and when He came to Peter and his company, He said to them, *Lay hold and handle me, and see that I am not a demon without body.* And straightway they touched Him, and they believed, being joined unto His flesh and His blood. Wherefore also they despised death, nay they were found superior to death. And after His resurrection He [both] ate with them and drank with them as one in the flesh, though spiritually He was united with the Father.

4. But these things I warn you, dearly beloved, knowing that ye yourselves are so minded. Howbeit I watch over you betimes to protect you from wild beasts in human form—men whom not only should ye not receive, but, if it were possible, not so much as meet [them]; only pray ye for them, if haply they may repent. This indeed is difficult, but Jesus Christ, our true life, hath power over it. For if these things were done by our Lord in semblance, then am I also a prisoner in semblance. And why then have I delivered myself over to death, unto fire, unto sword, unto wild beasts? But near to the sword, near to God; in company with wild beasts, in company with God. Only let it be in the name of Jesus Christ, so that we may suffer together with Him. I endure all things, seeing that He Himself enableth me, who is perfect Man.

5. But certain persons ignorantly deny Him, or rather have been denied by Him, being advocates of death rather than of the truth; and they have not been persuaded by the prophecies nor by the law of Moses, nay nor even to this very hour by the Gospel, nor by the sufferings of each of us severally; for they are of the same mind also concerning us. For what profit is it [to me], if a man praiseth me, but blasphemeth my Lord, not confessing that He was a bearer of flesh? Yet he that affirmeth not this, doth thereby deny Him altogether, being himself a bearer of a corpse. But their names, being unbelievers, I have not thought fit to record in writing; nay, far be it from me even to remember them, until they repent and return to the passion, which is our resurrection.

6. Let no man be deceived. Even the heavenly beings and the glory of the angels and the rulers visible and invisible, if they believe not in the blood of Christ [who is God], judgment awaiteth them also.

He that receiveth let him receive. Let not office puff up any man; for faith and love are all in all, and nothing is preferred before them. But mark ye those who hold strange doctrine touching the grace of Jesus Christ which came to us, how that they are contrary to the mind of God. They have no care for love, none for the widow, none for the orphan, none for the afflicted, none for the prisoner, none for the hungry or thirsty. They abstain from eucharist (thanksgiving) and prayer, because they allow not that the eucharist is the flesh of our Saviour Jesus Christ, which flesh suffered for our sins, and which the Father of His goodness raised up.

7. They therefore that gainsay the good gift of God perish by their questionings. But it were expedient for them to have love, that they may also rise again. It is therefore meet that ye should abstain from such, and not speak of them either privately or in public; but should give heed to the Prophets, and especially to the Gospel, wherein the passion is shown unto us and the resurrection is accomplished.

8. [But] shun divisions, as the beginning of evils. Do ye all follow your bishop, as Jesus Christ followed the Father, and the presbytery as the Apostles; and to the deacons pay respect, as to God's commandment. Let no man do aught of things pertaining to the Church apart from the bishop. Let that be held a valid eucharist which is under the bishop or one to whom he shall have committed it. Wheresoever the bishop shall appear, there let the people be; even as where Jesus may be, there is the universal Church. It is not lawful apart from the bishop either to baptize or to hold a love-feast; but whatsoever he shall approve, this is well-pleasing also to God; that everything which ye do may be sure and valid.

9. It is reasonable henceforth that we wake to soberness, while we have [still] time to repent and turn to God. It is good to recognise God and the bishop. He that honoureth the bishop is honoured of God; he that doeth aught without the knowledge of the bishop rendereth service to the devil. May all things therefore abound unto you in grace, for ye are worthy. Ye refreshed me in all things, and Jesus Christ shall refresh you. In my absence and in my presence ye cherished me. May God recompense you; for whose sake if ye endure all things, ye shall attain unto Him.

10. Philo and Rhaius Agathopus, who followed me in the cause of God, ye did well to receive as ministers of [Christ] God; who also give thanks to the Lord for you, because ye refreshed them in every

way. Nothing shall be lost to you. My spirit is devoted for you, as also are my bonds, which ye despised not, neither were ashamed of them. Nor shall He, who is perfect faithfulness, be ashamed of you, even Jesus Christ.

11. Your prayer sped forth unto the church which is in Antioch of Syria; whence coming a prisoner in most godly bonds I salute all men, though I am not worthy to belong to it, being the very last of them. By the Divine will was this vouchsafed to me, not of my own complicity, but by God's grace, which I pray may be given to me perfectly, that through your prayers I may attain unto God. Therefore that your work may be perfected both on earth and in heaven, it is meet that your church should appoint, for the honour of God, an ambassador of God that he may go as far as Syria and congratulate them because they are at peace, and have recovered their proper stature, and their proper bulk hath been restored to them. It seemed to me therefore a fitting thing that ye should send one of your own people with a letter, that he might join with them in giving glory for the calm which by God's will had overtaken them, and because they were already reaching a haven through your prayers. Seeing ye are perfect, let your counsels also be perfect; for if ye desire to do well, God is ready to grant the means.

12. The love of the brethren which are in Troas saluteth you; from whence also I write to you by the hand of Burrhus, whom ye sent with me jointly with the Ephesians your brethren. He hath refreshed me in all ways. And I would that all imitated him, for he is an ensample of the ministry of God. The Divine grace shall requite him in all things. I salute your godly bishop and your venerable presbytery [and] my fellow-servants the deacons, and all of you severally and in a body, in the name of Jesus Christ, and in His flesh and blood, in His passion and resurrection, which was both carnal and spiritual, in the unity of God and of yourselves. Grace to you, mercy, peace, patience, always.

13. I salute the households of my brethren with their wives and children, and the virgins who are called widows. I bid you farewell in the power of the Father. Philo, who is with me, saluteth you. I salute the household of Gavia, and I pray that she may be grounded in faith and love both of flesh and of spirit. I salute Alce, a name very dear to me, and Daphnus the incomparable, and Eutecnus, and all by name. Fare ye well in the grace of God.

7.

TO S. POLYCARP

IGNATIUS, who is also Theophorus, unto Polycarp who is bishop of the church of the Smyrnæans or rather who hath for his bishop God the Father and Jesus Christ, abundant greeting.

1. Welcoming thy godly mind which is grounded as it were on an immovable rock, I give exceeding glory that it hath been vouchsafed me to see thy blameless face, whereof I would fain have joy in God. I exhort thee in the grace wherewith thou art clothed to press forward in thy course and to exhort all men that they may be saved. Vindicate thine office in all diligence of flesh and of spirit. Have a care for union, than which there is nothing better. Bear all men, as the Lord also beareth thee. Suffer all men in love, as also thou doest. Give thyself to unceasing prayers. Ask for larger wisdom than thou hast. Be watchful, and keep thy spirit from slumbering. Speak to each man severally after the manner of God. Bear the maladies of all, as a perfect athlete. Where there is more toil, there is much gain.

2. If thou lovest good scholars, this is not thankworthy in thee. Rather bring the more pestilent to submission by gentleness. All wounds are not healed by the same salve. Allay sharp pains by fomentations. *Be thou prudent as the serpent* in all things *and guileless* always *as the dove.* Therefore art thou made of flesh and spirit, that thou mayest humour the things which appear before thine eyes; and as for the invisible things, pray thou that they may be revealed unto thee; that thou mayest be lacking in nothing, but mayest abound in every spiritual gift. The season requireth thee, as pilots require winds or as a storm-tossed mariner a haven, that it may attain unto God. Be sober, as God's athlete. The prize is incorruption and life eternal, concerning which thou also art persuaded. In all things I am devoted to thee—I and my bonds which thou didst cherish.

3. Let not those that seem to be plausible and yet teach strange doctrine dismay thee. Stand thou firm, as an anvil when it is smitten. It is the part of a great athlete to receive blows and be victorious. But especially must we for God's sake endure all things, that He also may endure us. Be thou more diligent than thou art. Mark the seasons.

Await Him that is above every season, the Eternal, the Invisible, who became visible for our sake, the Impalpable, the Impassible, who suffered for our sake, who endured in all ways for our sake.

4. Let not widows be neglected. After the Lord be thou their protector. Let nothing be done without thy consent; neither do thou anything without the consent of God, as indeed thou doest not. Be stedfast. Let meetings be held more frequently. Seek out all men by name. Despise not slaves, whether men or women. Yet let not these again be puffed up, but let them serve the more faithfully to the glory of God, that they may obtain a better freedom from God. Let them not desire to be set free at the public cost, lest they be found slaves of lust.

5. Flee evil arts, or rather hold thou discourse about these. Tell my sisters to love the Lord and to be content with their husbands in flesh and in spirit. In like manner also charge my brothers in the name of Jesus Christ to love their wives, *as the Lord loved the Church.* If any one is able to abide in chastity to the honour of the flesh of the Lord, let him so abide without boasting. If he boast, he is lost; and if it be known beyond the bishop, he is polluted. It becometh men and women too, when they marry, to unite themselves with the consent of the bishop, that the marriage may be after the Lord and not after concupiscence. Let all things be done to the honour of God.

6. Give ye heed to the bishop, that God also may give heed to you. I am devoted to those who are subject to the bishop, the presbyters, the deacons. May it be granted me to have my portion with them in the presence of God. Toil together one with another, struggle together, run together, suffer together, lie down together, rise up together, as God's stewards and assessors and ministers. Please the Captain in whose army ye serve, from whom also ye will receive your pay. Let none of you be found a deserter. Let your baptism abide with you as your shield; your faith as your helmet; your love as your spear; your patience as your body armour. Let your works be your deposits, that ye may receive your assets due to you. Be ye therefore long-suffering one with another in gentleness, as God is with you. May I have joy of you always.

7. Seeing that the church which is in Antioch of Syria hath peace, as it hath been reported to me, through your prayers, I myself also have been the more comforted since God hath banished my care; if so be I may through suffering attain unto God, that I may be found a disciple

through your intercession. It becometh thee, most blessed Polycarp, to call together a godly council and to elect some one among you who is very dear to you and zealous also, who shall be fit to bear the name of God's courier—to appoint him, I say, that he may go to Syria and glorify your zealous love unto the glory of God. A Christian hath no authority over himself, but giveth his time to God. This is God's work, and yours also, when ye shall complete it: for I trust in the Divine grace, that ye are ready for an act of well-doing which is meet for God. Knowing the fervour of your sincerity, I have exhorted you in a short letter.

8. Since I have not been able to write to all the churches, by reason of my sailing suddenly from Troas to Neapolis, as the Divine will enjoineth, thou shalt write to the churches in front, as one possessing the mind of God, to the intent that they also may do this same thing—let those who are able send messengers, and the rest letters by the persons who are sent by thee, that ye may be glorified by an ever memorable deed—for this is worthy of thee.

I salute all by name, and especially the wife of Epitropus with her whole household and her children's. I salute Attalus my beloved. I salute him that shall be appointed to go to Syria. Grace shall be with him always, and with Polycarp who sendeth him. I bid you farewell always in our God Jesus Christ, in whom abide ye in the unity and supervision of God. I salute Alce, a name very dear to me. Fare ye well in the Lord.

THE EPISTLE

OF

S. POLYCARP

THE EPISTLE OF S. POLYCARP

I

THE Epistle of Polycarp was written in reply to a communication from the Philippians. They had invited him to address words of exhortation to them (§ 3); they had requested him to forward by his own messenger the letter which they had addressed to the Syrian Church (§ 13); and they had asked him to send them any epistles of Ignatius which he might have in his hands (*ib.*).

This epistle is intimately connected with the letters and martyrdom of Ignatius himself. The Philippians had recently welcomed and escorted on their way certain saints who were in bonds (§ 1). From a later notice in the epistle it appears that Ignatius was one of these (§ 9). Two others besides are mentioned by name, Zosimus and Rufus (*ib.*). A not improbable conjecture makes these persons Bithynian Christians who had been sent by Pliny to Rome to be tried there and had joined Ignatius at Philippi. In this case they would be placed under the same escort with Ignatius, and proceed with him to Rome in the custody of the 'ten leopards' (Ign. *Rom.* 5). It is clear that Ignatius—probably by word of mouth—had given to the Philippians the same injunction which he gave to the churches generally (*Philad.* 10, *Smyrn.* 11, *Polyc.* 7), that they should send letters, and (where possible) representatives also, to congratulate the Church of Antioch on the restoration of peace. Hence the request of the Philippians, seconded by Ignatius himself, that Polycarp would forward their letter to Syria. It is plain likewise, that they had heard, either from Ignatius himself or from those about him, of the epistles which he had addressed to the Churches of Asia Minor, more especially to Smyrna. Hence their further petition that Polycarp would send them such of these letters as were in his possession. The visit of Ignatius had been recent—so recent indeed, that Polycarp, though he assumes that the saint has suffered martyrdom, is yet without any certain knowledge of the fact. He therefore asks the Philippians, who are some stages nearer to Rome than Smyrna, to communicate to him any information which they may have received respecting the saint and his companions (§ 13).

Beyond these references to Ignatius there is not much of personal matter in the letter. Polycarp refers to S. Paul's communications with the Philippians, both written and oral (§§ 3, 11). He mentions the fame of the Philippian Church in the primitive days of the Gospel, and he congratulates them on sustaining their early reputation (§§ 1, 11). Incidentally he states that the Philippians were converted to the Gospel before the Smyrnæans (§ 11)—a statement which entirely accords with the notices of the two churches in the New Testament.

The fair fame of the Philippian Church however had been sullied by the sin of one unworthy couple. Valens and his wife—the Ananias and Sapphira of the Philippian community—had been guilty of some act of greed, perhaps of fraud and dishonesty. Valens was one of their presbyters, and thus the church was more directly responsible for his crime. Polycarp expresses himself much grieved. Though the incident itself is only mentioned in one passage, it has plainly made a deep impression on him. The sin of avarice is denounced again and again in the body of the letter (§§ 2, 4, 6, 11).

The letter is sent by the hand of one Crescens. The sister of Crescens also, who purposes visiting Philippi, is commended to them (§ 14).

2

The authorities for the text are as follows.

(1) GREEK MANUSCRIPTS (G). These are nine in number (*Vaticanus* 859 [v], *Ottobonianus* 348 [o], *Florentinus Laur.* vii. 21 [f], *Parisiensis Graec.* 937 [p], *Casanatensis* G. v. 14 [c], *Theatinus* [t], *Neapolitanus Mus. Nat.* II. A. 17 [n], *Salmasianus* [s], *Andrius* [a]), and all belong to the same family, as appears from the fact that the Epistle of Polycarp runs on continuously into the Epistle of Barnabas without any break, the mutilated ending of Polycarp § 9 ἀποθανόντα καὶ δι' ἡμᾶς ὑπὸ being

followed by the mutilated beginning of Barnabas § 5 τὸν λαὸν τὸν και-
νὸν κ.τ.λ. Within this family however the MSS fall into two subdivisions : (1) *vopf*, all MSS in which the Epistle of Polycarp is attached
to the pseudo-Ignatian letters ; and (2) *ctna* (to which we may probably
add *s*), where it stands alone. In the first subdivision, *opf* have no
independent authority, being derived directly or indirectly from *v*. Of
the two subdivisions the former is slightly superior to the latter.

(2) LATIN VERSION (L). In the earlier part of the epistle this
version is sometimes useful for correcting the text of the extant Greek
MSS ; for, though very paraphrastic, it was made from an older form of
the Greek than these. But the two are closely allied, as appears from
the fact that this version is always found in connexion with the Latin
of the pseudo-Ignatian letters and seems to have been translated from
the same volume which contained them. For the latter part of the
epistle, from § 10 onward, it is the sole authority; with the exception
of portions of § 12, which are preserved in Syriac in passages of
Timotheus and Severus or elsewhere, and nearly the whole of § 13,
which is given by Eusebius in his *Ecclesiastical History*. The MSS of
which collations have been made for this part either by myself or by
others are nine in number (*Reginensis* 81 [r], *Trecensis* 412 [t], *Parisiensis* 1639, formerly *Colbertinus* 1039 [c], *Bruxellensis* 5510 [b], *Oxon.
Balliolensis* 229 [o], *Palatinus* 150 [p], *Florentinus Laur.* xxiii. 20 [f],
Vindobonensis 1068 [v], *Oxon. Magdalenensis* 78 [m]).

It will have been seen that, so far as regards the Greek and Latin
MSS, the Epistle of Polycarp is closely connected with the Long Recension of the Ignatian Epistles. This fact, if it had stood by itself, would
have thrown some discredit on the integrity of the text. It might have
been suspected that the same hand which interpolated the Ignatian
Epistles had tampered with this also. But the internal evidence, and
especially the allusiveness of the references to the Ignatian Epistles, is
decisive in favour of its genuineness. As regards external evidence,
not only does Irenæus, a pupil of Polycarp, allude to 'the very adequate
epistle of Polycarp written to the Philippians,' but the quotations of
Eusebius, Timotheus, and Severus, with the other Syriac fragments, are
a highly important testimony. They show that, wherever we have
opportunity of testing the text of the Greek and Latin copies, its general
integrity is vindicated.

THE EPISTLE OF S. POLYCARP

POLYCARP and the presbyters that are with him unto the Church of God which sojourneth at Philippi; mercy unto you and peace from God Almighty and Jesus Christ our Saviour be multiplied.

1. I rejoiced with you greatly in our Lord Jesus Christ, for that ye received the followers of the true Love and escorted them on their way, as befitted you—those men encircled in saintly bonds which are the diadems of them that be truly chosen of God and our Lord; and that the stedfast root of your faith which was famed from primitive times abideth until now and beareth fruit unto our Lord Jesus Christ, who endured to face even death for our sins, *whom God raised, having loosed the pangs of Hades; on whom, though ye saw Him not, ye believe with joy unutterable and full of glory;* unto which joy many desire to enter in; forasmuch as ye know that it is *by grace ye are saved, not of works,* but by the will of God through Jesus Christ.

2. *Wherefore gird up your loins and serve God in fear* and truth, forsaking the vain and empty talking and the error of the many, *for that ye have believed on Him that raised our Lord Jesus Christ from the dead and gave unto Him glory* and a throne on His right hand; unto whom all things were made subject that are in heaven and that are on the earth; to whom every creature that hath breath doeth service; who cometh as *judge of quick and dead;* whose blood God will require of them that are disobedient unto Him. Now *He that raised Him* from the dead *will raise us also;* if we do His will and walk in His commandments and love the things which He loved, abstaining from all unrighteousness, covetousness, love of money, evil speaking, false witness; *not rendering evil for evil or railing for railing* or blow for blow or cursing for cursing; but remembering the words which the Lord spake, as He taught; *Judge not that ye be not judged.*

Forgive, and it shall be forgiven to you. Have mercy that ye may receive mercy. With what measure ye mete, it shall be measured to you again; and again *Blessed are the poor and they that are persecuted for righteousness' sake, for theirs is the kingdom of God.*

3. These things, brethren, I write unto you concerning righteousness, not because I laid this charge upon myself, but because ye invited me. For neither am I, nor is any other like unto me, able to follow the wisdom of the blessed and glorious Paul, who when he came among you taught face to face with the men of that day the word which concerneth truth carefully and surely; who also, when he was absent, wrote a letter unto you, into the which if ye look diligently, ye shall be able to be builded up unto the faith given to you, *which is the mother of us all,* while hope followeth after and love goeth before—love toward God and Christ and toward our neighbour. For if any man be occupied with these, he hath fulfilled the commandment of righteousness; for he that hath love is far from all sin.

4. *But the love of money is the beginning of all troubles.* Knowing therefore that *we brought nothing into the world neither can we carry anything out,* let us arm ourselves with the armour of righteousness, and let us teach ourselves first to walk in the commandment of the Lord; and then our wives also, to walk in the faith that hath been given unto them and in love and purity, cherishing their own husbands in all truth and loving all men equally in all chastity, and to train their children in the training of the fear of God. Our widows must be sober-minded as touching the faith of the Lord, making intercession without ceasing for all men, abstaining from all calumny, evil speaking, false witness, love of money, and every evil thing, knowing that they are God's altar, and that all sacrifices are carefully inspected, and nothing escapeth Him either of their thoughts or intents or any of the secret things of the heart.

5. Knowing then that *God is not mocked,* we ought to walk worthily of His commandment and His glory. In like manner deacons should be blameless in the presence of His righteousness, as deacons of God and Christ and not of men; not calumniators, not double-tongued, not lovers of money, temperate in all things, compassionate, diligent, walking according to the truth of the Lord who became *a minister (deacon) of all.* For if we be well pleasing unto Him in this present world, we shall receive the future world also, according as He promised

us to raise us from the dead, and that if we conduct ourselves worthily of Him *we shall also reign with Him,* if indeed we have faith. In like manner also the younger men must be blameless in all things, caring for purity before everything and curbing themselves from every evil. For it is a good thing to refrain from lusts in the world, for every *lust warreth against the Spirit,* and *neither whoremongers nor effeminate persons nor defilers of themselves with men shall inherit the kingdom of God,* neither they that do untoward things. Wherefore it is right to abstain from all these things, submitting yourselves to the presbyters and deacons as to God and Christ. The virgins must walk in a blameless and pure conscience.

6. And the presbyters also must be compassionate, merciful towards all men, *turning back the sheep that are gone astray,* visiting all the infirm, not neglecting a widow or an orphan or a poor man : but *providing always for that which is honorable in the sight of God and of men,* abstaining from all anger, respect of persons, unrighteous judgment, being far from all love of money, not quick to believe anything against any man, not hasty in judgment, knowing that we all are debtors of sin. If then we entreat the Lord that He would forgive us, we also ought to forgive : for we are before the eyes of our Lord and God, and we must *all stand at the judgment-seat of Christ,* and *each man must give an account of himself.* Let us therefore so serve Him with fear and all reverence, as He himself gave commandment and the Apostles who preached the Gospel to us and the prophets who proclaimed beforehand the coming of our Lord ; being zealous as touching that which is good, abstaining from offences and from the false brethren and from them that bear the name of the Lord in hypocrisy, who lead foolish men astray.

7. For every one *who shall not confess that Jesus Christ is come in the flesh, is antichrist:* and whosoever shall not confess the testimony of the Cross, is of the devil ; and whosoever shall pervert the oracles of the Lord to his own lusts and say that there is neither resurrection nor judgment, that man is the first-born of Satan. Wherefore let us forsake the vain doing of the many and their false teachings, and turn unto the word which was delivered unto us from the beginning, *being sober unto prayer* and constant in fastings, entreating the all-seeing God with supplications that He *bring us not into temptation,* according as the Lord said, *The spirit indeed is willing, but the flesh is weak.*

8. Let us therefore without ceasing hold fast by our hope and by the earnest of our righteousness, which is Jesus Christ who *took up our sins in His own body upon the tree, who did no sin, neither was guile found in His mouth,* but for our sakes He endured all things, that we might live in Him. Let us therefore become imitators of His endurance; and if we should suffer for His name's sake, let us glorify Him. For He gave this example to us in His own person, and we believed this.

9. I exhort you all therefore to be obedient unto the word of righteousness and to practise all endurance, which also ye saw with your own eyes in the blessed Ignatius and Zosimus and Rufus, yea and in others also who came from among yourselves, as well as in Paul himself and the rest of the Apostles; being persuaded that all these *ran not in vain* but in faith and righteousness, and that they are in their due place in the presence of the Lord, with whom also they suffered. For they *loved not the present world,* but Him that died for our sakes and was raised by God for us.

10. Stand fast therefore in these things and follow the example of the Lord, *being firm in the faith* and *immovable, in love of the brotherhood kindly affectioned one to another,* partners with the truth, *forestalling one another* in the gentleness of the Lord, despising no man. *When ye are able to do good,* defer it not, for *Pitifulness delivereth from death. Be ye all subject one to another, having your conversation* unblameable *among the Gentiles, that from your good works* both ye may receive praise and the Lord may not be blasphemed in you. But *woe to him through whom the name of the Lord is blasphemed.* Therefore teach all men soberness, in which ye yourselves also walk.

11. I was exceedingly grieved for Valens, who aforetime was a presbyter among you, because he is so ignorant of the office which was given unto him. I warn you therefore that ye refrain from covetousness, and that ye be pure and truthful. Refrain from all evil. But he who cannot govern himself in these things, how doth he enjoin this upon another? If a man refrain not from covetousness, he shall be defiled by idolatry, and shall be judged as one of the Gentiles who *know not the judgment of the Lord. Nay, know we not, that the saints shall judge the world,* as Paul teacheth? But I have not found any such thing in you, neither have heard thereof, among whom the blessed Paul laboured, who were his *letters* in the beginning. For *he boasteth of you in* all those *churches* which alone at that time knew God; for we

knew Him not as yet. Therefore I am exceedingly grieved for him and for his wife, unto whom may the Lord grant true repentance. Be ye therefore yourselves also sober herein, and *hold not such as enemies,* but restore them as frail and erring members, that ye may save the whole body of you. For so doing, ye do edify one another.

12. For I am persuaded that ye are well trained in the sacred writings, and nothing is hidden from you. But to myself this is not granted. Only, as it is said in these scriptures, *Be ye angry and sin not,* and *Let not the sun set on your wrath.* Blessed is he that remembereth this; and I trust that this is in you. Now may the God and Father of our Lord Jesus Christ, and the eternal High-priest Himself, the [Son of] God Jesus Christ, build you up in faith and truth, and in all gentleness and in all avoidance of wrath and in forbearance and long suffering and in patient endurance and in purity; and may He grant unto you a lot and portion among His saints, and to us with you, and to all that are under heaven, who shall believe on our Lord and God Jesus Christ and on His Father *that raised Him from the dead. Pray for all the saints.* Pray also *for kings* and powers and princes, and *for them that persecute* and hate *you,* and for *the enemies of the cross,* that your fruit may be *manifest among all men,* that ye may be perfect in Him.

13. Ye wrote to me, both ye yourselves and Ignatius, asking that if any one should go to Syria he might carry thither the letters from you. And this I will do, if I get a fit opportunity, either I myself, or he whom I shall send to be ambassador on your behalf also. The letters of Ignatius which were sent to us by him, and others as many as we had by us, we send unto you, according as ye gave charge; the which are subjoined to this letter; from which ye will be able to gain great advantage. For they comprise faith and endurance and every kind of edification, which pertaineth unto our Lord. Moreover concerning Ignatius himself and those that were with him, if ye have any sure tidings, certify us.

14. I write these things to you by Crescens, whom I commended to you recently and now commend unto you: for he hath walked blamelessly with us; and I believe also with you in like manner. But ye shall have his sister commended, when she shall come to you. Fare ye well in the Lord Jesus Christ in grace, ye and all yours. Amen.

THE MARTYRDOM

OF

S. POLYCARP

THE MARTYRDOM OF POLYCARP

I

THE document which gives an account of Polycarp's martyrdom
is in the form of a letter addressed by the Church of Smyrna
to the Church of Philomelium.   It was however intended for much
wider circulation, and at the close (§ 20) directions are given to secure
its being so circulated.   The letter seems to have been written shortly
after the martyrdom itself, which happened A.D. 155 or 156.   It consists of two parts, (1) the main body of the letter ending with the
twentieth chapter, and (2) a number of supplementary paragraphs,
comprising the twenty-first and twenty-second chapters.   In point of
form these supplementary paragraphs are separable from the rest of the
letter.   Indeed, as Eusebius, our chief witness to the genuineness of
the documents, ends his quotations and paraphrases before he reaches
the close of the main body of the letter, we cannot say confidently
whether he had or had not the supplementary paragraphs.   The
genuineness of the two parts therefore must be considered separately.

For the genuineness of the main document there is abundant
evidence.   A quarter of a century after the occurrence Irenæus and
a little later Polycrates bear testimony to the fact of Polycarp's
martyrdom.   Further the Letter of the Gallican Churches (c. A.D. 177)
presents striking coincidences with the language of the Letter of the
Smyrnæans, and unless several points of resemblance are accidental,
Lucian in his account of Peregrinus Proteus (c. A.D. 165) must have
been acquainted with the document.   At the beginning of the fourth
century Eusebius directly refers to it in his Chronicon, and again in
his Ecclesiastical History (iv. 15), where he quotes and paraphrases
nearly the whole of it, intimating that it was the earliest written record

of a martyrdom with which he was acquainted. At the close of the same century the author of the Pionian Life of Polycarp inserts the letter in his work. The internal evidence likewise is clearly in favour of the genuineness; and the adverse argument based upon the miraculous element in the story falls to the ground when the incident of the dove (§ 16) is proved to be a later interpolation.

The supplementary paragraphs present a more difficult problem. They fall into three parts, separate in form the one from the other, and not improbably written by different hands; (i) The Chronological Appendix (§ 21); (ii) The Commendatory Postscript (§ 22. 1); (iii) The History of the Transmission (§ 22. 2, 3).

The first of these closes with a paragraph which is copied from the close of the Epistle of S. Clement, just as the opening of the Smyrnæan Letter is modelled on the opening of S. Clement's Epistle. The obligation being the same in kind at the beginning and at the end of the letter, the obvious inference is that they were penned by the same hand. And when the historical references contained in this appendix are found upon examination not only not to contradict history, but, as in the case of Philip the Trallian, to be confirmed by fresh accessions to our knowledge of the archæology and chronology of the age, the conclusion becomes irresistible that § 21 formed part of the original document.

The Commendatory Postscript is omitted in the Moscow MS and in the Latin version, but it may well have been a postscript added by the Philomelian Church, when they forwarded copies of the letter, as they were charged to do (§ 20), to churches more distant from Smyrna than themselves.

The History of the Transmission occurs in an expanded form in the Moscow MS, but in each edition it ends with a note purporting to be written by one Pionius. He tells us that he copied it from the transcript of the last-mentioned transcriber, and that Polycarp revealed its locality to him in a vision of which he promises to give an account in the sequel. Now the Acts are extant of a Pionius who was martyred under Decius (A.D. 250) while celebrating the birthday of Polycarp. There is also a Life of Polycarp extant (incorporating this very Letter of the Smyrnæans), which purports to have been written by this Pionius, but is manifestly the work of a forger of the fifth century. This life is incomplete, otherwise doubtless it would have contained the account of the vision of Pionius promised in the sequel. The writer of the Pionian Life is therefore the author of the History of the Transmission. One further fact remains to be recorded. Not only do the Pionian Life and the History of the Transmission appeal without scruple to ancient documents which have no existence. They abound largely in the supernatural. Now our extant MSS of the Smyrnæan Epistle have the Pionian postscript and therefore represent the Pionian edition of that Letter. Eusebius alone of all extant authorities is prior to the false Pionius and gives an independent text. Now our spurious Pionius was before all things a miracle-monger. Among other miracles he relates that on the eve of Polycarp's appointment to the episcopate a dove hovered round his head. So also in the Letter of the Smyrnæans a dove is found leaving his body when his spirit is wafted to heaven (§ 16). But this miracle appears only in the Pionian copies, not in Eusebius. Moreover, by the abruptness of its appearance an interpolation is suggested. Is it not the same dove which appears on the two occasions, and was it not uncaged and let fly by the same hand? We cannot resist the suspicion that our spurious Pionius was responsible for both these appearances.

2

The authorities for the text are threefold.

1. The GREEK MANUSCRIPTS [G], five in number, viz. (1) *Mosquensis* 160 (now 159) [m] which omits the first paragraph § 22 and amplifies the remaining part of this same chapter. This, though of the thirteenth century, is the most important of the Greek manuscripts. (2) *Barroccianus* 238 [b] in the Bodleian Library, an eleventh century MS from which Ussher derived his text. (3) *Paris. Bibl. Nat. Graec.* 1452 [p] of the tenth century, called by Halloix *Mediceus*. (4) *Vindob. Hist. Graec. Eccl.* iii. [v] an eleventh or early twelfth century MS betraying marks of an arbitrary literary revision; and (5) *S. Sep. Hierosol.* 1 fol. 136 [s] a tenth century MS of the same group as bpv, discovered quite recently in the Library of the Holy Sepulchre at Jerusalem by Professor Rendel Harris.

2. EUSEBIUS [E]. The extracts found in *Hist. Eccl.* iv. 15; not only the earliest, but also the most valuable authority.

3. The LATIN VERSION [L] in three forms; (*a*) as given in Rufinus' translation of Eusebius, which is probably the version of the martyrdom read, as we learn from Gregory of Tours that it was read, in the Churches of Gaul; (*b*) an independent Latin Version very loose and paraphrastic; (*c*) a combination of the two preceding forms. The MSS of the Latin Version are numerous.

There are also a Syriac Version and a Coptic Version in the Memphitic dialect; but both of these, like the Rufinian form, are made not from the document itself, but from the account in Eusebius. They do not therefore constitute fresh authorities.

LETTER OF THE SMYRNÆANS

LETTER OF THE SMYRNÆANS

THE CHURCH OF GOD which sojourneth at Smyrna to the Church of God which sojourneth in Philomelium and to all the brotherhoods of the holy and universal Church sojourning in every place ; mercy and peace and love from God the Father and our Lord Jesus Christ be multiplied.

1. We write unto you, brethren, an account of what befel those that suffered martyrdom and especially the blessed Polycarp, who stayed the persecution, having as it were set his seal upon it by his martyrdom. For nearly all the foregoing events came to pass that the Lord might show us once more an example of martyrdom which is conformable to the Gospel. For he lingered that he might be delivered up, even as the Lord did, to the end that we too might be imitators of him, *not looking* only *to that which concerneth ourselves, but also to that which concerneth our neighbours*. For it is the office of true and stedfast love, not only to desire that oneself be saved, but all the brethren also.

2. Blessed therefore and noble are all the martyrdoms which have taken place according to the will of God (for it behoveth us to be very scrupulous and to assign to God the power over all things). For who could fail to admire their nobleness and patient endurance and loyalty to the Master? seeing that when they were so torn by lashes that the mechanism of their flesh was visible even as far as the inward veins and arteries, they endured patiently, so that the very bystanders had pity and wept ; while they themselves reached such a pitch of bravery that none of them uttered a cry or a groan, thus showing to us all that at that hour the martyrs of Christ being tortured were absent from the flesh, or rather that the Lord was standing by and conversing with them. And giving heed unto the grace of Christ they despised the tortures of

this world, purchasing at the cost of one hour a release from eternal punishment. And they found the fire of their inhuman torturers cold : for they set before their eyes the escape from the eternal fire which is never quenched; while with the eyes of their heart they gazed upon the good things which are reserved for those that endure patiently, things *which neither ear hath heard nor eye hath seen, neither have they entered into the heart of man*, but were shown by the Lord to them, for they were no longer men but angels already. And in like manner also those that were condemned to the wild beasts endured fearful punishments, being made to lie on sharp shells and buffeted with other forms of manifold tortures, that the devil might, if possible, by the persistence of the punishment bring them to a denial; for he tried many wiles against them.

3. But thanks be to God; for He verily prevailed against all. For the right noble Germanicus encouraged their timorousness through the constancy which was in him; and he fought with the wild beasts in a signal way. For when the proconsul wished to prevail upon him and bade him have pity on his youth, he used violence and dragged the wild beast towards him, desiring the more speedily to obtain a release from their unrighteous and lawless life. So after this all the multitude, marvelling at the bravery of the God-beloved and God-fearing people of the Christians, raised a cry, 'Away with the atheists; let search be made for Polycarp.'

4. But one man, Quintus by name, a Phrygian newly arrived from Phrygia, when he saw the wild beasts, turned coward. He it was who had forced himself and some others to come forward of their own free will. This man the proconsul by much entreaty persuaded to swear the oath and to offer incense. For this cause therefore, brethren, we praise not those who deliver themselves up, since the Gospel doth not so teach us.

5. Now the glorious Polycarp at the first, when he heard it, so far from being dismayed, was desirous of remaining in town; but the greater part persuaded him to withdraw. So he withdrew to a farm not far distant from the city; and there he stayed with a few companions, doing nothing else night and day but praying for all men and for the churches throughout the world; for this was his constant habit. And while praying he falleth into a trance three days before his apprehension; and he saw his pillow burning with fire. And he turned and said unto those that were with him : 'It must needs be that I shall be burned alive.'

6. And as those that were in search of him persisted, he departed to another farm; and forthwith they that were in search of him came up; and not finding him, they seized two slave lads, one of whom confessed under torture; for it was impossible for him to lie concealed, seeing that the very persons who betrayed him were people of his own household. And the captain of the police, who chanced to have the very name, being called Herod, was eager to bring him into the stadium, that he himself might fulfil his appointed lot, being made a partaker with Christ, while they—his betrayers—underwent the punishment of Judas himself.

7. So taking the lad with them, on the Friday about the supper hour, the gendarmes and horsemen went forth with their accustomed arms, hastening *as against a robber*. And coming up in a body late in the evening, they found the man himself in bed in an upper chamber in a certain cottage; and though he might have departed thence to another place, he would not, saying, *The will of God be done*. So when he heard that they were come, he went down and conversed with them, the bystanders marvelling at his age and his constancy, and wondering how there should be so much eagerness for the apprehension of an old man like him. Thereupon forthwith he gave orders that a table should be spread for them to eat and drink at that hour, as much as they desired. And he persuaded them to grant him an hour that he might pray unmolested; and on their consenting, he stood up and prayed, being so full of the grace of God, that for two hours he could not hold his peace, and those that heard were amazed, and many repented that they had come against such a venerable old man.

8. But when at length he brought his prayer to an end, after remembering all who at any time had come in his way, small and great, high and low, and all the universal Church throughout the world, the hour of departure being come, they seated him on an ass and brought him into the city, it being a high sabbath. And he was met by Herod the captain of police and his father Nicetes, who also removed him to their carriage and tried to prevail upon him, seating themselves by his side and saying, 'Why what harm is there in saying, Cæsar is Lord, and offering incense', with more to this effect, 'and saving thyself?' But he at first gave them no answer. When however they persisted, he said, 'I am not going to do what ye counsel me.' Then they, failing to persuade him, uttered threatening words and made him dismount with speed, so that he bruised his shin, as he got down from the carriage.

And without even turning round, he went on his way promptly and with speed, as if nothing had happened to him, being taken to the stadium; there being such a tumult in the stadium that no man's voice could be so much as heard.

9.   But as Polycarp entered into the stadium, a voice came to him from heaven; 'Be strong, Polycarp, and play the man.' And no one saw the speaker, but those of our people who were present heard the voice. And at length, when he was brought up, there was a great tumult, for they heard that Polycarp had been apprehended. When then he was brought before him, the proconsul enquired whether he were the man. And on his confessing that he was, he tried to persuade him to a denial saying, 'Have respect to thine age,' and other things in accordance therewith, as it is their wont to say; 'Swear by the genius of Cæsar; repent and say, Away with the atheists.' Then Polycarp with solemn countenance looked upon the whole multitude of lawless heathen that were in the stadium, and waved his hand to them; and groaning and looking up to heaven he said, 'Away with the atheists.' But when the magistrate pressed him hard and said, 'Swear the oath, and I will release thee; revile the Christ,' Polycarp said, 'Fourscore and six years have I been His servant, and He hath done me no wrong. How then can I blaspheme my King who saved me?'

10.   But on his persisting again and saying, 'Swear by the genius of Cæsar,' he answered, 'If thou supposest vainly that I will swear by the genius of Cæsar, as thou sayest, and feignest that thou art ignorant who I am, hear thou plainly, I am a Christian. But if thou wouldest learn the doctrine of Christianity, assign a day and give me a hearing.' The proconsul said; 'Prevail upon the people.' But Polycarp said; 'As for thyself, I should have held thee worthy of discourse; for we have been taught to render, as is meet, to princes and authorities appointed by God such honour as does us no harm; but as for these, I do not hold them worthy, that I should defend myself before them.'

11.   Whereupon the proconsul said; 'I have wild beasts here and I will throw thee to them, except thou repent.' But he said, 'Call for them: for the repentance from better to worse is a change not permitted to us; but it is a noble thing to change from untowardness to righteousness.' Then he said to him again, 'I will cause thee to be consumed by fire, if thou despisest the wild beasts, unless thou repent.' But Polycarp said; 'Thou threatenest that fire which burneth for a season and after a little while is quenched: for thou art ignorant of the

fire of the future judgment and eternal punishment, which is reserved
for the ungodly.   But why delayest thou?   Come, do what thou wilt.'

12.   Saying these things and more besides, he was inspired with
courage and joy, and his countenance was filled with grace, so that not
only did it not drop in dismay at the things which were said to him,
but on the contrary the proconsul was astounded and sent his own
herald to proclaim three times in the midst of the stadium, 'Polycarp
hath confessed himself to be a Christian.'   When this was proclaimed
by the herald, the whole multitude both of Gentiles and of Jews who
dwelt in Smyrna cried out with ungovernable wrath and with a loud
shout, 'This is the teacher of Asia, the father of the Christians, the
puller down of our gods, who teacheth numbers not to sacrifice nor
worship.'   Saying these things, they shouted aloud and asked the
Asiarch Philip to let a lion loose upon Polycarp.   But he said that it
was not lawful for him, since he had brought the sports to a close.
Then they thought fit to shout out with one accord that Polycarp
should be burned alive.   For it must needs be that the matter of the
vision should be fulfilled, which was shown him concerning his pillow,
when he saw it on fire while praying, and turning round he said
prophetically to the faithful who were with him, 'I must needs be
burned alive.'

13.   These things then happened with so great speed, quicker than
words could tell, the crowds forthwith collecting from the workshops and
baths timber and faggots, and the Jews more especially assisting in this
with zeal, as is their wont.   But when the pile was made ready, divesting
himself of all his upper garments and loosing his girdle, he endeavoured
also to take off his shoes, though not in the habit of doing this before,
because all the faithful at all times vied eagerly who should soonest
touch his flesh.   For he had been treated with all honour for his holy
life even before his gray hairs came.   Forthwith then the instruments
that were prepared for the pile were placed about him; and as they
were going likewise to nail him to the stake, he said; 'Leave me as I
am; for He that hath granted me to endure the fire will grant me also
to remain at the pile unmoved, even without the security which ye seek
from the nails.'

14.   So they did not nail him, but tied him.   Then he, placing his
hands behind him and being bound to the stake, like a noble ram out
of a great flock for an offering, a burnt sacrifice made ready and acceptable to God, looking up to heaven said; 'O Lord God Almighty,

the Father of Thy beloved and blessed Son Jesus Christ, through whom we have received the knowledge of Thee, the God of angels and powers and of all creation and of the whole race of the righteous, who live in Thy presence; I bless Thee for that Thou hast granted me this day and hour, that I might receive a portion amongst the number of martyrs in the cup of [Thy] Christ unto resurrection of eternal life, both of soul and of body, in the incorruptibility of the Holy Spirit. May I be received among these in Thy presence this day, as a rich and acceptable sacrifice, as Thou didst prepare and reveal it beforehand, and hast accomplished it, Thou that art the faithful and true God. For this cause, yea and for all things, I praise Thee, I bless Thee, I glorify Thee, through the eternal and heavenly High-priest, Jesus Christ, Thy beloved Son, through whom with Him and the Holy Spirit be glory both now [and ever] and for the ages to come. Amen.'

15. When he had offered up the Amen and finished his prayer, the firemen lighted the fire. And, a mighty flame flashing forth, we to whom it was given to see, saw a marvel, yea and we were preserved that we might relate to the rest what happened. The fire, making the appearance of a vault, like the sail of a vessel filled by the wind, made a wall round about the body of the martyr; and it was there in the midst, not like flesh burning, but like [a loaf in the oven or like] gold and silver refined in a furnace. For we perceived such a fragrant smell, as if it were the wafted odour of frankincense or some other precious spice.

16. So at length the lawless men, seeing that his body could not be consumed by the fire, ordered an executioner to go up to him and stab him with a dagger. And when he had done this, there came forth [a dove and] a quantity of blood, so that it extinguished the fire; and all the multitude marvelled that there should be so great a difference between the unbelievers and the elect. In the number of these was this man, the glorious martyr Polycarp, who was found an apostolic and prophetic teacher in our own time, a bishop of the holy Church which is in Smyrna. For every word which he uttered from his mouth was accomplished and will be accomplished.

17. But the jealous and envious Evil One, the adversary of the family of the righteous, having seen the greatness of his martyrdom and his blameless life from the beginning, and how he was crowned with the crown of immortality and had won a reward which none could gainsay, managed that not even his poor body should be taken away

by us, although many desired to do this and to touch his holy flesh. So he put forward Nicetes, the father of Herod and brother of Alce, to plead with the magistrate not to give up his body, 'lest,' so it was said, 'they should abandon the crucified one and begin to worship this man'—this being done at the instigation and urgent entreaty of the Jews, who also watched when we were about to take it from the fire, not knowing that it will be impossible for us either to forsake at any time the Christ who suffered for the salvation of the whole world of those that are saved—suffered though faultless for sinners—nor to worship any other.   For Him, being the Son of God, we adore, but the martyrs as disciples and imitators of the Lord we cherish as they deserve for their matchless affection towards their own King and Teacher.   May it be our lot also to be found partakers and fellow-disciples with them.

18.   The centurion therefore, seeing the opposition raised on the part of the Jews, set him in the midst and burnt him after their custom. And so we afterwards took up his bones which are more valuable than precious stones and finer than refined gold, and laid them in a suitable place; where the Lord will permit us to gather ourselves together, as we are able, in gladness and joy, and to celebrate the birth-day of his martyrdom for the commemoration of those that have already fought in the contest, and for the training and preparation of those that shall do so hereafter.

19.   So it befel the blessed Polycarp, who having with those from Philadelphia suffered martyrdom in Smyrna—twelve in all—is especially remembered more than the others by all men, so that he is talked of even by the heathen in every place: for he showed himself not only a notable teacher, but also a distinguished martyr, whose martyrdom all desire to imitate, seeing that it was after the pattern of the Gospel of Christ.   Having by his endurance overcome the unrighteous ruler in the conflict and so received the crown of immortality, he rejoiceth in company with the Apostles and all righteous men, and glorifieth the Almighty God and Father, and blesseth our Lord Jesus Christ, the saviour of our souls and helmsman of our bodies and shepherd of the universal Church which is throughout the world.

20.   Ye indeed required that the things which happened should be shown unto you at greater length: but we for the present have certified you as it were in a summary through our brother Marcianus. When then ye have informed yourselves of these things, send the letter

about likewise to the brethren which are farther off, that they also may glorify the Lord, who maketh election from His own servants. Now unto Him that is able to bring us all by His grace and bounty unto His eternal kingdom, through His only-begotten Son Jesus Christ, be glory, honour, power, and greatness for ever. Salute all the saints. They that are with us salute you, and Euarestus, who wrote the letter, with his whole house.

21. Now the blessed Polycarp was martyred on the second day of the first part of the month Xanthicus, on the seventh before the kalends of March, on a great sabbath, at the eighth hour. He was apprehended by Herodes, when Philip of Tralles was high-priest, in the proconsulship of Statius Quadratus, but in the reign of the Eternal King Jesus Christ. To whom be the glory, honour, greatness, and eternal throne, from generation to generation. Amen.

22. (1) We bid you God speed, brethren, while ye walk by the word of Jesus Christ which is according to the Gospel; with whom be glory to God for the salvation of His holy elect; even as the blessed Polycarp suffered martyrdom, in whose footsteps may it be our lot to be found in the kingdom of Jesus Christ.

(2) This account Gaius copied from the papers of Irenæus, a disciple of Polycarp. The same also lived with Irenæus.

(3) And I Socrates wrote it down in Corinth from the copy of Gaius. Grace be with all men.

(4) And I Pionius again wrote it down from the aforementioned copy, having searched it out (for the blessed Polycarp showed me in a revelation, as I will declare in the sequel), gathering it together when it was now well nigh worn out by age, that the Lord Jesus Christ may gather me also with His elect into His heavenly kingdom; to whom be the glory with the Father and the Holy Spirit for ever and ever. Amen.

The three preceding paragraphs as read in the Moscow MS.

(2) This account Gaius copied from the papers of Irenæus. The same lived with Irenæus who had been a disciple of the holy Polycarp. For this Irenæus, being in Rome at the time of the martyrdom of the bishop Polycarp, instructed many; and many most excellent and orthodox treatises by him are in circulation. In these he makes

mention of Polycarp, saying that he was taught by him.   And he ably refuted every heresy, and handed down the catholic rule of the Church just as he had received it from the saint.   He mentions this fact also, that when Marcion, after whom the Marcionites are called, met the holy Polycarp on one occasion, and said 'Recognize us, Polycarp,' he said in reply to Marcion, 'Yes indeed, I recognize the firstborn of Satan.'   The following statement also is made in the writings of Irenæus, that on the very day and hour when Polycarp was martyred in Smyrna Irenæus being in the city of the Romans heard a voice as of a trumpet saying, ' Polycarp is martyred.'

(3)   From these papers of Irenæus then, as has been stated already, Gaius made a copy, and from the copy of Gaius Isocrates made another in Corinth.

(4)   And I Pionius again wrote it down from the copy of Isocrates, having searched for it in obedience to a revelation of the holy Polycarp, gathering it together, when it was well nigh worn out by age, that the Lord Jesus Christ may gather me also with His elect into His heavenly kingdom ; to whom be the glory with the Father and the Son and the Holy Spirit for ever and ever.   Amen.

THE DIDACHE,

OR

TEACHING OF THE APOSTLES

THE TEACHING OF THE APOSTLES

I

THE Didache is a church-manual of primitive Christianity or of some section of it. It is called 'The Teaching of the Apostles' or 'The Teaching of the Twelve Apostles.' The latter appears in the manuscript; but the former is the designation in several ancient writers who refer to it. It is therefore adopted as the title here. The manual consists of two parts: (1) a moral treatise founded on an ancient work called 'The Two Ways,' and setting forth the paths of righteousness and unrighteousness, of life and death respectively. This first part is not necessarily altogether of Christian origin; indeed there is reason to believe that some portions of it were known to the Jews, and perhaps also to the Greeks, though it has undoubtedly gathered by accretions. (2) The second part gives directions affecting church rites and orders. It treats of baptism, prayer and fasting, the eucharist and agape, the treatment of apostles and prophets, of bishops and deacons, the whole closing with a solemn warning to watchfulness in view of the second coming of Christ.

The work is obviously of very early date, as is shown by the internal evidence of language and subject-matter. Thus for instance the itinerant prophetic order has not yet been displaced by the permanent localized ministry, but exists side by side with it as in the lifetime of S. Paul (Eph. iv. 11, 1 Cor. xii. 28). Secondly, episcopacy has apparently not yet become universal; the word 'bishop' is still used as synonymous with 'presbyter,' and the writer therefore couples 'bishops' with 'deacons' (§ 15) as S. Paul does (1 Tim. iii. 1—8, Phil. i. 1) under similar circumstances. Thirdly, from the expression

121

in § 10 'after ye have been filled' it appears that the agape still remains part of the Lord's Supper. Lastly, the archaic simplicity of its practical suggestions is only consistent with the early infancy of a church. These indications point to the first or the beginning of the second century as the date of the work in its present form.

As regards the place of writing, opinion in the first instance had been strongly in favour of Egypt, because the Teaching was early quoted by Egyptian writers; but from the casual allusion in § 9 to the 'corn scattered upon the mountains' it will appear to have been written either in Syria or Palestine.

2

The Didache was discovered by Bryennios in the same MS with the complete copy of the Epistle of Clement mentioned above (p. 4) and called the Constantinopolitan or Hierosolymitan MS. Besides the Teaching and the Genuine and Spurious Epistles of Clement in full, this document contained Chrysostom's Synopsis of the Old and New Testament (incomplete), the Epistle of Barnabas, and the Long Recension of the Ignatian Epistles. The MS is dated A.D. 1056. But though a list of the contents of this document was announced by Bryennios in 1875, eight years elapsed before the Didache itself was published. Meanwhile, as a work of this name is mentioned by Eusebius and others among early apocryphal writings, a hope was excited in the minds of those interested in such studies that this might be the book alluded to, and that it would throw some light on the vexed question of the origin of the Apostolical Constitutions. When at length in 1883 it was given to the world, its interest and importance were proved to exceed the highest expectations. It has been generally admitted to be the work mentioned by Eusebius and also quoted by Clement of Alexandria as 'scripture.' It is the basis of the seventh book of the Apostolical Constitutions. In language and subject-matter it presents close affinities to many other early documents, notably the Ecclesiastical Canons and the Epistle of Barnabas. A fragment of a Latin translation has also been discovered by Gebhardt, and is printed below (p. 225). Thus though there is but one extant MS of the Didache in its present form, the incorporation of a great part of it into patristic writings and early church-manuals renders the problem of its origin and development a peculiarly interesting one.

THE TEACHING OF THE LORD TO THE GENTILES BY THE TWELVE APOSTLES.

1. THERE are two ways, one of life and one of death, and there is a great difference between the two ways. *The way of life is this.* First of all, *thou shalt love the God* that made thee; secondly, *thy neighbour as thyself. And all things whatsoever thou wouldest not have befal thyself, neither do thou unto another.* Now of these words the doctrine is this. *Bless them that curse you, and pray for* your enemies and fast for *them that persecute you; for what thank is it, if ye love them that love you? Do not even the Gentiles the same? But do ye love them that hate you,* and ye shall not have an enemy. Abstain thou from fleshly and bodily lusts. *If any man give thee a blow on thy right cheek, turn to him the other also,* and thou shalt be perfect; *if a man impress thee to go with him one mile, go with him twain; if a man take away thy cloak, give him thy coat also; if a man take away from thee that which is thine own, ask it not back,* for neither art thou able. *To every man that asketh of thee give, and ask not back;* for the Father desireth that gifts be given to all from His own bounties. Blessed is he that giveth according to the commandment; for he is guiltless. Woe to him that receiveth; for, if a man receiveth having need, he is guiltless; but he that hath no need shall give satisfaction why and wherefore he received; and being put in confinement he shall be examined concerning the deeds that he hath done, and *he shall not come out thence until he hath given back the last farthing.* Yea, as touching this also it is said; *Let thine alms sweat into thine hands, until thou shalt have learnt to whom to give.*

2. And this is the second commandment of the teaching. *Thou shalt do no murder, thou shalt not commit adultery,* thou shalt not corrupt boys, thou shalt not commit fornication, *thou shalt not steal,* thou shalt

not deal in magic, thou shalt do no sorcery, thou shalt not murder a child by abortion nor kill them when born, *thou shalt not covet thy neighbour's goods, thou shalt not perjure thyself, thou shalt not bear false witness*, thou shalt not speak evil, thou shalt not cherish a grudge, thou shalt not be double-minded nor double-tongued ; for the double tongue is a snare of death. Thy word shall not be false or empty, but fulfilled by action. Thou shalt not be avaricious nor a plunderer nor a hypocrite nor ill-tempered nor proud. Thou shalt not entertain an evil design against thy neighbour. *Thou shalt not hate* any man, *but some thou shalt reprove*, and for others thou shalt pray, *and others thou shalt love* more than thy life.

3. My child, flee from every evil and everything that resembleth it. Be not angry, for anger leadeth to murder, nor jealous nor contentious nor wrathful ; for of all these things murders are engendered. My child, be not lustful, for lust leadeth to fornication, neither foul-speaking neither with uplifted eyes ; for of all these things adulteries are engendered. My child, *be no dealer in omens*, since it leads to idolatry, nor an enchanter nor an astrologer nor a magician, neither be willing to look at them ; for from all these things idolatry is engendered. My child, be not a liar, since lying leads to theft, neither avaricious neither vainglorious ; for from all these things thefts are engendered. My child, be not a murmurer, since it leadeth to blasphemy, neither self-willed neither a thinker of evil thoughts ; for from all these things blasphemies are engendered. But be meek, since *the meek shall inherit the earth.* Be long-suffering and pitiful and guileless and *quiet* and kindly *and* always *fearing the words* which thou hast heard. Thou shalt not exalt thyself, neither shalt thou admit boldness into thy soul. Thy soul shall not cleave together with the lofty, but with the righteous and humble shalt thou walk. The accidents that befal thee thou shalt receive as good, knowing that nothing is done without God.

4. My child, *thou shalt remember him that speaketh unto thee the word of God* night and day, and shalt honour him as the Lord ; for whencesoever the Lordship speaketh, there is the Lord. Moreover thou shalt seek out day by day the persons of the saints, that thou mayest find rest in their words. Thou shalt not make a schism, but thou shalt pacify them that contend ; thou shalt judge righteously, thou shalt not make a difference in a person to reprove him for transgressions. Thou shalt not doubt whether a thing shall be or not be.

Be not thou found holding out thy hands to receive, but drawing them in as to giving. If thou hast ought passing through thy hands, thou shalt give a ransom for thy sins. Thou shalt not hesitate to give, neither shalt thou murmur when giving; for thou shalt know who is the good paymaster of thy reward. Thou shalt not turn away from him that is in want, but shalt make thy brother partaker in all things, and shalt not say *that anything is thine own.* For if ye are fellow-partakers in that which is imperishable, how much rather in the things which are perishable?

Thou shalt not withhold thy hand from thy son or from thy daughter, but from their youth thou shalt teach them the fear of God. Thou shalt not command thy bondservant or thine handmaid in thy bitterness, who trust in the same God as thyself, lest haply they should cease to fear the God who is over both of you; for He cometh, not to call men with respect of persons, but He cometh to those whom the Spirit hath prepared. But ye, servants, shall be subject unto your masters, as to a type of God, in shame and fear.

Thou shalt hate all hypocrisy, and everything that is not pleasing to the Lord. Thou shalt never forsake the commandments of the Lord; but shalt keep those things which thou hast received, neither adding to them nor taking away from them. In church thou shalt confess thy transgressions, and shalt not betake thyself to prayer with an evil conscience. This is the way of life.

5. But the way of death is this. First of all, it is evil and full of a curse; murders, adulteries, lusts, fornications, thefts, idolatries, magical arts, witchcrafts, plunderings, false witnessings, hypocrisies, doubleness of heart, treachery, pride, malice, stubbornness, covetousness, foul-speaking, jealousy, boldness, exaltation, boastfulness; persecutors of good men, hating truth, loving a lie, not perceiving the reward of righteousness, not *cleaving to the good* nor to righteous judgment, wakeful not for that which is good but for that which is evil; from whom gentleness and forbearance stand aloof; loving vain things, pursuing a recompense, not pitying the poor man, not toiling for him that is oppressed with toil, not recognizing Him that made them, murderers of children, corrupters of the creatures of God, turning away from him that is in want, oppressing him that is afflicted, advocates of the wealthy, unjust judges of the poor, altogether sinful. May ye be delivered, my children, from all these things.

6. See lest any man lead you astray from this way of righteousness, for he teacheth thee apart from God. For if thou art able to bear the

whole yoke of the Lord, thou shalt be perfect; but if thou art not able, do that which thou art able.

But concerning eating, bear that which thou art able; yet abstain by all means from meat sacrificed to idols; for it is the worship of dead gods.

7. But concerning baptism, thus shall ye baptize. Having first recited all these things, baptize *in the name of the Father and of the Son and of the Holy Spirit* in living (running) water. But if thou hast not living water, then baptize in other water; and if thou art not able in cold, then in warm. But if thou hast neither, then pour water on the head thrice in the name of the Father and of the Son and of the Holy Spirit. But before the baptism let him that baptizeth and him that is baptized fast, and any others also who are able; and thou shalt order him that is baptized to fast a day or two before.

8. And let not your fastings be with the hypocrites, for they fast on the second and the fifth day of the week; but do ye keep your fast on the fourth and on the preparation (the sixth) day. Neither pray ye *as the hypocrites,* but as the Lord commanded in His Gospel, *thus pray ye: Our Father, which art in heaven, hallowed be Thy name; Thy kingdom come; Thy will be done, as in heaven, so also on earth; give us this day our daily bread; and forgive us our debt, as we also forgive our debtors; and lead us not into temptation, but deliver us from the evil one;* for Thine is the power and the glory for ever and ever. Three times in the day pray ye so.

9. But as touching the eucharistic thanksgiving give ye thanks thus. First, as regards the cup: We give Thee thanks, O our Father, for the holy vine of Thy son David, which Thou madest known unto us through Thy Son Jesus; Thine is the glory for ever and ever. Then as regards the broken bread: We give Thee thanks, O our Father, for the life and knowledge which Thou didst make known unto us through Thy Son Jesus; Thine is the glory for ever and ever. As this broken bread was scattered upon the mountains and being gathered together became one, so may Thy Church be gathered together from the ends of the earth into Thy kingdom; for Thine is the glory and the power through Jesus Christ for ever and ever. But let no one eat or drink of this eucharistic thanksgiving, but they that have been baptized into the name of the Lord; for concerning this also the Lord hath said: *Give not that which is holy to the dogs.*

10. And after ye are satisfied thus give ye thanks: We give Thee

thanks, Holy Father, for Thy holy name, which Thou hast made to tabernacle in our hearts, and for the knowledge and faith and immortality, which Thou hast made known unto us through Thy Son Jesus; Thine is the glory for ever and ever. Thou, Almighty Master, didst create all things for Thy name's sake, and didst give food and drink unto men for enjoyment, that they might render thanks to Thee; but didst bestow upon us spiritual food and drink and eternal life through Thy Son. Before all things we give Thee thanks that Thou art powerful; Thine is the glory for ever and ever. Remember, Lord, Thy Church to deliver it from all evil and to perfect it in Thy love; and *gather it together from the four winds*—even the Church which has been sanctified—into Thy kingdom which Thou hast prepared for it; for Thine is the power and the glory for ever and ever. May grace come and may this world pass away. Hosanna to the God of David. If any man is holy, let him come; if any man is not, let him repent. Maran Atha. Amen.

But permit the prophets to offer thanksgiving as much as they desire.

11. Whosoever therefore shall come and teach you all these things that have been said before, receive him; but if the teacher himself be perverted and teach a different doctrine to the destruction thereof, hear him not; but if to the increase of righteousness and the knowledge of the Lord, receive him as the Lord.

But concerning the apostles and prophets, so do ye according to the ordinance of the Gospel. Let every apostle, when he cometh to you, be received as the Lord; but he shall not abide more than a single day, or if there be need, a second likewise; but if he abide three days, he is a false prophet. And when he departeth let the apostle receive nothing save bread, until he findeth shelter; but if he ask money, he is a false prophet. And any prophet speaking in the Spirit ye shall not try neither discern; for every sin shall be forgiven, but this sin shall not be forgiven. Yet not every one that speaketh in the Spirit is a prophet, but only if he have the ways of the Lord. From his ways therefore the false prophet and the prophet shall be recognized. And no prophet when he ordereth a table in the Spirit shall eat of it; otherwise he is a false prophet. And every prophet teaching the truth, if he doeth not what he teacheth, is a false prophet. And every prophet approved and found true, if he doeth ought as an outward mystery typical of the Church, and yet teacheth you not to do all that he himself doeth, shall not be judged before you; he hath his judgment in the presence of God; for in like manner also did the prophets of old time. And whosoever shall say in the Spirit, Give me silver or anything else, ye shall not listen to him; but if he tell you to give on behalf of others that are in want, let no man judge him.

12. But let every one *that cometh in the name of the Lord* be received; and then when ye have tested him ye shall know him, for ye shall have understanding on the right hand and on the left. If the comer is a traveller, assist him, so far as ye are able; but he shall not stay with you more than two or three days, if it be necessary. But if he wishes to settle with you, being a craftsman, let him work for and eat his bread. But if he has no craft, according to your wisdom provide how he shall live as a Christian among you, but not in idleness. If he will not do this, he is trafficking upon Christ. Beware of such men.

13. But every true prophet desiring to settle among you *is worthy of his food*. In like manner a true teacher *is* also *worthy*, like *the workman, of his food*. Every firstfruit then of the produce of the wine-vat and of the threshing-floor, of thy oxen and of thy sheep, thou shalt take and give as the firstfruit to the prophets; for they are your chief-priests. But if ye have not a prophet, give them to the poor. If thou makest bread, take the firstfruit and give according to the commandment. In like manner, when thou openest a jar of wine or of oil, take the firstfruit and give to the prophets; yea and of money and raiment and every possession take the firstfruit, as shall seem good to thee, and give according to the commandment.

14. And on the Lord's own day gather yourselves together and break bread and give thanks, first confessing your transgressions, that your sacrifice may be pure. And let no man, having his dispute with his fellow, join your assembly until they have been reconciled, that your sacrifice may not be defiled; for this sacrifice it is that was spoken of by the Lord; *In every place and at every time offer Me a pure sacrifice; for I am a great king, saith the Lord, and My name is wonderful among the nations.*

15. Appoint for yourselves therefore bishops and deacons worthy of the Lord, men who are meek and not lovers of money, and true and approved; for unto you they also perform the service of the prophets and teachers. Therefore despise them not; for they are your honourable men along with the prophets and teachers.

And reprove one another, not in anger but in peace, as ye find in the Gospel; and let no one speak to any that has gone wrong towards his neighbour, neither let him hear a word from you, until he repent. But your prayers and your almsgivings and all your deeds so do ye as ye find it in the Gospel of our Lord.

16. *Be watchful* for your life; *let your lamps not be quenched and your loins not ungirded, but be ye ready; for ye know not the hour in which our Lord cometh.* And ye shall gather yourselves together frequently, seeking what is fitting for your souls; for the whole time of your faith shall not profit you, if ye be not perfected at the last season. For in the last days *the false prophets* and corrupters shall be multiplied, and the sheep shall be turned into wolves, and love shall be turned into hate. For as lawlessness increaseth, *they shall hate one another and shall persecute and betray. And then* the world-deceiver *shall appear* as a son of God; *and shall work signs and wonders,* and the earth shall be delivered into his hands; and he shall do unholy things, which have never been since the world began. Then all created mankind shall come to the fire of testing, and many shall be offended and perish; *but they that endure* in their faith *shall be saved* by the Curse Himself. *And then shall the signs* of the truth *appear*; first a sign of a rift in the heaven, then a sign of a voice of a trumpet, and thirdly a resurrection of the dead; yet not of all, but as it was said : *The Lord shall come and all His saints with Him. Then shall* the world *see the Lord coming upon the clouds of heaven.*

THE EPISTLE

OF

BARNABAS

THE EPISTLE OF BARNABAS

I.

THE Epistle which bears the name of Barnabas stands alone in the literature of the early Church. The writer is an uncompromising antagonist of Judaism, but beyond this antagonism he has nothing in common with the Antijudaic heresies of the second century. Unlike Marcion, he postulates no opposition between the Old Testament and the New. On the contrary he sees Christianity everywhere in the Lawgiver and the Prophets, and treats them with a degree of respect which would have satisfied the most devout rabbi. He quotes them profusely as authoritative. Only he accuses the Jews of misunderstanding them from beginning to end, and intimates that the ordinances of circumcision, of the sabbath, of the distinctions of meats clean and unclean, were never intended to be literally observed, but had throughout a spiritual and mystical significance.

Who then was the writer of this Epistle? At the close of the second century Clement of Alexandria quotes it frequently, and ascribes it to the 'Apostle,' or the 'Prophet Barnabas,' identifying the author with 'Barnabas who himself also preached with the Apostle' (i.e. St Paul) 'in the ministry of the Gentiles.' Yet elsewhere he does not hesitate to criticize the work, and clearly therefore did not regard it as final and authoritative. A few years later, Origen cites the Epistle with the introductory words, 'It is written in the catholic (i.e. general) Epistle of Barnabas.' The earliest notices however are confined to the Alexandrian fathers, and the presumption is that it was written in Alexandria itself.

It will be observed that the writer nowhere claims to be the Apostle Barnabas; indeed his language is such as to suggest that he was wholly unconnected with the Apostles. The work therefore is in no sense apocryphal, if by apocryphal we mean fictitious. How the name of Barnabas came to be associated with it, it is impossible to say. An early tradition, or fiction, represents Barnabas as residing at Alexandria;

133

but this story might have been the consequence, rather than the cause, of the name attached to the letter. Possibly its author was some unknown namesake of the 'Son of Consolation.'

That Alexandria, the place of its earliest reception, was also the place of its birth, is borne out by the internal evidence of style and interpretation, which is Alexandrian throughout. The picture too which it presents of feuds between Jews and Christians is in keeping with the state of the population of that city, the various elements of which were continually in conflict. But the problem of the date is a more difficult one. The Epistle was certainly written after the first destruction of Jerusalem under Titus, to which it alludes; but, had it been composed after the war under Hadrian ending in the second devastation, it could hardly have failed to refer to that event. The possible limits therefore are A.D. 70 and A.D. 132. But within this period of sixty years the most various dates have been assigned to it. The conclusion depends mainly on the interpretation put upon two passages which treat of quotations from the prophets. (1) The first is in § 4, where Daniel vii. 7 sq is quoted as illustrating the great scandal or offence which, according to the writer, is at hand. The date will depend on the interpretation put upon the 'three kings in one' ($\tau\rho\epsilon\hat{\imath}s$ $\dot{\upsilon}\phi$' $\dot{\epsilon}\nu$ $\tau\hat{\omega}\nu$ $\beta\alpha\sigma\iota\lambda\dot{\epsilon}\omega\nu$), or 'three great horns in one' ($\dot{\upsilon}\phi$' $\dot{\epsilon}\nu$ $\tau\rho\dot{\iota}\alpha$ $\tau\hat{\omega}\nu$ $\mu\epsilon\gamma\dot{\alpha}\lambda\omega\nu$ $\kappa\epsilon\rho\dot{\alpha}\tau\omega\nu$) and 'the little excrescence' or 'offshoot horn' ($\mu\iota\kappa\rho\dot{\partial}\nu$ $\kappa\dot{\epsilon}\rho\alpha s$ $\pi\alpha\rho\alpha\phi\upsilon\dot{\alpha}\delta\iota\upsilon\nu$). And here no theory yet propounded appears quite satisfactory. Weizsäcker, who dates the Epistle in Vespasian's reign (A.D. 70—79), is compelled to consider that emperor as at once one of the great horns and the little horn; Hilgenfeld, who places it under Nerva (A.D. 96—98), arbitrarily omits Julius and Vitellius from the list of Cæsars, that he may make Domitian the tenth king; while both alike fail to recognize in Daniel's little horn a prophecy of Antichrist and therefore a persecuting emperor. Volkmar's date (A.D. 119—132), besides other serious objections, depends upon the enumeration of the three kings over and above the ten, whereas the language suggests that they were in some sense comprised within the ten. The solution, which follows, and which we are disposed to adopt provisionally, has not, we believe, been offered before. We enumerate the ten Cæsars in their natural sequence, with Weizsäcker, and arrive at Vespasian as the tenth. We regard the three Flavii as the three kings destined to be humiliated, with Hilgenfeld. We do not however with him contemplate them as three separate emperors, but explain the language as referring to the as-

sociation with himself by Vespasian of his two sons Titus and Domitian
in the exercise of supreme power.   So close a connexion of three in one
was never seen in the history of the empire, until a date too late to enter
into consideration.   The significance of this association is commemorated
in several types of coins, which exhibit Vespasian on the obverse and
Titus and Domitian on the reverse in various attitudes and with various
legends.   Lastly, with Volkmar, we interpret the little horn as symboliz-
ing Antichrist, and explain it by the expectation of Nero's reappearance
which we know to have been rife during the continuation of the
Flavian dynasty.   (2) The second passage is the interpretation in
§ 16 given to Isaiah xlix. 17, where it is foretold to the Jews that
'those who pulled down this temple themselves shall build it up,' and
the interpretation goes on to say that 'this is taking place ($\gamma \acute{\iota} \nu \epsilon \tau \alpha \iota$).
Because they went to war it was pulled down by their enemies; now
also the very subjects ($\acute{\upsilon} \pi \eta \rho \acute{\epsilon} \tau \alpha \iota$) of their enemies (the Romans) shall
build it up!'   This is taken by interpreters generally to refer to the
material temple at Jerusalem, and they explain it of the expectations
of the Jews at one epoch or another that the Romans would rebuild
the temple—the epoch generally chosen being the conquest of Hadrian,
at which point consequently very many place the writing of the Epistle.
This conflicts with any natural interpretation of the three horns and the
little horn.   But (i) no satisfactory evidence has been adduced that
Hadrian had any such intention, or that the Jews had any such expectation in his time; and (ii) there is the still more formidable objection
that this interpretation runs counter to the general teaching of this
writer, who reproaches the Jews with their material interpretations of
prophecy, and to the whole context, which is conceived in his usual
vein.   He explains at the outset that the Jews are wrong in setting
their hope on the material building.   Yet here, if this interpretation
be correct, he tells them to do this very thing.   Moreover, lest there
should be any mistake, he assures them that there *is* a temple, but this
temple of the Lord, predicted by the prophets, is a spiritual temple;
for it is either the Church of Christ, or the soul of the individual
believer, wherein the Lord dwells.   Whether with ℵ we read a second
$\kappa \alpha \grave{\iota}$ after $\alpha \acute{\upsilon} \tau o \grave{\iota}$ or not, this spiritual interpretation must be correct; but
the context suggests its omission.   Thus the passage has no bearing at
all on the date.   For these reasons we should probably place the date
of the so-called Epistle of Barnabas between A.D. 70—79; but the
ultimate decision must be affected by the view which shall commend

itself of the origin of those chapters, which the epistle has in common with the Teaching of the Apostles.

2.

The authorities for the text are as follows:

(I) GREEK MANUSCRIPTS.

1. The famous Sinaitic MS (ℵ) of the fourth century, where, in company with the Shepherd of Hermas, it occurs in a complete form, following the Apocalypse, as a sort of appendix to the sacred volume.

2. The Constantinopolitan MS (C) of Bryennios, an eleventh century document (see above, pp. 4, 216); here also the epistle is found complete.

3. The series of nine Greek MSS (G), all of one family, enumerated above, p. 166 sq; in this collection of manuscripts the first four chapters and part of the fifth are wanting.

There is also (II) a LATIN VERSION (L) extant in a MS of the ninth or tenth century (*Petropolitanus* Q. v. I. 39, formerly *Corbeiensis*). This MS omits the last four chapters, which apparently formed no part of the version in question.

Lastly, the quotations in Clement of Alexandria, comprising as they do portions of §§ 1, 4, 6, 9, 10, 11, 16, 21, and those passages in §§ 18—21 which this Epistle has in common with the Didache and other documents, open out additional considerations which must not be disregarded in the formation of the text.

THE EPISTLE OF BARNABAS

1.   I BID you greeting, sons and daughters, in the name of the Lord that loved us, in peace.

Seeing that the ordinances of God are great and rich unto you, I rejoice with an exceeding great and overflowing joy at your blessed and glorious spirits; so innate is the grace of the spiritual gift that ye have received. Wherefore also I the more congratulate myself hoping to be saved, for that I truly see the Spirit poured out among you from the riches of the fount of the Lord. So greatly did the much-desired sight of you astonish me respecting you. Being therefore persuaded of this, and being conscious with myself that having said much among you I know that the Lord journeyed with me on the way of righteousness, and am wholly constrained also myself to this, to love you more than my own soul (for great faith and love dwelleth in you through the hope of the life which is His)—considering this therefore, that, if it shall be my care to communicate to you some portion of that which I received, it shall turn to my reward for having ministered to such spirits, I was eager to send you a trifle, that along with your faith ye might have your knowledge also perfect. Well then, there are three ordinances of the Lord; †the hope of life, which is the beginning and end of our faith; and righteousness, which is the beginning and end of judgment; love shown in gladness and exultation, the testimony of works of righteousness†. For the Lord made known to us by His prophets things past and present, giving us likewise the firstfruits of the taste of things future. And seeing each of these things severally coming to pass, according as He spake, we ought to offer a richer and higher offering to the fear of Him. But I, not as though I were a teacher, but as one of yourselves, will show forth a few things, whereby ye shall be gladdened in the present circumstances.

2. Seeing then that the days are evil, and that the Active One himself has the authority, we ought to give heed to ourselves and to seek out the ordinances of the Lord. The aids of our faith then are fear and patience, and our allies are long-suffering and self-restraint. While these abide in a pure spirit in matters relating to the Lord, wisdom, understanding, science, knowledge rejoice with them. For He hath made manifest to us by all the prophets that He wanteth neither sacrifices nor whole burnt-offerings nor oblations, saying at one time; *What to Me is the multitude of your sacrifices, saith the Lord? I am full of whole burnt-offerings, and the fat of lambs and the blood of bulls and of goats I desire not, not though ye should come to be seen of Me. For who required these things at your hands? Ye shall continue no more to tread My court. If ye bring fine flour, it is vain; incense is an abomination to Me; your new moons and your sabbaths I cannot away with.* These things therefore He annulled, that the new law of our Lord Jesus Christ, being free from the yoke of constraint, might have its oblation not made by human hands. And He saith again unto them; *Did I command your fathers when they went forth from the land of Egypt to bring Me whole burnt-offerings and sacrifices? Nay, this was My command unto them, Let none of you bear a grudge of evil against his neighbour in his heart, and love you not a false oath.* So we ought to perceive, unless we are without understanding, the mind of the goodness of our Father; for He speaketh to us, desiring us not to go astray like them but to seek how we may approach Him. Thus then speaketh He to us; *The sacrifice unto God is a broken heart, the smell of a sweet savour unto the Lord is a heart that glorifies its Maker.* We ought therefore, brethren, to learn accurately concerning our salvation, lest the Evil One having effected an entrance of error in us should fling us away from our life.

3. He speaketh again therefore to them concerning these things; *Wherefore fast ye for Me, saith the Lord, so that your voice is heard this day crying aloud? This is not the fast which I have chosen, saith the Lord; not a man abasing his soul; not though ye should bend your neck as a hoop, and put on sackcloth and make your bed of ashes, not even so shall ye call a fast that is acceptable.* But unto us He saith; *Behold, this is the fast which I have chosen, saith the Lord; loosen every band of wickedness, untie the tightened cords of forcible contracts, send away the broken ones released and tear in pieces every unjust bond. Break thy bread to the hungry, and if thou seest one naked clothe him; bring the shelterless into thy house, and if thou seest a humble man, thou shalt*

not despise him, neither shall any one of thy household and of thine own seed. Then shall thy light break forth in the morning, and thy healing shall arise quickly, and righteousness shall go before thy face, and the glory of God shall environ thee. Then shalt thou cry out and God shall hear thee; while thou art still speaking, He shall say, 'Lo, I am here'; if thou shalt take away from thee the yoke and the stretching forth of the finger and the word of murmuring, and shalt give thy bread to the hungry heartily, and shalt pity the abased soul. To this end therefore, my brethren, He that is long-suffering, foreseeing that the people whom He had prepared in His well-beloved would believe in simplicity, manifested to us before-hand concerning all things, that we might not as novices shipwreck ourselves upon their law.

4. It behoves us therefore to investigate deeply concerning the present, and to search out the things which have power to save us. Let us therefore flee altogether from all the works of lawlessness, lest the works of lawlessness overpower us; and let us loathe the error of the present time, that we may be loved for that which is to come. Let us give no relaxation to our soul that it should have liberty to consort with sinners and wicked men, lest haply we be made like unto them. The last offence is at hand, concerning which the scripture speaketh, as Enoch saith. For to this end the Master hath cut the seasons and the days short, that His beloved might hasten and come to His inheritance. And the prophet also speaketh on this wise; *Ten reigns shall reign upon the earth, and after them shall arise a little king, who shall bring low three of the kings under one.* In like manner Daniel speaketh concerning the same; *And I saw the fourth beast to be wicked and strong and more intractable than all the beasts of the earth, and how there arose from him ten horns, and from these a little horn an excrescence, and how that it abased under one three of the great horns.* Ye ought therefore to understand. Moreover I ask you this one thing besides, as being one of yourselves and loving you all in particular more than my own soul, to give heed to yourselves now, and not to liken yourselves to certain persons who pile up sin upon sin, saying that our covenant remains to them also. Ours it is; but they lost it in this way for ever, when Moses had just received it. For the scripture saith; *And Moses was in the mountain fasting forty days and forty nights, and he received the covenant from the Lord, even tables of stone written with the finger of the hand of the Lord.* But they lost it by turning unto idols. For thus saith the Lord; *Moses, Moses, come down quickly; for thy people whom thou*

broughtest out of the land of Egypt hath done unlawfully. And Moses understood, and threw the two tables from his hands; and their covenant was broken in pieces, that the covenant of the beloved Jesus might be sealed unto our hearts in the hope which springeth from faith in Him. But though I would fain write many things, not as a teacher, but as becometh one who loveth you not to fall short of that which we possess, I was anxious to write to you, being your devoted slave. Wherefore let us take heed in these last days. For the whole time of our faith shall profit us nothing, unless we now, in the season of lawlessness and in the offences that shall be, as becometh sons of God, offer resistance, that the Black One may not effect an entrance. Let us flee from all vanity, let us entirely hate the works of the evil way. Do not entering in privily stand apart by yourselves, as if ye were already justified, but assemble yourselves together and consult concerning the common welfare. For the scripture saith; *Woe unto them that are wise for themselves, and understanding in their own sight.* Let us become spiritual, let us become a temple perfect unto God. As far as in us lies, let us exercise ourselves in the fear of God, [and] let us strive to keep His commandments, that we may rejoice in His ordinances. The Lord judgeth the world without respect of persons; each man shall receive according to his deeds. If he be good, his righteousness shall go before him in the way; if he be evil, the recompense of his evil-doing is before him; lest perchance, if we relax as men that are called, we should slumber over our sins, and the prince of evil receive power against us and thrust us out from the kingdom of the Lord. Moreover understand this also, my brothers. When ye see that after so many signs and wonders wrought in Israel, even then they were abandoned, let us give heed, lest haply we be found, as the scripture saith, *many called but few chosen.*

5. For to this end the Lord endured to deliver His flesh unto corruption, that by the remission of sins we might be cleansed, which cleansing is through the blood of His sprinkling. For the scripture concerning Him containeth some things relating to Israel, and some things relating to us. And it speaketh thus; *He was wounded for our transgressions, and He hath been bruised for our sins; by His stripes we were healed. As a sheep He was led to the slaughter, and as a lamb that is dumb before his shearer.* We ought therefore to be very thankful unto the Lord, for that He both revealed unto us the past, and made us wise in the present, and as regards the future we are not without understanding. Now the scripture saith; *Not unjustly is the net spread*

for the birds. He meaneth this that a man shall justly perish, who having the knowledge of the way of righteousness forceth himself into the way of darkness. There is yet this also, my brethren ; if the Lord endured to suffer for our souls, though He was Lord of the whole world, unto whom God said from the foundation of the world, *Let us make man after our image and likeness,* how then did He endure to suffer at the hand of men? Understand ye. The prophets, receiving grace from Him, prophesied concerning Him. But He Himself endured that He might destroy death and show forth the resurrection of the dead, for that He must needs be manifested in the flesh ; that at the same time He might redeem the promise made to the fathers, and by preparing the new people for Himself might show, while He was on earth, that having brought about the resurrection He will Himself exercise judgment. Yea and further, He preached teaching Israel and performing so many wonders and miracles, and He loved him exceedingly. And when He chose His own apostles who were to proclaim His Gospel, who that He might show that *He came not to call the righteous but sinners* were sinners above every sin, then He manifested Himself to be the Son of God. For if He had not come in the flesh neither would men have looked upon Him and been saved, forasmuch as when they look upon the sun that shall cease to be, which is the work of His own hands, they cannot face its rays. Therefore the Son of God came in the flesh to this end, that He might sum up the complete tale of their sins against those who persecuted and slew His prophets. To this end therefore He endured. For God saith of the wounds of His flesh that they came from them ; *When they shall smite their own shepherd, then shall the sheep of the flock be lost.* But He Himself desired so to suffer ; for it was necessary for Him to suffer on a tree. For he that prophesied said concerning Him, *Spare My soul from the sword;* and, *Pierce My flesh with nails, for the congregations of evil-doers have risen up against Me.* And again He saith ; *Behold I have given My back to stripes, and My cheeks to smitings, and My face did I set as a hard rock.*

6. When then He gave the commandment, what saith He ? *Who is he that disputeth with Me? Let him oppose Me. Or who is he that goeth to law with Me? Let him draw nigh unto the servant of the Lord. Woe unto you, for ye all shall wax old as a garment, and the moth shall consume you.* And again the prophet saith, seeing that as a hard stone He was ordained for crushing ; *Behold I will put into the foundations of Zion a stone very precious, elect, a chief corner-stone, honourable.* Then again

what saith He; *And whosoever shall set his hope on Him, shall live for ever.* Is our hope then set upon a stone? Far be it. But it is because the Lord hath set His flesh in strength. For He saith; *And He set Me as a hard rock.* And the prophet saith again; *The stone which the builders rejected, this became the head of the corner.* And again He saith; *This is the great and wonderful day, which the Lord made.* I write to you the more simply, that ye may understand, I who am the offscouring of your love. What then saith the prophet again? *The assembly of evil-doers gathered about Me, they surrounded Me as bees surround a comb;* and; *For My garment they cast a lot.* Forasmuch then as He was about to be manifested in the flesh and to suffer, His suffering was manifested beforehand. For the prophet saith concerning Israel; *Woe unto their soul, for they have counselled evil counsel against themselves saying, Let us bind the righteous one, for he is unprofitable for us.* What saith the other prophet Moses unto them? *Behold, these things saith the Lord God; enter into the good land which the Lord sware unto Abraham, Isaac and Jacob, and inherit it, a land flowing with milk and honey.* But what saith knowledge? Understand ye. Set your hope on Him who is about to be manifested to you in the flesh, even Jesus. For man is earth suffering; for from the face of the earth came the creation of Adam. What then saith He? *Into the good land, a land flowing with milk and honey.* Blessed is our Lord, brethren, who established among us wisdom and understanding of His secret things. For the prophet speaketh a parable concerning the Lord. Who shall comprehend, save he that is wise and prudent and that loveth his Lord? Forasmuch then as He renewed us in the remission of sins, He made us to be a new type, so that we should have the soul of children, as if He were re-creating us. For the scripture saith concerning us, how He saith to the Son; *Let us make man after our image and after our likeness, and let them rule over the beasts of the earth and the fowls of the heaven and the fishes of the sea.* And the Lord said when He saw the fair creation of us men; *Increase and multiply and fill the earth.* These words refer to the Son. Again I will shew thee how the Lord speaketh concerning us. He made a second creation at the last; and the Lord saith; *Behold I make the last things as the first.* In reference to this then the prophet preached; *Enter into a land flowing with milk and honey, and be lords over it.* Behold then we have been created anew, as He saith again in another prophet; *Behold, saith the Lord, I will take out from these,* that is to say, from those whom the Spirit of the

Lord foresaw, *their stony hearts, and will put into them hearts of flesh ;* for He Himself was to be manifested in the flesh and to dwell in us. For a holy temple unto the Lord, my brethren, is the abode of our heart. For the Lord saith again ; *For wherein shall I appear unto the Lord my God and be glorified ? I will make confession unto Thee in the assembly of my brethren, and I will sing unto Thee in the midst of the assembly of the saints.* We therefore are they whom He brought into the good land. What then is the milk and the honey ? Because the child is first kept alive by honey, and then by milk. So in like manner we also, being kept alive by our faith in the promise and by the word, shall live and be lords of the earth. Now we have already said above ; *And let them increase and multiply and rule over the fishes.* But who is he that is able [now] to rule over beasts and fishes and fowls of the heaven ; for we ought to perceive that to rule implieth power, so that one should give orders and have dominion. If then this cometh not to pass now, assuredly He spake to us for the hereafter, when we ourselves shall be made perfect so that we may become heirs of the covenant of the Lord.

7. Understand therefore, children of gladness, that the good Lord manifested all things to us beforehand, that we might know to whom we ought in all things to render thanksgiving and praise. If then the Son of God, being Lord and future Judge of quick and dead, suffered that His wound might give us life, let us believe that the Son of God could not suffer except for our sakes. But moreover when crucified He had vinegar and gall given Him to drink. Hear how on this matter the priests of the temple have revealed. Seeing that there is a commandment in scripture, *Whosoever shall not observe the fast shall surely die,* the Lord commanded, because He was in His own person about to offer the vessel of His Spirit a sacrifice for our sins, that the type also which was given in Isaac who was offered upon the altar should be fulfilled. What then saith He in the prophet? *And let them eat of the goat that is offered at the fast for all their sins.* Attend carefully ; *And let all the priests alone eat the entrails unwashed with vinegar.* Wherefore ? Since ye are to give Me, who am to offer My flesh for the sins of My new people, gall with vinegar to drink, eat ye alone, while the people fasteth and waileth in sackcloth and ashes ; that He might shew that He must suffer at their hands. Attend ye to the commandments which He gave. *Take two goats, fair and alike, and offer them, and let the priest take the one for a whole burnt-offering for sins.* But the

other one—what must they do with it? *Accursed*, saith He, *is the one.* Give heed how the type of Jesus is revealed. *And do ye all spit upon it and goad it, and place scarlet wool about its head, and so let it be cast into the wilderness.* And when it is so done, he that taketh the goat into the wilderness leadeth it, and taketh off the wool, and putteth it upon the branch which is called Rachia, the same whereof we are wont to eat the shoots when we find them in the country. Of this briar alone is the fruit thus sweet. What then meaneth this? Give heed. *The one for the altar, and the other accursed.* And moreover the accursed one crowned. For they shall see Him in that day wearing the long scarlet robe about His flesh, and shall say, Is not this He, Whom once we crucified and set at nought and spat upon; verily this was He, Who then said that He was the Son of God. For how is He like the goat? For this reason it says *the goats shall be fair and alike,* that, when they shall see Him coming then, they may be astonished at the likeness of the goat. Therefore behold the type of Jesus that was to suffer. But what meaneth it, that they place the wool in the midst of the thorns? It is a type of Jesus set forth for the Church, since whosoever should desire to take away the scarlet wool it behoved him to suffer many things owing to the terrible nature of the thorn, and through affliction to win the mastery over it. Thus, He saith, they that desire to see Me, and to attain unto My kingdom, must lay hold on Me through tribulation and affliction.

8. But what think ye meaneth the type, where the commandment is given to Israel that those men, whose sins are full grown, offer an heifer and slaughter and burn it, and then that the children take up the ashes, and cast them into vessels, and twist the scarlet wool on a tree (see here again is the type of the cross and the scarlet wool), and the hyssop, and that this done the children should sprinkle the people one by one, that they may be purified from their sins? Understand ye how in all plainness it is spoken unto you; the calf is Jesus, the men that offer it, being sinners, are they that offered Him for the slaughter. †After this it is no more men (who offer); the glory is no more for sinners.† The children who sprinkle are they that preached unto us the forgiveness of sins and the purification of our heart, they to whom, being twelve in number for a testimony unto the tribes (for there are twelve tribes of Israel), He gave authority over the Gospel, that they should preach it. But wherefore are the children that sprinkle three in number? For a testimony unto Abraham, Isaac and Jacob, because

these are mighty before God.   Then there is the placing the wool on
the tree.   This means that the kingdom of Jesus is on the cross, and
that they who set their hope on Him shall live for ever.   And why is
there the wool and the hyssop at the same time?   Because in His
kingdom there shall be evil and foul days, in which we shall be saved;
for he who suffers pain in the flesh is healed through the foulness of the
hyssop.   Now to us indeed it is manifest that these things so befel for
this reason, but to them they were dark, because they heard not the
voice of the Lord.

9.   Furthermore He saith concerning the ears, how that it is our
heart which He circumcised.   The Lord saith in the prophet; *With
the hearing of the ears they listened unto Me.*   And again He saith; *They
that are afar off shall hear with their ears, and shall perceive what I
have done.*   And; *Be ye circumcised in your hearts*, saith the Lord.
And again He saith; *Hear, O Israel, for thus saith the Lord thy God.
Who is he that desireth to live for ever, let him hear with his ears the
voice of My servant.*   And again He saith; *Hear, O heaven, and give
ear, O earth, for the Lord hath spoken these things for a testimony.*   And
again He saith; *Hear the word of the Lord, ye rulers of this people.*
And again He saith; *Hear, O my children, the voice of one crying in the
wilderness.*   Therefore He circumcised our ears, that hearing the word
we might believe.   But moreover the circumcision, in which they have
confidence, is abolished; for He hath said that a circumcision not of
the flesh should be practised.   But they transgressed, for an evil angel
taught them cleverness.   He saith unto them; *Thus saith the Lord
your God* (so I find the commandment); *sow not upon thorns, be
ye circumcised to your Lord.*   And what saith He?   *Be ye circumcised
in the hardness of your heart; and then ye will not harden your neck.*
Take this again; *Behold, saith the Lord, all the Gentiles are uncircumcised in their foreskin, but this people is uncircumcised in their
hearts.*   But thou wilt say; In truth the people hath been circumcised for a seal.   Nay, but so likewise is every Syrian and Arabian
and all the priests of the idols.   Do all those then too belong to their
covenant?   Moreover the Egyptians also are included among the
circumcised.   Learn therefore, children of love, concerning all things
abundantly, that Abraham, who first appointed circumcision, looked
forward in the spirit unto Jesus, when he circumcised having received
the ordinances of three letters.   For the scripture saith; *And Abraham
circumcised of his household eighteen males and three hundred.*   What

then was the knowledge given unto him? Understand ye that He saith *the eighteen* first, and then after an interval *three hundred*. In the eighteen I stands for ten, H for eight. Here thou hast JESUS (IHΣOYΣ). And because the cross in the T was to have grace, He saith also *three hundred*. So He revealeth Jesus in the two letters, and in the remaining one the cross. He who placed within us the innate gift of His covenant knoweth; no man hath ever learnt from me a more genuine word; but I know that ye are worthy.

10. But forasmuch as Moses said; *Ye shall not eat swine nor eagle nor falcon nor crow nor any fish which hath no scale upon it,* he received in his understanding three ordinances. Yea and further He saith unto them in Deuteronomy; *And I will lay as a covenant upon this people My ordinances.* So then it is not a commandment of God that they should not bite with their teeth, but Moses spake it in spirit. Accordingly he mentioned the swine with this intent. Thou shalt not cleave, saith he, to such men who are like unto swine; that is, when they are in luxury they forget the Lord, but when they are in want they recognize the Lord, just as the swine when it eateth knoweth not his lord, but when it is hungry it crieth out, and when it has received food again it is silent. *Neither shalt thou eat eagle nor falcon nor kite nor crow.* Thou shalt not, He saith, cleave unto, or be likened to, such men who know not how to provide food for themselves by toil and sweat, but in their lawlessness seize what belongeth to others, and as if they were walking in guilelessness watch and search about for some one to rob in their rapacity, just as these birds alone do not provide food for themselves, but sit idle and seek how they may eat the meat that belongeth to others, being pestilent in their evil-doings. *And thou shalt not eat,* saith He, *lamprey nor polypus nor cuttle fish.* Thou shalt not, He meaneth, become like unto such men, who are desperately wicked, and are already condemned to death, just as these fishes alone are accursed and swim in the depths, not swimming on the surface like the rest, but dwell on the ground beneath the deep sea. Moreover *thou shalt not eat the hare.* Why so? Thou shalt not be found a corrupter of boys, nor shalt thou become like such persons; for the hare gaineth one passage in the body every year; for according to the number of years it lives it has just so many orifices. Again, *neither shalt thou eat the hyena;* thou shalt not, saith He, become an adulterer or a fornicator, neither shalt thou resemble such persons. Why so? Because this animal changeth its nature year by year, and becometh at

one time male and at another female. Moreover He hath hated the weasel also and with good reason. Thou shalt not, saith He, become such as those men of whom we hear as working iniquity with their mouth for uncleanness, neither shalt thou cleave unto impure women who work iniquity with their mouth. For this animal conceiveth with its mouth. Concerning meats then Moses received three decrees to this effect and uttered them in a spiritual sense; but they accepted them according to the lust of the flesh, as though they referred to eating. And David also receiveth knowledge of the same three decrees, and saith; *Blessed is the man who hath not gone in the counsel of the ungodly*—even as the fishes go in darkness into the depths; *and hath not stood in the path of sinners*—just as they who pretend to fear the Lord sin like swine; *and hath not sat on the seat of the destroyers*— as the birds that are seated for prey. Ye have now the complete lesson concerning eating. Again Moses saith; *Ye shall eat everything that divideth the hoof and cheweth the cud.* What meaneth he? He that receiveth the food knoweth Him that giveth him the food, and being refreshed appeareth to rejoice in him. Well said he, having regard to the commandment. What then meaneth he? Cleave unto those that fear the Lord, with those who meditate in their heart on the distinction of the word which they have received, with those who tell of the ordinances of the Lord and keep them, with those who know that meditation is a work of gladness and who chew the cud of the word of the Lord. But why that which divideth the hoof? Because the righteous man both walketh in this world, and at the same time looketh for the holy world to come. Ye see how wise a lawgiver Moses was. But whence should they perceive or understand these things? Howbeit we having justly perceived the commandments tell them as the Lord willed. To this end He circumcised our ears and hearts, that we might understand these things.

11. But let us enquire whether the Lord took care to signify beforehand concerning the water and the cross. Now concerning the water it is written in reference to Israel, how that they would not receive the baptism which bringeth remission of sins, but would build for themselves. For the prophet saith; *Be astonished, O heaven, and let the earth shudder the more at this, for this people hath done two evil things; they abandoned Me the fountain of life, and they digged for themselves a pit of death. Is My holy mountain of Sinai a desert rock? for ye shall be as the fledglings of a bird, which flutter aloft when deprived of their nest.* And

again the prophet saith; *I will go before thee, and level mountains and crush gates of brass and break in pieces bolts of iron, and I will give thee treasures dark, concealed, unseen, that they may know that I am the Lord God.* And; *Thou shalt dwell in a lofty cave of a strong rock.* And; *His water shall be sure; ye shall see the King in glory, and your soul shall meditate on the fear of the Lord.* And again He saith in another prophet; *And He that doeth these things shall be as the tree that is planted by the parting streams of waters, which shall yield his fruit at his proper season, and his leaf shall not fall off, and all things whatsoever he doeth shall prosper. Not so are the ungodly, not so, but are as the dust which the wind scattereth from the face of the earth. Therefore ungodly men shall not stand in judgment, neither sinners in the counsel of the righteous; for the Lord knoweth the way of the righteous, and the way of the ungodly shall perish.* Ye perceive how He pointed out the water and the cross at the same time. For this is the meaning; Blessed are they that set their hope on the cross, and go down into the water; for He speaketh of the reward *at his proper season;* then, saith He, I will repay. But now what saith He? *His leaves shall not fall off;* He meaneth by this that every word, which shall come forth from you through your mouth in faith and love, shall be for the conversion and hope of many. And again another prophet saith; *And the land of Jacob was praised above the whole earth.* He meaneth this; He glorifieth the vessel of His Spirit. Next what saith He? *And there was a river streaming from the right hand, and beautiful trees rose up from it; and whosoever shall eat of them shall live for ever.* This He saith, because we go down into the water laden with sins and filth, and rise up from it bearing fruit in the heart, resting our fear and hope on Jesus in the spirit. *And whosoever shall eat of these shall live for ever;* He meaneth this; whosoever, saith He, shall hear these things spoken and shall believe, shall live for ever.

12. In like manner again He defineth concerning the cross in another prophet, who saith; *And when shall these things be accomplished? saith the Lord. Whensoever a tree shall be bended and stand upright, and whensoever blood shall drop from a tree.* Again thou art taught concerning the cross, and Him that was to be crucified. And He saith again in Moses, when war was waged against Israel by men of another nation, and that He might remind them when the war was waged against them that for their sins they were delivered unto death; the Spirit saith to the heart of Moses, that he should make a type of

the cross and of Him that was to suffer, that unless, saith He, they shall
set their hope on Him, war shall be waged against them for ever.
Moses therefore pileth arms one upon another in the midst of the
encounter, and standing on higher ground than any he stretched out his
hands, and so Israel was again victorious.   Then, whenever he lowered
them, they were slain with the sword.   Wherefore was this? That they
might learn that they cannot be saved, unless they should set their hope
on Him.   And again in another prophet He saith; *The whole day long
have I stretched out My hands to a disobedient people that did gainsay My
righteous way*.   Again Moses maketh a type of Jesus, how that He must
suffer, and that He Himself whom they shall think to have destroyed
shall make alive in an emblem when Israel was falling.   For the Lord
caused all manner of serpents to bite them, and they died (forasmuch
as the transgression was wrought in Eve through the serpent), that He
might convince them that by reason of their transgression they should
be delivered over to the affliction of death.   Yea and further though
Moses gave the commandment; *Ye shall not have a molten or a carved
image for your God*, yet he himself made one that he might shew them
a type of Jesus.   So Moses maketh a brazen serpent, and setteth it up
conspicuously, and summoneth the people by proclamation.   When
therefore they were assembled together they entreated Moses that
he should offer up intercession for them that they might be healed.
And Moses said unto them; Whensoever, said he, one of you shall be
bitten, let him come to the serpent which is placed on the tree, and let
him believe and hope that the serpent being himself dead can make
alive; and forthwith he shall be saved.   And so they did.   Here again
thou hast in these things also the glory of Jesus, how that in Him and
unto Him are all things.   What again saith Moses unto Jesus (Joshua)
the son of Nun, when he giveth him this name, as being a prophet,
that all the people might give ear to him alone, because the Father
revealeth all things concerning His Son Jesus?   Moses therefore saith
to Jesus the son of Nun, giving him this name, when he sent him as a
spy on the land; *Take a book in thy hands, and write what the Lord
saith, how that the Son of God shall cut up by the roots all the house of
Amalek in the last days*.   Behold again it is Jesus, not a son of man, but
the Son of God, and He was revealed in the flesh in a figure.   Since
then men will say that Christ is the son of David, David himself
prophesieth being afraid and understanding the error of sinners; *The
Lord said unto my Lord, Sit thou on My right hand until I set thine*

enemies for a footstool under Thy feet. And again thus saith Isaiah; *The Lord said unto my Christ the Lord, of whose right hand I laid hold, that the nations should give ear before Him, and I will break down the strength of kings.* See how David calleth Him Lord, and calleth Him not Son.

13. Now let us see whether this people or the first people hath the inheritance, and whether the covenant had reference to us or to them. Hear then what the scripture saith concerning the people; *And Isaac prayed concerning Rebecca his wife, for she was barren. And she conceived. Then Rebecca went out to enquire of the Lord. And the Lord said unto her; Two nations are in thy womb, and two peoples in thy belly, and one people shall vanquish another people, and the greater shall serve the less.* Ye ought to understand who Isaac is, and who Rebecca is, and in whose case He hath shewn that the one people is greater than the other. And in another prophecy Jacob speaketh more plainly to Joseph his son, saying; *Behold, the Lord hath not bereft me of thy face; bring me thy sons, that I may bless them.* And he brought Ephraim and Manasseh, desiring that Manasseh should be blessed, because he was the elder; for Joseph led him to the right hand of his father Jacob. But Jacob saw in the spirit a type of the people that should come afterwards. And what saith He? *And Jacob crossed his hands, and placed his right hand on the head of Ephraim, the second and younger, and blessed him. And Joseph said unto Jacob, Transfer thy right hand to the head of Manasseh, for he is my first-born son. And Jacob said to Joseph, I know it, my son, I know it; but the greater shall serve the less. Yet this one also shall be blessed.* Mark in whose cases He ordained that this people should be first and heir of the covenant. If then besides this He also recorded it through Abraham, we attain the completion of our knowledge. What then saith he to Abraham when he alone believed, and was ascribed for righteousness? *Behold I have made thee, Abraham, a father of nations that believe in God in uncircumcision.*

14. Yea verily, but as regards the covenant which He sware to the fathers to give it to the people let us see whether He hath actually given it. He hath given it, but they themselves were not found worthy to receive it by reason of their sins. For the prophet saith; *And Moses was fasting in Mount Sinai forty days and forty nights, that he might receive the covenant of the Lord to give to the people. And [Moses] received from the Lord the two tables which were written by the finger of the hand of the Lord in the spirit.* And Moses took them, and brought

them down to give them to the people. And the Lord said unto Moses; *Moses, Moses, come down quickly; for thy people, whom thou leddest forth from the land of Egypt, hath done wickedly. And Moses perceived that they had made for themselves again molten images, and he cast them out of his hands and the tables of the covenant of the Lord were broken in pieces.* Moses received them, but they themselves were not found worthy. But how did we receive them? Mark this. Moses received them being a servant, but the Lord himself gave them to us to be the people of His inheritance, having endured patiently for our sakes. But He was made manifest, in order that at the same time they might be perfected in their sins, and we might receive the covenant through Him who inherited it, even the Lord Jesus, who was prepared beforehand hereunto, that appearing in person He might redeem out of darkness our hearts which had already been paid over unto death and delivered up to the iniquity of error, and thus establish the covenant in us through the word. For it is written how the Father chargeth Him to deliver us from darkness, and to prepare a holy people for Himself. Therefore saith the prophet; *I the Lord thy God called thee in righteousness, and I will lay hold of thy hand and will strengthen thee, and I have given thee to be a covenant of the race, a light to the Gentiles, to open the eyes of the blind, and to bring forth them that are bound from their fetters, and them that sit in darkness from their prison house.* We perceive then whence we were ransomed. Again the prophet saith; *Behold, I have set Thee to be a light to the Gentiles, that Thou shouldest be for salvation unto the ends of the earth; thus saith the Lord that ransomed thee, even God.* Again the prophet saith; *The Spirit of the Lord is upon Me, wherefore He anointed Me to preach good tidings to the humble; He hath sent Me to heal them that are broken-hearted, to preach release to the captives and recovery of sight to the blind, to proclaim the acceptable year of the Lord and the day of recompense, to comfort all that mourn.*

15. Moreover concerning the sabbath likewise it is written in the Ten Words, in which He spake to Moses face to face on Mount Sinai; *And ye shall hallow the sabbath of the Lord with pure hands and with a pure heart.* And in another place He saith; *If My sons observe the sabbath, then I will bestow My mercy upon them.* Of the sabbath He speaketh in the beginning of the creation; *And God made the works of His hands in six days, and He ended on the seventh day, and rested on it, and He hallowed it.* Give heed, children, what this meaneth; *He ended in six days.* He meaneth this, that in six thousand years the Lord shall bring

all things to an end; for the day with Him signifieth a thousand years; and this He himself beareth me witness, saying; *Behold, the day of the Lord shall be as a thousand years.* Therefore, children, in six days, that is in six thousand years, everything shall come to an end. *And He rested on the seventh day.* This He meaneth; when His Son shall come, and shall abolish the time of the Lawless One, and shall judge the ungodly, and shall change the sun and the moon and the stars, then shall He truly rest on the seventh day. Yea and furthermore He saith; *Thou shalt hallow it with pure hands and with a pure heart.* If therefore a man is able now to hallow the day which God hallowed, though he be pure in heart, we have gone utterly astray. But if after all then and not till then shall we truly rest and hallow it, when we shall ourselves be able to do so after being justified and receiving the promise, when iniquity is no more and all things have been made new by the Lord, we shall be able to hallow it then, because we ourselves shall have been hallowed first. Finally He saith to them; *Your new moons and your sabbaths I cannot away with.* Ye see what is His meaning; it is not your present sabbaths that are acceptable [unto Me], but the sabbath which I have made, in the which, when I have set all things at rest, I will make the beginning of the eighth day which is the beginning of another world. Wherefore also we keep the eighth day for rejoicing, in the which also Jesus rose from the dead, and having been manifested ascended into the heavens.

16. Moreover I will tell you likewise concerning the temple, how these wretched men being led astray set their hope on the building, and not on their God that made them, as being a house of God. For like the Gentiles almost they consecrated Him in the temple. But what saith the Lord abolishing the temple? Learn ye. *Who hath measured the heaven with a span, or hath measured the earth with his hand? Have not I, saith the Lord? The heaven is My throne and the earth the footstool of My feet. What manner of house will ye build for Me? Or what shall be My resting-place?* Ye perceive that their hope is vain. Furthermore He saith again; *Behold they that pulled down this temple themselves shall build it.* So it cometh to pass; for because they went to war it was pulled down by their enemies. Now also the very servants of their enemies shall build it up. Again, it was revealed how the city and the temple and the people of Israel should be betrayed. For the scripture saith; *And it shall be in the last days, that the Lord shall deliver up the sheep of the pasture and the fold and the tower*

thereof to destruction. And it came to pass as the Lord spake. But let us enquire whether there be any temple of God. There is; in the place where He Himself undertakes to make and finish it. For it is written; *And it shall come to pass, when the week is being accomplished, the temple of God shall be built gloriously in the name of the Lord.* I find then that there is a temple. How then shall it be built in the name of the Lord? Understand ye. Before we believed on God, the abode of our heart was corrupt and weak, a temple truly built by hands; for it was full of idolatry and was a house of demons, because we did whatsoever was contrary to God. *But it shall be built in the name of the Lord.* Give heed then that the temple of the Lord may be built gloriously. How? Understand ye. By receiving the remission of our sins and hoping on the Name we became new, created afresh from the beginning. Wherefore God dwelleth truly in our habitation within us. How? The word of His faith, the calling of His promise, the wisdom of the ordinances, the commandments of the teaching, He Himself prophesying in us, He Himself dwelling in us, opening for us who had been in bondage unto death the door of the temple, which is the mouth, and giving us repentance leadeth us to the incorruptible temple. For he that desireth to be saved looketh not to the man, but to Him that dwelleth and speaketh in him, being amazed at this that he has never at any time heard these words from the mouth of the speaker, nor himself ever desired to hear them. This is the spiritual temple built up to the Lord.

17. So far as it was possible with all simplicity to declare it unto you, my soul hopeth that I have not omitted anything [of the matters pertaining unto salvation and so failed in my desire]. For if I should write to you concerning things immediate or future, ye would not understand them, because they are put in parables. So much then for this.

18. But let us pass on to another lesson and teaching. There are two ways of teaching and of power, the one of light and the other of darkness; and there is a great difference between the two ways. For on the one are stationed the light-giving angels of God, on the other the angels of Satan. And the one is Lord from all eternity and unto all eternity, whereas the other is Lord of the season of iniquity that now is.

19. This then is the way of light, if any one desiring to travel on the way to his appointed place would be zealous in his works. The

knowledge then which is given to us whereby we may walk therein is as follows. Thou shalt love Him that made thee, thou shalt fear Him that created thee, thou shalt glorify Him that redeemed thee from death; thou shalt be simple in heart and rich in spirit; thou shalt not cleave to those who walk in the way of death; thou shalt hate everything that is not pleasing to God; thou shalt hate all hypocrisy; thou shalt never forsake the commandments of the Lord. Thou shalt not exalt thyself, but shalt be lowly-minded in all things. Thou shalt not assume glory to thyself. Thou shalt not entertain a wicked design against thy neighbour; thou shalt not admit boldness into thy soul. Thou shalt not commit fornication, *thou shalt not commit adultery*, thou shalt not corrupt boys. The word of God shall not come forth from thee where any are unclean. Thou shalt not make a difference in a person to reprove him for a transgression. Thou shalt be meek, thou shalt be *quiet*, thou shalt be *fearing the words* which thou hast heard. Thou shalt not bear a grudge against thy brother. Thou shalt not doubt whether a thing shall be or not be. *Thou shalt not take the name of the Lord in vain.* Thou shalt love thy neighbour more than thine own soul. Thou shalt not murder a child by abortion, nor again shalt thou kill it when it is born. Thou shalt not withhold thy hand from thy son or thy daughter, but from their youth thou shalt teach them the fear of God. Thou shalt not be found coveting thy neighbour's goods; thou shalt not be found greedy of gain. Neither shalt thou cleave with thy soul to the lofty, but shalt walk with the humble and righteous. The accidents that befal thee thou shalt receive as good, knowing that nothing is done without God. Thou shalt not be double-minded nor double-tongued. Thou shalt be subject unto thy masters as to a type of God in shame and fear. Thou shalt not command in bitterness thy bondservant or thine handmaid who set their hope on the same God, lest haply they should cease to fear the God who is over both of you; for He came not to call with respect of persons, but to call those whom the Spirit had prepared. Thou shalt make thy neighbour partake in all things, and shalt not say *that anything is thine own.* For if ye are fellow-partakers in that which is imperishable, how much rather shall ye be in the things which are perishable. Thou shalt not be hasty with thy tongue, for the mouth is a snare of death. So far as thou art able, thou shalt be pure for thy soul's sake. *Be not thou found holding out thy hands to receive, and drawing them in to give.* Thou shalt love as the apple of thine eye every one *that speaketh unto thee the word of the Lord. Thou shalt remember* the day of judgment night and day, and thou shalt seek out day by day the persons of the saints, either labouring by word and going to exhort them and meditating how thou mayst save souls by thy word, or thou shalt work with thy hands for a ransom for thy sins. Thou shall not hesitate to give, neither shalt thou murmur when giving, but thou shalt know who is the good paymaster of thy reward. Thou shalt keep those things which thou hast received, neither adding to them nor taking away from them. Thou shalt utterly hate the Evil One. Thou shalt judge righteously. Thou shalt not make a schism, but thou shalt pacify them that contend by bringing them together. Thou shalt confess thy sins. Thou shalt not betake thyself to prayer with an evil conscience. This is the way of light.

20. But the way of the Black One is crooked and full of a curse. For it is a way of eternal death with punishment wherein are the things that destroy men's souls—idolatry, boldness, exaltation of power, hypocrisy, doubleness of heart, adultery, murder, plundering, pride, transgression, treachery, malice, stubbornness, witchcraft, magic, covetousness, absence of the fear of God; persecutors of good men, hating the truth, loving lies, not perceiving the reward of righteousness, not *cleaving to the good* nor to righteous judgment, paying no heed to the widow and the orphan, wakeful not for the fear of God but for that which is evil; men from whom gentleness and forbearance stand aloof and far off; loving vain things, pursuing a recompense, not pitying the poor man, not toiling for him that is oppressed with toil, ready in slander, not recognizing Him that made them, murderers of children, corrupters of the creatures of God, turning away from him that is in want, oppressing him that is afflicted, advocates of the wealthy, unjust judges of the poor, sinful in all things.

21. It is good therefore to learn the ordinances of the Lord, as many as have been written above, and to walk in them. For he that doeth these things shall be glorified in the kingdom of God; whereas he that chooseth their opposites shall perish together with his works. For this cause is the resurrection, for this the recompense. I entreat those of you who are in higher station, if ye will receive any counsel of good advice from me, keep amongst you those to whom ye may do good. Fail not. The day is at hand, in which everything shall be destroyed together with the Evil One. *The Lord is at hand and His reward.* Again and again I entreat you; be good lawgivers one to another; continue faithful counsellors to yourselves; take away from

you all hypocrisy. And may God, who is Lord of the whole world, give you wisdom, judgment, learning, knowledge of His ordinances, patience. And be ye taught of God, seeking diligently what the Lord requireth of you, and act that ye may be found in the day of judgment. But if you have any remembrance of good, call me to mind when ye practise these things, that both my desire and my watchfulness may lead to some good result. I entreat you asking it as a favour. So long as the good vessel (of the body) is with you, be lacking in none of these things, but search them out constantly, and fulfil every commandment; for they deserve it. For this reason I was the more eager to write to you so far as I was able, that I might give you joy. Fare ye well, children of love and peace. The Lord of glory and of every grace be with your spirit.

THE SHEPHERD

OF

HERMAS

THE SHEPHERD OF HERMAS

THIS work is entitled in the most ancient notices 'The Shepherd', or 'The Shepherd of Hermas'. Hermas is both the narrator and the hero of the narrative. The Shepherd is the divine teacher, who communicates to Hermas, either by precept or by allegory, the lessons which are to be disseminated for the instruction of the Church. Later confusions, which identify Hermas with the Pastor, find no countenance in the work itself. Hermas' own personal and family history are interwoven from time to time into the narrative, and made subservient to the moral purposes of the work. In this case it resembles the *Divina Commedia*, though history plays a much less important part here than in Dante's great poem.

The structure of the work is seriously impaired by the common division into three parts or books, *Visions*, *Mandates*, and *Similitudes*, as if they stood on the same level. It may be convenient to use this mode of division for purposes of reference alone; but we must not suffer it to dominate our conception of the work. The *Visions* are introductory, and the Shepherd does not appear until their close. He delivers his message to Hermas in two parts, (1) *Mandates* or Precepts, (2) *Similitudes* or Parables, i.e., moral lessons taught by allegory.

The person first introduced in the book is one Rhoda (*Vis*. i. 1), to whom Hermas had been sold when brought from Rome as a slave. Her part is somewhat the same as Beatrice's in Dante's poem. She appears to him in the heavens as he is on his way to Cumæ, and reproaches him with his not altogether blameless passion for her. Having thus aroused his conscience, she withdraws. Then he sees before him an aged woman whom (considering the place) he not unnaturally mistakes for the Sibyl (*Vis*. ii. 4), but who proves to be the Church. The object of the *Visions* indeed seems to be to place before the reader the conception of the Church under the guise of an aged woman, whose features become more youthful at each successive appearance. Thus the lessons of a smitten and penitent conscience, of the Church growing and spreading (the Church Militant), lastly, of the Church purified by suffering (the Church Triumphant), and the terrors of the judgment, occupy the four *Visions* properly so called. Hermas is enjoined to write down all that he hears. One copy of his book he is to send to Clement, who is charged with making it known to foreign cities; another to Grapte, whose business it is to instruct the widows and orphans, and he himself, together with the presbyters, is to read it to the people of 'this city', i.e., Rome (*Vis.* ii. 4).

The fifth *Vision* is different in kind from the preceding four, and indeed is designated, not a Vision (ὅρασις), but a Revelation (ἀποκάλυψις). Hermas is now in his own house. The appearance is no longer the representation of the Church, but a man of glorious visage in a pastoral habit, who has been sent to dwell with him, and teach him to the end of his days. He is 'the Shepherd, the angel of repentance', who delivers to him certain Mandates and Similitudes, which he is ordered to write down, and which form the two remaining books—the main part of the work.

The teaching of the Shepherd then is contained in the twelve *Mandates* and the ten *Similitudes* which follow. But the tenth and last of the latter is not strictly a parable like the rest. It contains a final chapter, summing up the function of the Shepherd and his heavenly associates, in the work of perfecting the instruction of Hermas.

2.

The geographical setting of the narrative has its centre in Rome, where evidently the work itself was written. Hermas' home in the city, the road to Cumæ, the *Via Campana*,—these are the localities mentioned by name. There is one exception. Arcadia is chosen as the subject of a Similitude (*Sim.* ix.), the last properly so called, because the mountains visible from a central height by their character and position afford a good subject for the concluding parable, the component elements of the Church (see J. A. Robinson, *The Athos*

Codex of the Shepherd of Hermas, p. 30, where the views of Rendel Harris are discussed and further developed and modified). As he was brought to Rome, and sold as a slave there, Arcadia may have been his native place.

3.

The *date* is uncertain. The work is found in general circulation in the Eastern and Western Churches, soon after the middle of the second century. About this time also it must have been translated into Latin. It is quoted by Irenæus in Gaul, by Tertullian in Africa, by Clement and Origen in Alexandria. All these fathers—even Tertullian, before he became a Montanist—either cite it as scripture, or assign to it a special authority as in some sense inspired and quasi-canonical. The same inference as to its early influence may be drawn from the denunciation of Tertullian, who—now become a Montanist—rejects it as repulsive to his puritan tendencies (*de Pudic.* 10), and the author of the *Muratorian Canon* (c. A.D. 180), who denies it a place among either the prophets or the apostles, though apparently allowing it to be read privately for edification. Its canonicity moreover had been the subject of discussion in more than one council, when Tertullian wrote (*l. c.*, not before A.D. 212).

With the date is closely connected the question of *authorship*. On this point there are two ancient traditions.

(1) The author of the 'Shepherd' was the same Hermas, who is greeted by S. Paul as a member of the Roman Church, A.D. 58 (Rom. xvi. 14). This is the view adopted by Origen (IV. p. 683) in his commentary on the passage, where he speaks of the book as 'a very useful scripture, and in my opinion divinely inspired'; but, as he introduces this view of the authorship with 'ut puto' it is plain that he does not fall back on any historical tradition in support of his opinion. His influence had great weight with subsequent writers.

(2) It was written by one Hermas, the brother of pope Pius I (c. A.D. 140—155) during the episcopate of the latter. This is stated in the *Muratorian Canon* (c. A.D. 180) 'sedente cathedram urbis Romae ecclesiae Pio episcopo fratre eius'. This statement, however, is not consistent with the mention of Clement as a contemporary. If it be true, either some other Clement is meant, or the original Greek of the

Canon, of which only the Latin is extant, cannot have stated that Pius was actually bishop at the time when it was written.

This tradition appears likewise in one or two subsequent writings, which however are perhaps not independent. It is somewhat discredited by the fact that its motive in depreciating the value of the work, as being quite recent and having no claim to be read in the Church like the writings of the Apostles and prophets, appears in the context[1].

(3)   Besides these two traditional views, a third and intermediate Hermas, not otherwise known, is postulated as the author about A.D. 90—100, to meet the difficulty about Clement. This is the view of several recent critics (Zahn, *Hirt des Hermas* p. 14 sq, followed by Caspari and others). The notices of the Christian ministry, and of the condition of the Church generally, seem to be consistent with either the second or the third view, though they suggest the earlier date rather than the later (*Vis.* ii. 2, 4, iii. 5, 9, *Sim.* ix. 27).

On the whole we may, though not without diffidence, adopt (2) the ancient tradition, which is definite and claims to be almost contemporary, as the safest guide; though confessedly (3) the modern suggestion has stronger support from internal evidence, such as it is.

The Æthiopic version, which identifies the author with S. Paul, ought to be regarded as a blunder, rather than a tradition founded on Acts xiv. 12 τὸν δὲ Παῦλον Ἑρμῆν.

4.

The authorities for the text are as follows :

I.   GREEK MANUSCRIPTS.

1.   The celebrated Sinaitic MS (א) of the fourth century, where, after a gap caused by the loss of six leaves, the Shepherd follows

---

[1] These words are illustrated by the fact that (a) in the Codex Sinaiticus (א) the Shepherd (a fragment, see below, p. 295) appears at the end of the volume, following on the Epistle of Barnabas, which again follows the Apocalypse and the books of the Canonical New Testament ; (b) in the list appended to the Codex Claromontanus (VIth Cent.) again it follows the New Testament proper, of which the closing books are 'Revelation of John', 'Acts', and is succeeded by the apocryphal 'Acts of Paul', and 'Revelation of Peter'; (c) in several MSS of the Latin version it appears in different parts of the Old Testament.

the Epistle of Barnabas at the end of the volume. Unfortunately, however, only a fragment, roughly speaking the first quarter of the text, survives, the manuscript, after several lacunæ, breaking off finally in the middle of *Mand.* iv. 3.

2. The Athos MS (A), written in a very small and cramped hand of the fourteenth century. This consists of three leaves now in the University Library at Leipsic, and six leaves still remaining in the Monastery of Gregory on Mount Athos. The portion of the manuscript now at Leipsic was in 1855 brought from Mount Athos by the famous forger Simonides, who sold it to the University there, as well as what purported to be a copy of six other leaves of the same document. This copy was subsequently edited by Anger. The existence, however, of the original manuscript was questioned until 1880, when Dr Lambros rediscovered it at Mount Athos. His collation of the readings of these six leaves was in 1888 published by J. A. Robinson (*The Athos Codex of the Shepherd of Hermas*). Like the Sinaitic, this manuscript is incomplete, having lost a leaf at the end; but from *Mand.* iv. 3 to *Sim.* ix. 30 (where it fails us), that is to say, for nearly three fourths of the whole work, it is our sole Greek authority for the text.

Besides Simonides' *apographon* mentioned above, another copy was subsequently found among his papers after his arrest, and published by Tischendorf. The publication of Dr Lambros' collation shows us that, whereas the *apographon* edited by Anger was a forgery, the second apographon was truly described as being a transcript of the Athos MS. In passages therefore where the Athos codex has become damaged and illegible between 1855 and 1880, this apographon (A^s) has a certain value.

II. VERSIONS.

1. Latin Versions. These are two in number, (*a*) the so-called *Old Latin Version* (L$_1$), which exists in about twenty manuscripts, the mutual relation of which has not yet been made quite clear. From this version Faber Stapulensis published his *editio princeps* in 1513. (*b*) The *Palatine Version* (L$_2$), found in one manuscript of the fourteenth century, and in 1857 published in full by Dressel. Both these versions give us the text virtually complete.

2. Æthiopic Version (E). This exists in a manuscript discovered in 1847 in the monastery of Guindaguinde by A. d'Abbadie, who procured a transcript, but did not realise the full importance of his

discovery. At length at Dillmann's earnest request he published the text with a Latin translation in 1860. This version likewise contains the Pastor complete.

The mutual relations and comparative value of our authorities are matters of considerable dispute; but a comparison of the early chapters, where the Greek of the Sinaitic MS exists, shows us that ℵ generally agrees with L_1 L_2 against AE, the close connexion of this latter pair of authorities being noticeable throughout. Again, within these groups, L_2 appears to preserve a purer text than L_1, and E than A.

III. PATRISTIC QUOTATIONS.

Besides these direct authorities for the text, the Shepherd of Hermas is quoted in the Greek by Clement of Alexandria and Origen, while considerable passages have been incorporated into the texts of Antiochus the Monk and ps-Athanasius.

THE SHEPHERD OF HERMAS

THE master, who reared me, had sold me to one Rhoda in Rome. After many years, I met her again, and began to love her as a sister. After a certain time I saw her bathing in the river Tiber; and I gave her my hand, and led her out of the river. So, seeing her beauty, I reasoned in my heart, saying, 'Happy were I, if I had such an one to wife both in beauty and in character.' I merely reflected on this and nothing more. After a certain time, as I was journeying to Cumæ, and glorifying God's creatures for their greatness and splendour and power, as I walked I fell asleep. And a Spirit took me, and bore me away through a pathless tract, through which no man could pass: for the place was precipitous, and broken into clefts by reason of the waters. When then I had crossed the river, I came into the level country, and knelt down, and began to pray to the Lord and to confess my sins. Now, while I prayed, the heaven was opened, and I see the lady, whom I had desired, greeting me from heaven, saying, 'Good morrow, Hermas.' And, looking at her, I said to her, 'Lady, what doest *thou* here?' Then she answered me, 'I was taken up, that I might convict thee of thy sins before the Lord.' I said to her, 'Dost thou now convict me?' 'Nay, not so,' said she, 'but hear the words, that I shall say to thee. God, Who dwelleth in the heavens, and created out of nothing the things which are, and increased and multiplied them for His holy Church's sake, is wroth with thee, for that thou didst sin against me.' I answered her and said, 'Sin against thee? In what way? Did I ever speak an unseemly word unto thee? Did I not always regard thee as a goddess? Did I not always respect thee as a sister? How couldst thou falsely charge me, lady, with such villainy and uncleanness?' Laughing she saith unto me, 'The desire after evil entered into thine heart. Nay, thinkest thou not that it is an evil deed for a righteous man, if the evil desire should enter into his heart? It is indeed a sin and a great one too,' saith she; 'for the righteous man entertaineth righteous purposes. While then his purposes are righteous, his repute stands stedfast in the heavens, and he finds the Lord easily propitiated in all that he does. But they that entertain evil purposes in their hearts, bring upon themselves death and captivity, especially they that claim for themselves this present world, and boast in its riches, and cleave not to the good things that are to come. Their souls shall rue it, seeing that they have no hope, but have abandoned themselves and their life. But do thou pray unto God, and He shall heal thine own sins, and those of thy whole house, and of all the saints.'

2. As soon as she had spoken these words the heavens were shut; and I was given over to horror and grief. Then I said within myself, 'If this sin is recorded against me, how can I be saved? Or how shall I propitiate God for my sins which are full-blown? Or with what words shall I entreat the Lord that He may be propitious unto me?' While I was advising and discussing these matters in my heart, I see before me a great white chair of snow-white wool; and there came an aged lady in glistening raiment, having a book in her hands, and she sat down alone, and she saluted me, 'Good morrow, Hermas.' Then I, grieved and weeping, said, 'Good morrow, lady.' And she said to me, 'Why so gloomy, Hermas, thou that art patient and good-tempered, and art always smiling? Why so downcast in thy looks, and far from cheerful?' And I said to her, 'Because of an excellent lady's saying that I had sinned against her.' Then she said, 'Far be this thing from the servant of God! Nevertheless the thought did enter into thy heart concerning her. Now to the servants of God such a purpose bringeth sin. For it is an evil and mad purpose to overtake a devout spirit that hath been already approved, that it should desire an evil deed, and especially if it be Hermas the temperate, who abstaineth from every evil desire, and is full of all simplicity and of great guilelessness.

3. 'Yet it is not for this that God is wroth with thee, but that thou mayest convert thy family, that hath done wrong against the Lord and against you their parents. But out of fondness for thy children thou didst not admonish thy family, but didst suffer it to become fearfully corrupt. Therefore the Lord is wroth with thee. But He will heal all thy past sins, which have been committed in thy family; for by reason of their sins and iniquities thou hast been corrupted by the affairs of this world. But the great mercy of the Lord had pity on thee and thy

family, and will strengthen thee, and establish thee in His glory. Only be not thou careless, but take courage, and strengthen thy family. For as the smith hammering his work conquers the task which he wills, so also doth righteous discourse repeated daily conquer all evil. Cease not therefore to reprove thy children; for I know that if they shall repent with all their heart, they shall be written in the books of life with the saints.' After these words of hers had ceased, she saith unto me, 'Wilt thou listen to me as I read?' Then say I, 'Yes, lady.' She saith to me, 'Be attentive, and hear the glories of God.' I listened with attention and with wonder to that which I had no power to remember; for all the words were terrible, such as man cannot bear. The last words however I remembered, for they were suitable for us and gentle. 'Behold, the God of Hosts, Who by His invisible and mighty power and by His great wisdom created the world, and by His glorious purpose clothed His creation with comeliness, and by His strong word fixed the heaven, and founded the earth upon the waters, and by His own wisdom and providence formed His holy Church, which also He blessed—behold, He removeth the heavens and the mountains and the hills and the seas, and all things are made level for His elect, that He may fulfil to them the promise which He promised with great glory and rejoicing, if so be that they shall keep the ordinances of God, which they received, with great faith.'

4. When then she finished reading and arose from her chair, there came four young men, and they took away the chair, and departed towards the East. Then she calleth me unto her, and she touched my breast, and saith to me, 'Did my reading please thee?' And I say unto her, 'Lady, these last words please me, but the former were difficult and hard.' Then she spake to me, saying, 'These last words are for the righteous, but the former are for the heathen and the rebellious.' While she yet spake with me, two men appeared, and took her by the arms, and they departed, whither the chair also had gone, towards the East. And she smiled as she departed and, as she was going, she saith to me, 'Play the man, Hermas.'

VISION 2.

1. I was on the way to Cumæ, at the same season as last year, and I called to mind my last year's vision as I walked; and again a Spirit taketh me, and carrieth me away to the same place as last year. When then I arrived at the place, I fell upon my knees, and began to pray to

the Lord, and to glorify His name, for that he counted me worthy, and made known unto me my former sins. But after I had risen up from prayer, I behold before me the aged lady, whom also I had seen last year, walking and reading a little book. And she saith to me, 'Canst thou report these things to the elect of God?' I say unto her, 'Lady, I cannot recollect so much; but give me the little book, that I may copy it.' 'Take it,' saith she, 'and be sure and return it to me.' I took it, and retiring to a certain spot in the country I copied it letter for letter: for I could not make out the syllables. When then I had finished the letters of the book, suddenly the book was snatched out of my hand; but by whom I did not see.

2. Now after fifteen days, when I had fasted and entreated the Lord earnestly, the knowledge of the writing was revealed to me. And this is what was written:—

'Thy seed, Hermas, have sinned against God, and have blasphemed the Lord, and have betrayed their parents through great wickedness, yea, they have got the name of betrayers of parents, and yet they did not profit by their betrayal; and they still further added to their sins wanton deeds and reckless wickedness; and so the measure of their transgressions was filled up. But make these words known to all thy children, and to thy wife who shall be as thy sister; for she too refraineth not from using her tongue, wherewith she doeth evil. But, when she hears these words, she will refrain, and will find mercy. After that thou hast made known unto them all these words, which the Master commanded me that they should be revealed unto thee, then all their sins which they sinned aforetime are forgiven to them; yea, and to all the saints that have sinned unto this day, if they repent with their whole heart, and remove double-mindedness from their heart. For the Master sware by His own glory, as concerning His elect; that if, now that this day has been set as a limit, sin shall hereafter be committed, they shall not find salvation; for repentance for the righteous hath an end; the days of repentance are accomplished for all the saints; whereas for the Gentiles there is repentance until the last day. Thou shalt therefore say unto the rulers of the Church, that they direct their paths in righteousness, that they may receive in full the promises with abundant glory. Ye therefore that work righteousness be stedfast, and be not double-minded, that ye may have admission with the holy angels. Blessed are ye, as many as endure patiently the great tribulation that cometh, and as many as shall not deny their life. For the

Lord sware concerning His Son, that those who denied their Lord should be rejected from their life, even they that are now about to deny Him in the coming days; but to those who denied Him aforetime, to them mercy was given of His great lovingkindness.

3. 'But do thou, Hermas, no longer bear a grudge against thy children, neither suffer thy sister to have her way, so that they may be purified from their former sins. For they shall be chastised with a righteous chastisement, unless thou bear a grudge against them thyself. The bearing of a grudge worketh death. But thou, Hermas, hast had great tribulations of thine own, by reason of the transgressions of thy family, because thou hadst no care for them. For thou wast neglectful of them, and wast mixed up with thine evil transactions. But herein is thy salvation, in that thou didst not depart from the living God, and in thy simplicity and thy great continence. These have saved thee, if thou abidest therein; and they save all who do such things, and walk in guilelessness and simplicity. These men prevail over all wickedness, and continue unto life eternal. Blessed are all they that work righteousness. They shall never be destroyed. But thou shalt say to Maximus, "Behold tribulation cometh (upon thee), if thou think fit to deny a second time. *The Lord is nigh unto them that turn unto Him*, as it is written in Eldad and Modat, who prophesied to the people in the wilderness."'

4. Now, brethren, a revelation was made unto me in my sleep by a youth of exceeding fair form, who said to me, 'Whom thinkest thou the aged woman, from whom thou receivedst the book, to be?' I say, 'The Sibyl.' 'Thou art wrong,' saith he, 'she is not.' 'Who then is she?' I say. 'The Church,' saith he. I said unto him, 'Wherefore then is she aged?' 'Because,' saith he, 'she was created before all things; therefore is she aged; and for her sake the world was framed.' And afterwards I saw a vision in my house. The aged woman came, and asked me, if I had already given the book to the elders. I said that I had not given it. 'Thou hast done well,' she said, 'for I have words to add. When then I shall have finished all the words, it shall be made known by thy means to all the elect. Thou shalt therefore write two little books, and shalt send one to Clement, and one to Grapte. So Clement shall send to the foreign cities, for this is his duty; while Grapte shall instruct the widows and the orphans. But thou shalt read (the book) to this city along with the elders that preside over the Church.

Vision 3.

The third vision, which I saw, brethren, was as follows. After fasting often, and entreating the Lord to declare unto me the revelation which He promised to show me by the mouth of the aged woman, that very night the aged woman was seen of me, and she said to me, ' Seeing that thou art so importunate and eager to know all things, come into the country where thou abidest, and about the fifth hour I will appear, and will show thee what thou oughtest to see.' I asked her, saying, ' Lady, to what part of the country?' ' Where thou wilt,' saith she. I selected a beautiful and retired spot; but before I spoke to her and named the spot, she saith to me, ' I will come, whither thou willest.' I went then, brethren, into the country, and I counted up the hours, and came to the place where I appointed her to come, and I see an ivory couch placed there, and on the couch there lay a linen cushion, and on the cushion was spread a coverlet of fine linen of flax.

When I saw these things so ordered, and no one in the place, I was amazed, and a fit of trembling seized me, and my hair stood on end ; and a fit of shuddering came upon me, because I was alone. When then I recovered myself, and remembered the glory of God, and took courage, I knelt down and confessed my sins to the Lord once more, as I had done on the former occasion.

Then she came with six young men, the same whom I had seen before, and she stood by me, and listened attentively to me, as I prayed and confessed my sins to the Lord.   And she touched me, and said : ' Hermas, make an end of constantly entreating for thy sins ; entreat also for righteousness, that thou mayest take some part forthwith to thy family.'   Then she raiseth me by the hand, and leadeth me to the couch, and saith to the young men, ' Go ye, and build.'   And after the young men had retired and we were left alone, she saith to me, ' Sit down here.'   I say to her, ' Lady, let the elders sit down first.'   ' Do as I bid thee,' saith she, ' sit down.'   When then I wanted to sit down on the right side, she would not allow me, but beckoned me with her hand that I should sit on the left side.   As then I was musing thereon, and was sad because she would not permit me to sit on the right side, she saith to me, ' Art thou sad, Hermas?   The place on the right side is for others, even for those who have already been well-pleasing to God, and have suffered for the Name's sake.   But thou lackest much that thou shouldest sit with them; but as thou abidest in thy simplicity, even so continue, and thou shalt sit with them, thou and as many as shall have done their deeds, and have suffered what they suffered.'

2. 'What did they suffer?' say I. 'Listen,' saith she. 'Stripes, imprisonments, great tribulations, crosses, wild beasts, for the Name's sake. Therefore to them belongs the right side of the Holiness—to them, and to all who shall suffer for the Name. But for the rest is the left side. Howbeit, to both, to them that sit on the right, and to them that sit on the left, are the same gifts, and the same promises, only they sit on the right and have a certain glory. Thou indeed art very desirous to sit on the right with them, but thy shortcomings are many; yet thou shalt be purified from thy shortcomings; yea, and all that are not double-minded shall be purified from all their sins unto this day.'

When she had said this, she wished to depart; but, falling at her feet, I entreated her by the Lord that she would show me the vision which she promised. Then she again took me by the hand, and raiseth me, and seateth me on the couch at the left hand, while she herself sat on the right. And lifting up a certain glistening rod, she saith to me, 'Seest thou a great thing?' I say to her, 'Lady, I see nothing.' She saith to me, 'Look thou; dost thou not see in front of thee a great tower being builded upon the waters, of glistening square stones?' Now the tower was being builded foursquare by the six young men that came with her. And countless other men were bringing stones, some of them from the deep, and others from the land, and were handing them to the six young men. And they took them and builded. The stones that were dragged from the deep they placed in every case, just as they were, into the building, for they had been shaped, and they fitted in their joining with the other stones; and they adhered so closely one with another that their joining could not possibly be detected; and the building of the tower appeared as if it were built of one stone. But of the other stones which were brought from the dry land, some they threw away, and some they put into the building; and others they broke in pieces, and threw to a distance from the tower. Now many other stones were lying round the tower, and they did not use them for the building; for some of them were mildewed, and others had cracks in them, and others were too short, and others were white and round, and did not fit into the building. And I saw other stones thrown to a distance from the tower, and coming to the way, and yet not staying in the way, but rolling to where there was no way; and others falling into the fire and burning there; and others falling near the waters, and yet not able to

roll into the water, although they desired to roll and to come to
the water.

3. When she had shown me these things, she wished to hurry away.
I say to her, 'Lady, what advantage is it to me to have seen these things,
and yet not to know what the things mean?'   She answered and said
unto me, 'Thou art an over-curious fellow, in desiring to know all that
concerns the tower.'   'Yea, lady,' I said, 'that I may announce it to
my brethren, and that they [may be the more gladdened and] when
they hear [these things] may know the Lord in great glory.'   Then said
she, 'Many shall hear; but when they hear, some of them shall be glad,
and others shall weep.   Yet even these latter, if they hear and repent,
shall likewise be glad.   Hear thou therefore the parables of the tower;
for I will reveal all things unto thee.   And trouble me no more about
revelation; for these revelations have an end, seeing that they have
been completed.   Nevertheless thou wilt not cease asking for revelations;
for thou art shameless.

'The tower, which thou seest building, is myself, the Church, which
was seen of thee both now and aforetime.   Ask, therefore, what thou
willest concerning the tower, and I will reveal it unto thee, that thou
mayest rejoice with the saints.'   I say unto her, 'Lady, since thou didst
hold me worthy once for all, that thou shouldest reveal all things to me,
reveal them.'   Then she saith to me, 'Whatsoever is possible to be
revealed to thee, shall be revealed.   Only let thy heart be with God,
and doubt not in thy mind about that which thou seest.'   I asked her,
'Wherefore is the tower builded upon waters, lady?'   'I told thee so
before,' said she, 'and indeed thou dost enquire diligently.   So by thy
enquiry thou discoverest the truth.   Hear then why the tower is builded
upon waters; it is because your life is saved and shall be saved by water.
But the tower has been founded by the word of the Almighty and
Glorious Name, and is strengthened by the unseen power of the Master.'

4. I answered and said unto her, 'Lady, this thing is great and
marvellous.   But the six young men that build, who are they, lady?'

'These are the holy angels of GOD, that were created first of all, unto
whom the Lord delivered all His creation to increase and to build it,
and to be masters of all creation.   By their hands therefore the building
of the tower will be accomplished.'   'And who are the others who are
bringing the stones?'   'They also are holy angels of God; but these
six are superior to them.   The building of the tower then shall be accomplished, and all alike shall rejoice in the (completed) circle of the tower,

and shall glorify God that the building of the tower was accomplished.' I enquired of her, saying, 'Lady, I could wish to know concerning the end of the stones, and their power, of what kind it is.' She answered and said unto me, 'It is not that thou of all men art especially worthy that it should be revealed to thee; for there are others before thee, and better than thou art, unto whom these visions ought to have been revealed. But that the name of God may be glorified, it hath been revealed to thee, and shall be revealed, for the sake of the doubtful-minded, who question in their hearts whether these things are so or not. Tell them that all these things are true, and that there is nothing beside the truth, but that all are stedfast, and valid, and established on a firm foundation.

5. 'Hear now concerning the stones that go to the building. The stones that are squared and white, and that fit together in their joints, these are the apostles and bishops and teachers and deacons, who walked after the holiness of God, and exercised their office of bishop and teacher and deacon in purity and sanctity for the elect of God, some of them already fallen on sleep, and others still living. And because they always agreed with one another, they both had peace among themselves and listened one to another. Therefore their joinings fit together in the building of the tower.' 'But they that are dragged from the deep, and placed in the building, and that fit together in their joinings with the other stones that are already builded in, who are they?' 'These are they that suffered for the name of the Lord.' 'But the other stones that are brought from the dry land, I would fain know who these are, lady.' She said, 'Those that go to the building, and yet are not hewn, these the Lord hath approved because they walked in the uprightness of the Lord, and rightly performed His commandments.' 'But they that are brought and placed in the building, who are they?' 'They are young in the faith, and faithful; but they are warned by the angels to do good, because wickedness was found in them.' 'But those whom they rejected and threw away, who are they?' 'These have sinned, and desire to repent, therefore they were not cast to a great distance from the tower, because they will be useful for the building, if they repent. They then that shall repent, if they repent, will be strong in the faith, if they repent now while the tower is building. But if the building shall be finished, they have no more any place, but shall be castaways. This privilege only they have, that they lie near the tower.

6. 'But wouldst thou know about them that are broken in pieces, and cast away far from the tower? These are the sons of lawlessness. They received the faith in hypocrisy, and no wickedness was absent from them. Therefore they have not salvation, for they are not useful for building by reason of their wickednesses. Therefore they were broken up and thrown far away by reason of the wrath of the Lord, for they excited Him to wrath. But the rest whom thou hast seen lying in great numbers, not going to the building, of these they that are mildewed are they that knew the truth, but did not abide in it, nor cleave to the saints. Therefore they are useless.'

'But they that have the cracks, who are they?' 'These are they that have discord in their hearts against one another, and are not at peace among themselves; who have an appearance of peace, but when they depart from one another, their wickednesses abide in their hearts. These are the cracks which the stones have. But they that are broken off short, these have believed, and have their greater part in righteousness, but have some parts of lawlessness; therefore they are too short, and are not perfect.'

'But the white and round stones, which did not fit into the building, who are they, lady?' She answered and said to me, 'How long art thou foolish and stupid, and enquirest everything, and understandest nothing? These are they that have faith, but have also riches of this world. When tribulation cometh, they deny their Lord by reason of their riches and their business affairs.' And I answered and said unto her, 'When then, lady, will they be useful for the building?' 'When,' she replied, 'their wealth, which leadeth their souls astray, shall be cut away, then will they be useful for God. For just as the round stone, unless it be cut away, and lose some portion of itself, cannot become square, so also they that are rich in this world, unless their riches be cut away, cannot become useful to the Lord. Learn first from thyself. When thou hadst riches, thou wast useless; but now thou art useful and profitable unto life. Be ye useful unto God, for thou thyself also art taken from the same stones.

7. 'But the other stones which thou sawest cast far away from the tower and falling into the way and rolling out of the way into the regions where there is no way, these are they that have believed, but by reason of their double heart they abandon their true way. Thus thinking that they can find a better way, they go astray and are sore distressed, as they walk about in the regions where there is no

way.   But they that fall into the fire and are burned, these are they
that finally rebelled from the living God, and it no more entered into
their hearts to repent by reason of the lusts of their wantonness and
of the wickednesses which they wrought.   But the others, which fall
near the waters and yet cannot roll into the water, wouldest thou know
who are they?   These are they that heard the word, and would be
baptized unto the name of the Lord.   Then, when they call to their
remembrance the purity of the truth, they change their minds, and go
back again after their evil desires.'   So she finished the explanation of
the tower.   Still importunate, I asked her further, whether for all these
stones that were rejected and would not fit into the building of the tower
there was repentance, and they had a place in this tower.   'They can
repent,' she said, 'but they cannot be fitted into this tower.   Yet they
shall be fitted into another place much more humble, but not until they
have undergone torments, and have fulfilled the days of their sins.
And they shall be changed for this reason, because they participated in
the Righteous Word; and then shall it befal them to be relieved from
their torments, if the evil deeds, that they have done, come into
their heart; but if these come not into their heart, they are not saved
by reason of the hardness of their hearts.'

8.   When then I ceased asking her concerning all these things, she
saith to me; 'Wouldest thou see something else?'   Being very desirous
of beholding, I was greatly rejoiced that I should see it.   She looked
upon me, and smiled, and she saith to me, 'Seest thou seven women
round the tower?'   'I see them, lady,' say I.   'This tower is supported
by them by commandment of the Lord.   Hear now their employments.
The first of them, the woman with the strong hands, is called Faith;
through her are saved the elect of God.   And the second, that is girded
about and looketh like a man, is called Continence; she is the daughter
of Faith.   Whosoever then shall follow her, becometh happy in his life,
for he shall refrain from all evil deeds, believing that, if he refrain from
every evil desire, he shall inherit eternal life.'   'And the others, lady,
who be they?'   'They are daughters one of the other.   The name of
the one is Simplicity, of the next, Knowledge, of the next, Guilelessness,
of the next, Reverence, of the next, Love.   When then thou shalt do all
the works of their mother, thou canst live.'   'I would fain know, lady,'
I say, 'what power each of them possesseth.'   'Listen then,' saith she, 'to
the powers which they have.   Their powers are mastered each by the
other, and they follow each other, in the order in which they were born.

From Faith is born Continence, from Continence Simplicity, from Simplicity Guilelessness, from Guilelessness Reverence, from Reverence Knowledge, from Knowledge Love. Their works then are pure and reverent and divine. Whosoever therefore shall serve these women, and shall have strength to master their works, shall have his dwelling in the tower with the saints of God.' Then I asked her concerning the seasons, whether the consummation is even now. But she cried aloud, saying, 'Foolish man, seest thou not that the tower is still a-building? Whensoever therefore the tower shall be finished building, the end cometh ; but it shall be built up quickly. Ask me no more questions : this reminder is sufficient for you and for the saints, and is the renewal of your spirits. But it was not revealed to thyself alone, but in order that thou mightest show these things unto all. After three days—for thou must understand first, and I charge thee, Hermas, first with these words, which I am about to speak to thee—(I charge thee to) tell all these things into the ears of the saints, that hearing them and doing them they may be purified from their wickednesses, and thyself also with them.

9. 'Hear me, my children. I brought you up in much simplicity and guilelessness and reverence, through the mercy of the Lord, Who instilled righteousness into you, that ye might be justified and sanctified from all wickedness and all crookedness. But ye will not to cease from your wickedness. Now then hear me and be at peace among yourselves, and have regard one to another, and assist one another, and do not partake of the creatures of God alone in abundance, but share them also with those that are in want. For some men through their much eating bring weakness on the flesh, and injure their flesh : whereas the flesh of those who have nought to eat is injured by their not having sufficient nourishment, and their body is ruined. This exclusiveness therefore is hurtful to you that have and do not share with them that are in want. Look ye to the judgment that cometh. Ye then that have more than enough, seek out them that are hungry, while the tower is still unfinished ; for after the tower is finished, ye will desire to do good, and will find no place for it. Look ye therefore, ye that exult in your wealth, lest they that are in want shall moan, and their moaning shall go up unto the Lord, and ye with your [abundance of] good things be shut outside the door of the tower. Now therefore I say unto you that are rulers of the Church, and that occupy the chief seats ; be not ye like unto the sorcerers. The sorcerers indeed carry their

drugs in boxes, but ye carry your drug and your poison in your heart. Ye are case-hardened, and ye will not cleanse your hearts and mix your wisdom together in a clean heart, that ye may obtain mercy from the Great King. Look ye therefore, children, lest these divisions of yours deprive you of your life. How is it that ye wish to instruct the elect of the Lord, while ye yourselves have no instruction? Instruct one another therefore, and have peace among yourselves, that I also may stand gladsome before the Father, and give an account concerning you all to your Lord.'

10. When then she ceased speaking with me, the six young men, who were building, came, and took her away to the tower, and other four lifted the couch, and took it also away to the tower. I saw not the face of these, for they were turned away. And, as she went, I asked her to reveal to me concerning the three forms, in which she had appeared to me. She answered and said to me; 'As concerning these things thou must ask another, that they may be revealed to thee.' Now she was seen of me, brethren, in my first vision of last year, as a very aged woman and seated on a chair. In the second vision her face was youthful, but her flesh and her hair were aged, and she spake to me standing; and she was more gladsome than before. But in the third vision she was altogether youthful and of exceeding great beauty, and her hair alone was aged; and she was gladsome exceedingly and seated on a couch. Touching these things I was very greatly anxious to learn this revelation. And I see the aged woman in a vision of the night, saying to me, ' Every enquiry needs humility. Fast therefore, and thou shalt receive what thou askest from the Lord.' So I fasted one day; and that very night there appeared unto me a young man, and he saith to me, 'Seeing that thou askest me revelations offhand with entreaty, take heed lest by thy much asking thou injure thy flesh. Sufficient for, thee are these revelations. Canst thou see mightier revelations than those thou hast seen?' I say unto him in reply, ' Sir, this one thing alone I ask, concerning the three forms of the aged woman, that a complete revelation may be vouchsafed me.' He saith to me in answer, ' How long are ye without understanding? It is your double-mindedness that maketh you of no understanding, and because your heart is not set towards the Lord.' I answered and said unto him again, 'From thee, Sir, we shall learn the matters more accurately.'

11. ' Listen,' saith he, 'concerning the three forms, of which thou enquirest. In the first vision wherefore did she appear to thee an aged

woman and seated on a chair? Because your spirit was aged, and already decayed, and had no power by reason of your infirmities and acts of double-mindedness. For as aged people, having no longer hope of renewing their youth, expect nothing else but to fall asleep, so ye also, being weakened with the affairs of this world, gave yourselves over to repining, and cast not your cares on the Lord; but your spirit was broken, and ye were aged by your sorrows.' 'Wherefore then she was seated on a chair, I would fain know, Sir.' 'Because every weak person sits on a chair by reason of his weakness, that the weakness of his body may be supported. So thou hast the symbolism of the first vision.

12. 'But in the second vision thou sawest her standing, and with her countenance more youthful and more gladsome than before; but her flesh and her hair aged. Listen to this parable also,' saith he. 'Imagine an old man, who has now lost all hope of himself by reason of his weakness and his poverty, and expecteth nothing else save the last day of his life. Suddenly an inheritance is left him. He heareth the news, riseth up and full of joy clothes himself with strength, and no longer lieth down, but standeth up, and his spirit, which was now broken by reason of his former circumstances, is renewed again, and he no longer sitteth, but taketh courage; so also was it with you, when ye heard the revelation which the Lord revealed unto you. For He had compassion on you, and renewed your spirits, and ye laid aside your maladies, and strength came to you, and ye were made powerful in the faith, and the Lord rejoiced to see you put on your strength. And therefore He showed you the building of the tower; yea, and other things also shall He show you, if with your whole heart ye be at peace among yourselves.

13. 'But in the third vision ye saw her younger and fair and gladsome, and her form fair. For just as when to some mourner cometh some piece of good tidings, immediately he forgetteth his former sorrows, and admitteth nothing but the tidings which he hath heard, and is strengthened thenceforth unto that which is good, and his spirit is renewed by reason of the joy which he hath received; so also ye have received a renewal of your spirits by seeing these good things. And whereas thou sawest her seated on a couch, the position is a firm one; for the couch has four feet and standeth firmly; for the world too is upheld by means of four elements. They then that have fully repented shall be young again, and founded firmly, seeing that they have re-

pented with their whole heart. There thou hast the revelation entire and complete. Thou shalt ask nothing more as touching revelation; but if anything be lacking still, it shall be revealed unto thee.'

[Vision 4.]

1. The fourth vision which I saw, brethren, twenty days after the former vision which came unto me, for a type of the impending tribulation. I was going into the country by the Campanian Way. From the high road, it is about ten stades; and the place is easy for travelling. While then I am walking alone, I entreat the Lord that He will accomplish the revelations and the visions which He showed me through His holy Church, that He may strengthen me and may give repentance to His servants which have stumbled, that His great and glorious Name may be glorified, for that He held me worthy that He should show me His marvels. And as I gave glory and thanksgiving to Him, there answered me as it were the sound of a voice, ' Be not of doubtful mind, Hermas.' I began to question in myself and to say, ' How can I be of doubtful mind, seeing that I am so firmly founded by the Lord, and have seen glorious things?' And I went on a little, brethren, and behold, I see a cloud of dust rising as it were to heaven, and I began to say within myself, 'Can it be that cattle are coming, and raising a cloud of dust?' for it was just about a stade from me. As the cloud of dust waxed greater and greater, I suspected that it was something supernatural. Then the sun shone out a little, and behold, I see a huge beast like some sea-monster, and from its mouth fiery locusts issued forth. And the beast was about a hundred feet in length, and its head was as it were of pottery. And I began to weep, and to entreat the Lord that He would rescue me from it. And I remembered the word which I had heard, ' Be not of doubtful mind, Hermas.' Having therefore, brethren, put on the faith of the Lord and called to mind the mighty works that He had taught me, I took courage and gave myself up to the beast. Now the beast was coming on with such a rush, that it might have ruined a city. I come near it, and, huge monster as it was, it stretcheth itself on the ground, and merely put forth its tongue, and stirred not at all until I had passed by it. And the beast had on its head four colours; black, then fire and blood colour, then gold, then white.

2. Now after I had passed the beast, and had gone forward about thirty feet, behold, there meeteth me a virgin arrayed as if she were going forth from a bride-chamber, all in white and with white sandals, veiled up to her forehead, and her head-covering consisted of a turban, and her hair was white. I knew from the former visions that it was the Church, and I became more cheerful. She saluteth me, saying, 'Good morrow, my good man'; and I saluted her in turn, 'Lady, good morrow.' She answered and said unto me, 'Did nothing meet thee?' I say unto her, 'Lady, such a huge beast, that could have destroyed whole peoples : but, by the power of the Lord and by His great mercy, I escaped it.' 'Thou didst escape it well,' saith she, 'because thou didst cast thy care upon God, and didst open thy heart to the Lord, believing that thou canst be saved by nothing else but by His great and glorious Name. Therefore the Lord sent His angel, which is over the beasts, whose name is Segri, and *shut its mouth, that it might not hurt thee.* Thou hast escaped a great tribulation by reason of thy faith, and because, though thou sawest so huge a beast, thou didst not doubt in thy mind. Go therefore, and declare to the elect of the Lord His mighty works, and tell them that this beast is a type of the great tribulation which is to come. If therefore ye prepare yourselves beforehand, and repent (and turn) unto the Lord with your whole heart, ye shall be able to escape it, if your heart be made pure and without blemish, and if for the remaining days of your life ye serve the Lord blamelessly. Cast your cares upon the Lord and He will set them straight. Trust ye in the Lord, ye men of doubtful mind, for He can do all things, yea, He both turneth away His wrath from you, and again He sendeth forth His plagues upon you that are of doubtful mind. Woe to them that hear these words and are disobedient; it were better for them that they had not been born.'

3. I asked her concerning the four colours, which the beast had upon its head. Then she answered me and said, 'Again thou art curious about such matters.' 'Yes, lady,' said I, 'make known unto me what these things are.' 'Listen,' said she ; 'the black is this world in which ye dwell; and the fire and blood colour showeth that this world must perish by blood and fire ; and the golden part are ye that have escaped from this world. For as the gold is tested by the fire and is made useful, so ye also [that dwell in it] are being tested in yourselves. Ye then that abide and pass through the fire will be purified by it. For as the gold loses its dross, so ye also shall cast away all sorrow and

tribulation, and shall be purified, and shall be useful for the building of the tower. But the white portion is the coming age, in which the elect of God shall dwell; because the elect of God shall be without spot and pure unto life eternal. Wherefore cease not thou to speak in the ears of the saints. Ye have now the symbolism also of the tribulation which is coming in power. But if ye be willing, it shall be nought. Remember ye the things that are written beforehand.' With these words she departed, and I saw not in what direction she departed; for a noise was made; and I turned back in fear, thinking that the beast was coming.

Revelation 5.

As I prayed in the house, and sat on the couch, there entered a man glorious in his visage, in the garb of a shepherd, with a white skin wrapped about him, and with a wallet on his shoulders and a staff in his hand. And he saluted me, and I saluted him in return. And he immediately sat down by my side, and he saith unto me, 'I was sent by the most holy angel, that I might dwell with thee the remaining days of thy life.' I thought he came to tempt me, and I say unto him, 'Why, who art thou? For I know,' say I, 'unto whom I was delivered.' He saith to me, 'Dost thou not recognise me?' 'No,' I say. 'I,' saith he, 'am the shepherd, unto whom thou wast delivered.' While he was still speaking, his form was changed, and I recognised him as being the same, to whom I was delivered; and straightway I was confounded, and fear seized me, and I was altogether overwhelmed with distress that I had answered him so wickedly and senselessly. But he answered and said unto me, 'Be not confounded, but strengthen thyself in my commandments which I am about to command thee. For I was sent,' saith he, 'that I might show thee again all the things which thou didst see before, merely the heads which are convenient for you. First of all, write down my commandments and my parables; and the other matters thou shalt write down as I shall show them to thee. The reason why,' saith he, 'I command thee to write down first the commandments and parables is, that thou mayest read them off-hand, and mayest be able to keep them.' So I wrote down the commandments and parables, as he commanded me. If then, when ye hear them, ye keep them and walk in them, and do them with a pure heart, ye shall receive from the Lord all things that He promised you; but if, when ye hear them, ye do not repent, but still add to your sins, ye shall receive from the Lord the opposite. All these the shepherd, the angel of repentance, commanded me so to write.

Mandate the First.

'First of all, believe that God is One, even He Who created all things and set them in order, and brought all things from non-existence into being, Who comprehendeth all things, being alone incomprehensible. Believe Him therefore, and fear Him, and in this fear be continent. Keep these things, and thou shalt cast off all wickedness from thyself, and shalt clothe thyself with every excellence of righteousness, and shalt live unto God, if thou keep this commandment.'

Mandate the Second.

He saith to me; 'Keep simplicity and be guileless, and thou shalt be as little children, that know not the wickedness which destroyeth the life of men. First of all, speak evil of no man, neither take pleasure in listening to a slanderer. Otherwise thou that hearest too shalt be responsible for the sin of him that speaketh the evil, if thou believest the slander, which thou hearest; for in believing it thou thyself also wilt have a grudge against thy brother. So then shalt thou be responsible for the sin of him that speaketh the evil. Slander is evil; it is a restless demon, never at peace, but always having its home among factions. Refrain from it therefore, and thou shalt have success at all times with all men. But clothe thyself in reverence, wherein is no evil stumbling-block, but all things are smooth and gladsome. Work that which is good, and of thy labours, which God giveth thee, give to all that are in want freely, not questioning to whom thou shalt give, and to whom thou shalt not give. Give to all; for to all God desireth that there should be given of His own bounties. They then that receive shall render an account to God why they received it, and to what end; for they that receive in distress shall not be judged, but they that receive by false pretence shall pay the penalty. He then that giveth is guiltless; for as he received from the Lord the ministration to perform it, he hath performed it in sincerity, by making no distinction to whom to give or not to give. This ministration then, when sincerely performed, becomes glorious in the sight of God. He therefore that ministereth thus sincerely shall live unto God. Therefore keep this commandment, as I have told thee, that thine own repentance and that of thy household may be found to be sincere, and [thy] heart pure and undefiled.'

Mandate the Third.

Again he saith to me; 'Love truth, and let nothing but truth proceed out of thy mouth, that the Spirit which God made to dwell in this flesh, may be found true in the sight of all men; and thus shall the Lord, Who dwelleth in thee, be glorified; for the Lord is true in every word, and with Him there is no falsehood. They therefore that speak lies set the Lord at nought, and become robbers of the Lord, for they do not deliver up to Him the deposit which they received. For they received of Him a spirit free from lies. This if they shall return a lying spirit, they have defiled the commandment of the Lord and have become robbers.' When then I heard these things, I wept bitterly. But seeing me weep he saith, 'Why weepest thou?' 'Because, Sir,' say I, 'I know not if I can be saved.' 'Why so?' saith he. 'Because, Sir,' I say, 'never in my life spake I a true word, but I always lived deceitfully with all men and dressed up my falsehood as truth before all men; and no man ever contradicted me, but confidence was placed in my word. How then, Sir,' say I, 'can I live, seeing that I have done these things?' 'Your supposition,' he saith, 'is right and true, for it behoved thee as a servant of God to walk in truth, and no complicity with evil should abide with the Spirit of truth, nor bring grief to the Spirit which is holy and true.' 'Never, Sir,' say I, 'heard I clearly words such as these.' 'Now then,' saith he, 'thou hearest. Guard them, that the former falsehoods also which thou spakest in thy business affairs may themselves become credible, now that these are found true; for they too can become trustworthy. If thou keep these things, and from henceforward speak nothing but truth, thou shalt be able to secure life for thyself. And whosoever shall hear this command, and abstain from falsehood, that most pernicious habit, shall live unto God.'

Mandate the Fourth.

1. 'I charge thee,' saith he, 'to keep purity, and let not a thought enter into thy heart concerning another's wife, or concerning fornication, or concerning any such like evil deeds; for in so doing thou committest a great sin. But remember thine own wife always, and thou shalt never go wrong. For should this desire enter into thine heart, thou wilt go wrong, and should any other as evil as this, thou committest sin. For this desire in a servant of God is a great sin; and if any man doeth this evil deed, he worketh out death for himself. Look to it

therefore. Abstain from this desire; for, where holiness dwelleth, there lawlessness ought not to enter into the heart of a righteous man.' I say to him, 'Sir, permit me to ask thee a few more questions.' 'Say on,' saith he. 'Sir,' say I, 'if a man who has a wife that is faithful in the Lord detect her in adultery, doth the husband sin in living with her?' 'So long as he is ignorant,' saith he, 'he sinneth not; but if the husband know of her sin, and the wife repent not, but continue in her fornication, and her husband live with her, he makes himself responsible for her sin and an accomplice in her adultery.' 'What then, Sir,' say I, 'shall the husband do, if the wife continue in this case?' 'Let him divorce her,' saith he, 'and let the husband abide alone: but if after divorcing his wife he shall marry another, he likewise committeth adultery.' 'If then, Sir,' say I, 'after the wife is divorced, she repent and desire to return to her own husband, shall she not be received?' 'Certainly,' saith he, 'if the husband receiveth her not, he sinneth and bringeth great sin upon himself; nay, one who hath sinned and repented must be received, yet not often; for there is but one repentance for the servants of God. For the sake of her repentance therefore the husband ought not to marry. This is the manner of acting enjoined on husband and wife. Not only,' saith he, 'is it adultery, if a man pollute his flesh, but whosoever doeth things like unto the heathen committeth adultery. If therefore in such deeds as these likewise a man continue and repent not, keep away from him, and live not with him. Otherwise, thou also art a partaker of his sin. For this cause ye were enjoined to remain single, whether husband or wife; for in such cases repentance is possible. I,' said he, 'am not giving an excuse that this matter should be concluded thus, but to the end that the sinner should sin no more. But as concerning his former sin, there is One Who is able to give healing; it is He Who hath authority over all things.'

2. I asked him again, saying, 'Seeing that the Lord held me worthy that thou shouldest always dwell with me, suffer me still to say a few words, since I understand nothing, and my heart has been made dense by my former deeds. Make me to understand, for I am very foolish, and I apprehend absolutely nothing.' He answered and said unto me, 'I,' saith he, 'preside over repentance, and I give understanding to all who repent. Nay, thinkest thou not,' saith he, 'that this very act of repentance is understanding? To repent is great understanding,' saith he. 'For the man that hath sinned understandeth that he hath done evil before the Lord, and the deed which he hath done entereth into his

heart, and he repenteth, and doeth no more evil, but doeth good lavishly, and humbleth his own soul and putteth it to torture because it sinned. Thou seest then that repentance is great understanding.' 'It is on this account therefore, Sir,' say I, 'that I enquire everything accurately of thee; first, because I am a sinner; secondly, because I know not what deeds I must do that I may live, for my sins are many and various.' 'Thou shalt live,' saith he, 'if thou keep my commandments and walk in them; and whosoever shall hear these commandments and keep them, shall live unto God.'

3. 'I will still proceed, Sir,' say I, 'to ask a further question.' 'Speak on,' saith he. 'I have heard, Sir,' say I, 'from certain teachers, that there is no other repentance, save that which took place when we went down into the water and obtained remission of our former sins.' He saith to me; 'Thou hast well heard; for so it is. For he that hath received remission of sins ought no longer to sin, but to dwell in purity. But, since thou enquirest all things accurately, I will declare unto thee this also, so as to give no excuse to those who shall hereafter believe, or those who have already believed, on the Lord. For they that have already believed, or shall hereafter believe, have not repentance for sins, but have only remission of their former sins. To those then that were called before these days the Lord has appointed repentance. For the Lord, being a discerner of hearts and foreknowing all things, perceived the weakness of men and the manifold wiles of the devil, how that he will be doing some mischief to the servants of God, and will deal wickedly with them. The Lord then, being very compassionate, had pity on His handiwork, and appointed this (opportunity of) repentance, and to me was given the authority over this repentance. But I say unto you,' saith he, 'if after this great and holy calling any one, being tempted of the devil, shall commit sin, he hath only one (opportunity of) repentance. But if he sin off-hand and repent, repentance is unprofitable for such a man; for he shall live with difficulty.' I say unto him, 'I was quickened into life again, when I heard these things from thee so precisely. For I know that, if I shall add no more to my sins, I shall be saved.' 'Thou shalt be saved,' he saith, 'thou and all, as many as shall do these things.'

4. I asked him again, saying, 'Sir, since once thou dost bear with me, declare unto me this further matter also.' 'Say on,' saith he. 'If a wife, Sir,' say I, 'or, it may be, a husband fall asleep, and one of them marry, doth the one that marrieth sin?' 'He sinneth not,' saith he, 'but if he remain single, he investeth himself with more exceeding honour

and with great glory before the Lord; yet even if he should marry, he sinneth not. Preserve purity and holiness therefore, and thou shalt live unto God. All these things, which I speak and shall hereafter speak unto thee, guard from this time forward, from the day when thou wast committed unto me, and I will dwell in thy house. But for thy former transgressions there shall be remission, if thou keepest my commandments. Yea, and all shall have remission, if they keep these my commandments, and walk in this purity.'

Mandate the Fifth.

1. 'Be thou long-suffering and understanding,' he saith, 'and thou shalt have the mastery over all evil deeds, and shalt work all righteousness. For if thou art long-suffering, the Holy Spirit that abideth in thee shall be pure, not being darkened by another evil spirit, but dwelling in a large room shall rejoice and be glad with the vessel in which he dwelleth, and shall serve God with much cheerfulness, having prosperity in himself. But if any angry temper approach, forthwith the Holy Spirit, being delicate, is straitened, not having [the] place clear, and seeketh to retire from the place; for he is being choked by the evil spirit, and has no room to minister unto the Lord, as he desireth, being polluted by angry temper. For the Lord dwelleth in long-suffering, but the devil in angry temper. Thus that both the spirits then should be dwelling together is inconvenient and evil for that man in whom they dwell. For if you take a little wormwood, and pour it into a jar of honey, is not the whole of the honey spoiled, and all that honey ruined by a very small quantity of wormwood? For it destroyeth the sweetness of the honey, and it no longer hath the same attraction for the owner, because it is rendered bitter and hath lost its use. But if the wormwood be not put into the honey, the honey is found sweet and becomes useful to its owner. Thou seest [then] that long-suffering is very sweet, beyond the sweetness of honey, and is useful to the Lord, and He dwelleth in it. But angry temper is bitter and useless. If then angry temper be mixed with long-suffering, long-suffering is polluted and the man's intercession is no longer useful to God.' 'I would fain know, Sir,' say I, 'the working of angry temper, that I may guard myself from it.' 'Yea, verily,' saith he, 'if thou guard not thyself from it—thou and thy family—thou hast lost all thy hope. But guard thyself from it; for I am with thee. Yea,

and all men shall hold aloof from it, as many as have repented with their whole heart. For I will be with them and will preserve them; for they all were justified by the most holy angel.

2. 'Hear now,' saith he, 'the working of angry temper, how evil it is, and how it subverteth the servants of God by its own working, and how it leadeth them astray from righteousness. But it doth not lead astray them that are full in the faith, nor can it work upon them, because the power of the Lord is with them; but them that are empty and double-minded it leadeth astray. For when it seeth such men in prosperity it insinuates itself into the heart of the man, and for no cause whatever the man or the woman is embittered on account of worldly matters, either about meats, or some triviality, or about some friend, or about giving or receiving, or about follies of this kind. For all these things are foolish and vain and senseless and inexpedient for the servants of God. But long-suffering is great and strong, and has a mighty and vigorous power, and is prosperous in great enlargement, gladsome, exultant, free from care, glorifying the Lord at every season, having no bitterness in itself, remaining always gentle and tranquil. This long-suffering therefore dwelleth with those whose faith is perfect. But angry temper is in the first place foolish, fickle and senseless; then from foolishness is engendered bitterness, and from bitterness wrath, and from wrath anger, and from anger spite; then spite being composed of all these evil elements becometh a great sin and incurable. For when all these spirits dwell in one vessel, where the Holy Spirit also dwelleth, that vessel cannot contain them, but overfloweth. The delicate spirit therefore, as not being accustomed to dwell with an evil spirit nor with harshness, departeth from a man of that kind, and seeketh to dwell with gentleness and tranquillity. Then, when it hath removed from that man, in whom it dwells, that man becometh emptied of the righteous spirit, and henceforward, being filled with the evil spirits, he is unstable in all his actions, being dragged about hither and thither by the evil spirits, and is altogether blinded and bereft of his good intent. Thus then it happeneth to all persons of angry temper. Refrain therefore from angry temper, the most evil of evil spirits. But clothe thyself in long-suffering, and resist angry temper and bitterness, and thou shalt be found in company with the holiness which is beloved of the Lord. See then that thou never neglect this commandment; for if thou master this commandment, thou shalt be able likewise to keep the remaining commandments, which I am about to give thee. Be strong in them and

endowed with power; and let all be endowed with power, as many as desire to walk in them.'

Mandate the Sixth.

1. 'I charged thee,' saith he, 'in my first commandment to guard faith and fear and temperance.' 'Yes, Sir,' say I. 'But now,' saith he, 'I wish to show thee their powers also, that thou mayest understand what is the power and effect of each one of them. For their effects are twofold. Now they are prescribed alike to the righteous and the unrighteous. Do thou therefore trust righteousness, but trust not unrighteousness; for the way of righteousness is straight, but the way of unrighteousness is crooked. But walk thou in the straight [and level] path, and leave the crooked one alone. For the crooked way has no tracks, but only pathlessness and many stumbling-stones, and is rough and thorny. So it is therefore harmful to those who walk in it. But those who walk in the straight way walk on the level and without stumbling: for it is neither rough nor thorny. Thou seest then that it is more expedient to walk in this way.' 'I am pleased, Sir,' say I, 'to walk in this way.' 'Thou shalt walk,' he saith, 'yea, and whosoever shall turn unto the Lord with his whole heart shall walk in it.

2. 'Hear now,' saith he, 'concerning faith. There are two angels with a man, one of righteousness and one of wickedness.' 'How then, Sir,' say I, 'shall I know their workings, seeing that both angels dwell with me?' 'Hear,' saith he, 'and understand their workings. The angel of righteousness is delicate and bashful and gentle and tranquil. When then this one enters into thy heart, forthwith he speaketh with thee of righteousness, of purity, of holiness, and of contentment, of every righteous deed and of every glorious virtue. When all these things enter into thy heart, know that the angel of righteousness is with thee. [These then are the works of the angel of righteousness.] Trust him therefore and his works. Now see the works of the angel of wickedness also. First of all, he is quick-tempered and bitter and senseless, and his works are evil, overthrowing the servants of God. Whenever then he entereth into thy heart, know him by his works.' 'How I shall discern him, Sir,' I reply, 'I know not.' 'Listen,' saith he. 'When a fit of angry temper or bitterness comes upon thee, know that he is in thee. Then the desire of much business and the costliness of many viands and drinking bouts and of many drunken fits and of various

luxuries which are unseemly, and the desire of women, and avarice, and haughtiness and boastfulness, and whatsoever things are akin and like to these—when then these things enter into thy heart, know that the angel of wickedness is with thee.   Do thou therefore, recognising his works, stand aloof from him, and trust him in nothing, for his works are evil and inexpedient for the servants of God.   Here then thou hast the workings of both the angels.   Understand them, and trust the angel of righteousness.   But from the angel of wickedness stand aloof, for his teaching is evil in every matter ; for though one be a man of faith, and the desire of this angel enter into his heart, that man, or that woman, must commit some sin.   And if again a man or a woman be exceedingly wicked, and the works of the angel of righteousness come into that man's heart, he must of necessity do something good.   Thou seest then,' saith he, ' that it is good to follow the angel of righteousness, and to bid farewell to the angel of wickedness.   This commandment declareth what concerneth faith, that thou mayest trust the works of the angel of righteousness, and doing them mayest live unto God. But believe that the works of the angel of wickedness are difficult ; so by not doing them thou shalt live unto God.'

Mandate the Seventh.

' Fear the Lord,' saith he, ' and keep His commandments.   So keeping the commandments of God thou shalt be powerful in every deed, and thy doing shall be incomparable.   For whilst thou fearest the Lord, thou shalt do all things well.   But this is the fear wherewith thou oughtest to be afraid, and thou shalt be saved.   But fear not the devil ; for, if thou fear the Lord, thou shalt be master over the devil, for there is no power in him.   [For] in whom is no power, neither is there fear of him ; but in whom power is glorious, of him is fear like-wise.   For every one that hath power hath fear, whereas he that hath no power is despised of all.   But fear thou the works of the devil, for they are evil.   While then thou fearest the Lord, thou wilt fear the works of the devil, and wilt not do them, but abstain from them. Fear therefore is of two kinds.   If thou desire to do evil, fear the Lord, and thou shalt not do it.   If again thou desire to do good, fear the Lord and thou shalt do it.   Therefore the fear of the Lord is powerful and great and glorious.   Fear the Lord then, and thou shalt live unto Him ; yea, and as many of them that keep His command-ments as shall fear Him, shall live unto God.'   ' Wherefore, Sir,' say I, 'didst thou say concerning those that keep His commandments, "They shall live unto God"?' 'Because,' saith he, 'every creature feareth the Lord, but not every one keepeth His commandments. Those then that fear Him and keep His commandments, they have life unto God; but they that keep not His commandments have no life in them.'

MANDATE THE EIGHTH.

'I told thee,' saith he, 'that the creatures of God are twofold; for temperance also is twofold. For in some things it is right to be temperate, but in other things it is not right.' 'Make known unto me, Sir,' say I, 'in what things it is right to be temperate, and in what things it is not right.' 'Listen,' saith he. 'Be temperate as to what is evil, and do it not; but be not temperate as to what is good, but do it. For if thou be temperate as to what is good, so as not to do it, thou committest a great sin; but if thou be temperate as to what is evil, so as not to do it, thou doest great righteousness. Be temperate therefore in abstaining from all wickedness, and do that which is good.' 'What kinds of wickedness, Sir,' say I, 'are they from which we must be temperate and abstain?' 'Listen,' saith he; 'from adultery and fornication, from the lawlessness of drunkenness, from wicked luxury, from many viands and the costliness of riches, and vaunting and haughtiness and pride, and from falsehood and evil-speaking and hypocrisy, malice and all blasphemy. These works are the most wicked of all in the life of men. From these works therefore the servant of God must be temperate and abstain; for he that is not temperate so as to abstain from these cannot live unto God. Listen then to what follows upon these.' 'Why, are there still other evil deeds, Sir?' say I. 'Aye,' saith he, 'there are many, from which the servant of God must be temperate and abstain; theft, falsehood, deprivation, false witness, avarice, evil desire, deceit, vain-glory, boastfulness, and whatsoever things are like unto these. Thinkest thou not that these things are wrong, yea, very wrong,' [saith he,] 'for the servants of God? In all these things he that serveth God must exercise temperance. Be thou temperate, therefore, and refrain from all these things, that thou mayest live unto God, and be enrolled among those who exercise self-restraint in them. These then are the things from which thou shouldest restrain thyself. Now hear,' saith he, 'the things, in which thou shouldest not exercise self-restraint, but do them. Exercise no self-restraint in that which is good, but do it.' 'Sir,' say I, 'show me the power of the good also, that I may walk in them and serve them, that doing them it may be possible for me to be saved.' 'Hear,' saith he, 'the works of the good likewise, which thou must do, and towards which thou must exercise no self-restraint. First of all, there is faith, fear of the Lord, love, concord, words of righteousness, truth, patience ; nothing is better than these in the life of men. If a man keep these, and exercise not self-restraint from them, he becomes blessed in his life. Hear now what follow upon these; to minister to widows, to visit the orphans and the needy, to ransom the servants of God from their afflictions, to be hospitable (for in hospitality benevolence from time to time has a place), to resist no man, to be tranquil, to show yourself more submissive than all men, to reverence the aged, to practise righteousness, to observe brotherly feeling, to endure injury, to be long-suffering, to bear no grudge, to exhort those who are sick at soul, not to cast away those that have stumbled from the faith, but to convert them and to put courage into them, to reprove sinners, not to oppress debtors and indigent persons, and whatsoever actions are like these. Do these things,' saith he, 'seem to thee to be good?' 'Why, what, Sir,' say I, 'can be better than these?' 'Then walk in them,' saith he, 'and abstain not from them, and thou shalt live unto God. Keep this commandment therefore. If thou do good and abstain not from it, thou shalt live unto God ; yea, and all shall live unto God who act so. And again if thou do not evil, and abstain from it, thou shalt live unto God ; yea, and all shall live unto God, who shall keep these commandments, and walk in them.'

MANDATE THE NINTH.

He saith to me ; 'Remove from thyself a doubtful mind and doubt not at all whether to ask of God, saying within thyself, "How can I ask a thing of the Lord and receive it, seeing that I have committed so many sins against Him?" Reason not thus, but turn to the Lord with thy whole heart, and ask of Him nothing wavering, and thou shalt know His exceeding compassion, that He will surely not abandon thee, but will fulfil the petition of thy soul. For God is not as men who bear a grudge, but Himself is without malice and hath compassion on His creatures. Do thou therefore cleanse thy heart from all the vanities of this life, and from the things mentioned before ; and ask of the Lord, and thou shalt receive all things, and shalt lack nothing of all thy petitions, if thou ask of the Lord nothing wavering. But if thou waver in thy heart, thou shalt surely receive none of thy petitions. For they that waver towards God, these are the doubtful-minded, and they never obtain any of their petitions. But they that are complete in the faith make all their petitions trusting in the Lord, and they receive, because they ask without wavering, nothing doubting; for every doubtful-minded man, if he repent not, shall hardly be saved. Cleanse therefore thy heart from doubtful-mindedness, and put on faith, for it is strong, and trust God that thou wilt receive all thy petitions which thou askest; and if after asking anything of the Lord, thou receive thy petition somewhat tardily, be not of doubtful mind because thou didst not receive the petition of thy soul at once. For assuredly it is by reason of some temptation or some transgression, of which thou art ignorant, that thou receivest thy petition so tardily. Do thou therefore cease not to make thy soul's petition, and thou shalt receive it. But if thou grow weary, and doubt as thou askest, blame thyself and not Him that giveth unto thee. See to this doubtful-mindedness; for it is evil and senseless, and uprooteth many from the faith, yea, even very faithful and strong men. For indeed this doubtful-mindedness is a daughter of the devil, and worketh great wickedness against the servants of God. Therefore despise doubtful-mindedness and gain the mastery over it in everything, clothing thyself with faith which is strong and powerful. For faith promiseth all things, accomplisheth all things; but doubtful-mindedness, as having no confidence in itself, fails in all the works which it doeth. Thou seest then,' saith he, 'that faith is from above from the Lord, and hath great power; but doubtful-mindedness is an earthly spirit from the devil, and hath no power. Do thou therefore serve that faith which hath power, and hold aloof from the doubtful-mindedness which hath no power; and thou shalt live unto God; yea, and all those shall live unto God who are so minded.'

MANDATE THE TENTH.

1. 'Put away sorrow from thyself,' saith he, 'for she is the sister of doubtful-mindedness and of angry temper.' 'How, Sir,' say I, 'is she the sister of these? For angry temper seems to me to be one thing, doubtful-mindedness another, sorrow another.' 'Thou art a foolish fellow,' saith he, '[and] perceivest not that sorrow is more evil than all the spirits, and is most fatal to the servants of God, and beyond all the spirits destroys a man, and crushes out the Holy Spirit, and yet again saves it.' 'I, Sir,' say I, 'am without understanding, and I understand

not these parables.   For how it can crush out and again save, I do not comprehend.'   'Listen,' saith he.   'Those who have never investigated concerning the truth, nor enquired concerning the deity, but have merely believed, and have been mixed up in business affairs and riches and heathen friendships, and many other affairs of this world—as many, I say, as devote themselves to these things, comprehend not the parables of the deity; for they are darkened by these actions, and are corrupted and become barren.   As good vineyards, when they are treated with neglect, are made barren by the thorns and weeds of various kinds, so men who after they have believed fall into these many occupations which were mentioned before, lose their understanding and comprehend nothing at all concerning righteousness; for if they hear concerning the deity and truth, their mind is absorbed in their occupations, and they perceive nothing at all.   But they that have the fear of God, and investigate concerning deity and truth, and direct their heart towards the Lord, perceive and understand everything that is said to them more quickly, because they have the fear of the Lord in themselves; for where the Lord dwelleth, there too is great understanding.   Cleave therefore unto the Lord, and thou shalt understand and perceive all things.

2.   'Hear now, senseless man,' saith he, 'how sorrow crusheth out the Holy Spirit, and again saveth it.   When the man of doubtful mind sets his hand to any action, and fails in it owing to his doubtful-mindedness, grief at this entereth into the man, and grieveth the Holy Spirit, and crusheth it out.   Then again when angry temper cleaveth to a man concerning any matter, and he is much embittered, again sorrow entereth into the heart of the man that was ill-tempered, and he is grieved at the deed which he hath done, and repenteth that he did evil.   This sadness therefore seemeth to bring salvation, because he repented at having done the evil.   So both the operations sadden the Spirit; first, the doubtful mind saddens the Spirit, because it succeeded not in its business, and the angry temper again, because it did what was evil.   Thus both are saddening to the Holy Spirit, the doubtful mind and the angry temper.   Put away therefore from thyself sadness, and afflict not the Holy Spirit that dwelleth in thee, lest haply He intercede with God [against thee], and depart from thee.   For the Spirit of God, that was given unto this flesh, endureth not sadness neither constraint.

3.   'Therefore clothe thyself in cheerfulness, which hath favour with God always, and is acceptable to Him, and rejoice in it.   For every

cheerful man worketh good, and thinketh good, and despiseth sadness; but the sad man is always committing sin.   In the first place he committeth sin, because he grieveth the Holy Spirit, which was given to the man being a cheerful spirit; and in the second place, by grieving the Holy Spirit he doeth lawlessness, in that he doth not intercede with neither confess unto God.   For the intercession of a sad man hath never at any time power to ascend to the altar of God.'   'Wherefore,' say I, 'doth not the intercession of him that is saddened ascend to the altar?'   'Because,' saith he, 'sadness is seated at his heart. Thus sadness mingled with the intercession doth not suffer the intercession to ascend pure to the altar.   For as vinegar when mingled with wine in the same (vessel) hath not the same pleasant taste, so likewise sadness mingled with the Holy Spirit hath not the same intercession. Therefore cleanse thyself from this wicked sadness, and thou shalt live unto God; yea, and all they shall live unto God, who shall cast away sadness from themselves and clothe themselves in all cheerfulness.'

MANDATE THE ELEVENTH.

He shewed me men seated on a couch, and another man seated on a chair.   And he saith to me, 'Seest thou those that are seated on the couch?'   'I see them, Sir,' say I.   'These,' saith he, 'are faithful, but he that sitteth on the chair is a false prophet who destroyeth the mind of the servants of God—I mean, of the doubtful-minded, not of the faithful.   These doubtful-minded ones then come to him as to a soothsayer and enquire of him what shall befall them.   And he, the false prophet, having no power of a divine Spirit in himself, speaketh with them according to their enquiries [and according to the lusts of their wickedness], and filleth their souls as they themselves wish.   For being empty himself he giveth empty answers to empty enquirers; for whatever enquiry may be made of him, he answereth according to the emptiness of the man.   But he speaketh also some true words; for the devil filleth him with his own spirit, if so be he shall be able to break down some of the righteous.   So many therefore as are strong in the faith of the Lord, clothed with the truth, cleave not to such spirits, but hold aloof from them; but as many as are doubters and frequently change their minds, practise soothsaying like the Gentiles, and bring upon themselves greater sin by their idolatries.   For he that consulteth a false prophet on any matter is an idolater and emptied of the truth, and senseless.   For no Spirit given of God needeth to be consulted; but, having the power of deity, speaketh all things of itself, because it is from above, even from the power of the divine Spirit. But the spirit which is consulted, and speaketh according to the desires of men, is earthly and fickle, having no power; and it speaketh not at all, unless it be consulted.' 'How then, Sir,' say I, 'shall a man know who of them is a prophet, and who a false prophet?' 'Hear,' saith he, 'concerning both the prophets; and, as I shall tell thee, so shalt thou test the prophet and the false prophet. By his life test the man that hath the divine Spirit. In the first place, he that hath the [divine] Spirit, which is from above, is gentle and tranquil and humble-minded, and abstaineth from all wickedness and vain desire of this present world, and holdeth himself inferior to all men, and giveth no answer to any man when enquired of, nor speaketh in solitude (for neither doth the Holy Spirit speak when a man wisheth Him to speak); but the man speaketh then when God wisheth him to speak. When then the man who hath the divine Spirit cometh into an assembly of righteous men, who have faith in a divine Spirit, and intercession is made to God by the gathering of those men, then the angel of the prophetic spirit, who is attached to him, filleth the man, and the man, being filled with the Holy Spirit, speaketh to the multitude, according as the Lord willeth. In this way then the Spirit of the deity shall be manifest. This then is the greatness of the power as touching the Spirit of the deity of the Lord. Hear now,' saith he, 'concerning the earthly and vain spirit, which hath no power but is foolish. In the first place, that man who seemeth to have a spirit exalteth himself, and desireth to have a chief place, and straightway he is impudent and shameless and talkative and conversant in many luxuries and in many other deceits, and receiveth money for his prophesying, and if he receiveth not, he prophesieth not. Now can a divine Spirit receive money and prophesy? It is not possible for a prophet of God to do this, but the spirit of such prophets is earthly. In the next place, it never approacheth an assembly of righteous men; but avoideth them, and cleaveth to the doubtful-minded and empty, and prophesieth to them in corners, and deceiveth them, speaking all things in emptiness to gratify their desires; for they too are empty whom it answereth. For the empty vessel placed together with the empty is not broken, but they agree one with the other. But when he comes into an assembly full of righteous men who have a Spirit of deity, and intercession is made from them, that man is emptied, and the earthly spirit fleeth from him in fear, and that man is struck dumb and is altogether broken in pieces, being unable to utter a word. For, if you pack wine or oil into a closet, and place an empty vessel among them, and again desire to unpack the closet, the vessel which you placed there empty, empty in like manner you will find it. Thus also the empty prophets, whenever they come unto the spirits of righteous men, are found just such as they came. I have given thee the life of both kinds of prophets. Therefore test, by his life and his works, the man who says that he is moved by the Spirit. But do thou trust the Spirit that cometh from God, and hath power; but in the earthly and empty spirit put no trust at all; for in it there is no power, for it cometh from the devil. Listen [then] to the parable which I shall tell thee. Take a stone, and throw it up to heaven—see if thou canst reach it; or again, take a squirt of water, and squirt it up to heaven—see if thou canst bore through the heaven.' 'How, Sir,' say I, 'can these things be? For both these things which thou hast mentioned are beyond our power.' 'Well then,' saith he, 'just as these things are beyond our power, so likewise the earthly spirits have no power and are feeble. Now take the power which cometh from above. The hail is a very small grain, and yet, when it falleth on a man's head, what pain it causeth! Or again, take a drop which falls on the ground from the tiles, and bores through the stone. Thou seest then that the smallest things from above falling on the earth have great power. So likewise the divine Spirit coming from above is powerful. This Spirit therefore trust, but from the other hold aloof.'

MANDATE THE TWELFTH.

1. He saith to me; 'Remove from thyself all evil desire, and clothe thyself in the desire which is good and holy; for clothed with this desire thou shalt hate the evil desire, and shalt bridle and direct it as thou wilt. For the evil desire is wild, and only tamed with difficulty; for it is terrible, and by its wildness is very costly to men; more especially if a servant of God get entangled in it, and have no understanding, he is put to fearful costs by it. But it is costly to such men as are not clothed in the good desire, but are mixed up with this life. These men then it hands over to death.' 'Of what sort, Sir,' say I, 'are the works of the evil desire, which hand over men to death? Make them known to me, that I may hold aloof from them.' 'Listen,' [saith he,] 'through what works the evil desire bringeth death to the servants of God.

2. 'Before all is desire for the wife or husband of another, and for extravagance of wealth, and for many needless dainties, and for drinks and other luxuries, many and foolish. For every luxury is foolish and vain for the servants of God. These desires then are evil, and bring death to the servants of God. For this evil desire is a daughter of the devil. Ye must, therefore, abstain from the evil desires, that so abstaining ye may live unto God. But as many as are mastered by them, and resist them not, are done to death utterly; for these desires are deadly. But do thou clothe thyself in the desire of righteousness, and, having armed thyself with the fear of the Lord, resist them. For the fear of God dwelleth in the good desire. If the evil desire shall see thee armed with the fear of God and resisting itself, it shall flee far from thee, and shall no more be seen of thee, being in fear of thine arms. Do thou therefore, when thou art crowned for thy victory over it, come to the desire of righteousness, and deliver to her the victor's prize which thou hast received, and serve her, according as she herself desireth. If thou serve the good desire, and art subject to her, thou shalt have power to master the evil desire, and to subject her, according as thou wilt.'

3. 'I would fain know, Sir,' say I, 'in what ways I ought to serve the good desire.' 'Listen,' saith he; 'practise righteousness and virtue, truth and the fear of the Lord, faith and gentleness, and as many good deeds as are like these. Practising these thou shalt be well-pleasing as a servant of God, and shalt live unto Him; yea, and every one who shall serve the good desire shall live unto God.'

So he completed the twelve commandments, and he saith to me; 'Thou hast these commandments; walk in them, and exhort thy hearers that their repentance may become pure for the rest of the days of their life. This ministration, which I give thee, fulfil thou with all diligence to the end, and thou shalt effect much. For thou shalt find favour among those who are about to repent, and they shall obey thy words. For I will be with thee, and will compel them to obey thee.'

I say to him; 'Sir, these commandments are great and beautiful and glorious, and are able *to gladden the heart of* the *man* who is able to observe them. But I know not whether these commandments can be kept by a man, for they are very hard.' He answered and said unto me; 'If thou set it before thyself that they can be kept, thou wilt easily keep them, and they will not be hard; but if it once enter into thy heart that they cannot be kept by a man, thou wilt not keep them. But now I say unto thee; if thou keep them not, but neglect them, thou shalt not have salvation, neither thy children nor thy household, since thou hast already pronounced judgment against thyself that these commandments cannot be kept by a man.'

4. And these things he said to me very angrily, so that I was confounded, and feared him exceedingly; for his form was changed, so that a man could not endure his anger. And when he saw that I was altogether disturbed and confounded, he began to speak more kindly [and cheerfully] to me, and he saith; 'Foolish fellow, void of understanding and of doubtful mind, perceivest thou not the glory of God, how great and mighty and marvellous it is, how that He created the world for man's sake, and subjected all His creation to man, and gave all authority to him, that he should be master over all things under the heaven? If then,' [he saith,] 'man is lord of all the creatures of God and mastereth all things, cannot he also master these commandments? Aye,' saith he, 'the man that hath the Lord in his heart can master [all things and] all these commandments. But they that have the Lord on their lips, while their heart is hardened, and are far from the Lord, to them these commandments are hard and inaccessible. Therefore do ye, who are empty and fickle in the faith, set your Lord in your heart, and ye shall perceive that nothing is easier than these commandments, nor sweeter, nor more gentle. Be ye converted, ye that walk after the commandments of the devil, (the commandments which are so) difficult and bitter and wild and riotous; and fear not the devil, for there is no power in him against you. For I will be with you, I, the angel of repentance, who have the mastery over him. The devil hath fear alone, but his fear hath no force. Fear him not therefore; and he will flee from you.'

5. I say to him, 'Sir, listen to a few words from me.' 'Say what thou wilt,' saith he. 'Man, Sir,' I say, 'is eager to keep the commandments of God, and there is no one that asketh not of the Lord, that he may be strengthened in His commandments, and be subject to them; but the devil is hard and overmastereth them.' 'He cannot,' saith he, 'overmaster the servants of God, who set their hope on Him with their whole heart. The devil can wrestle with them, but he cannot overthrow them. If then ye resist him, he will be vanquished, and will flee from you disgraced. But as many,' saith he, 'as are utterly empty, fear the devil as if he had power. When a man has filled amply sufficient jars with good wine, and among these jars a few are quite empty, he comes to the jars, and does not examine the full

ones, for he knows that they are full; but he examineth the empty ones, fearing lest they have turned sour. For empty jars soon turn sour, and the taste of the wine is spoilt. So also the devil cometh to all the servants of God tempting them. As many then as are complete in the faith, oppose him mightily, and he departeth from them, not having a place where he can find an entrance. So he cometh next to the empty ones, and finding a place goeth into them, and further he doeth what he willeth in them, and they become submissive slaves to him.

6. 'But I, the angel of repentance, say unto you; Fear not the devil; for I was sent,' saith he, 'to be with you who repent with your whole heart, and to strengthen you in the faith. Believe, therefore, on God, ye who by reason of your sins have despaired of your life, and are adding to your sins, and weighing down your life; for if ye turn unto the Lord with your whole heart, and work righteousness the remaining days of your life, and serve Him rightly according to His will, He will give healing to your former sins, and ye shall have power to master the works of the devil. But of the threatening of the devil fear not at all; for he is unstrung, like the sinews of a dead man. Hear me therefore, and fear Him, *Who is able* to do all things, *to save and to destroy*, and observe these commandments, and ye shall live unto God.' I say to him, 'Sir, now am I strengthened in all the ordinances of the Lord, because thou art with me; and I know that thou wilt crush all the power of the devil, and we shall be masters over him, and shall prevail over all his works. And I hope, Sir, that I am now able to keep these commandments which thou hast commanded, the Lord enabling me.' 'Thou shalt keep them,' saith he, 'if thy heart be found pure with the Lord; yea, and all shall keep them, as many as shall purify their hearts from the vain desires of this world, and shall live unto God.'

PARABLES WHICH HE SPAKE WITH ME.

He saith to me; 'Ye know that ye, who are the servants of God, are dwelling in a foreign land; for your city is far from this city. If then ye know your city, in which ye shall dwell, why do ye here prepare fields and expensive displays and buildings and dwelling-chambers which are superfluous? He, therefore, that prepareth these things for this city does not purpose to return to his own city. O foolish and double-minded and miserable man, perceivest thou not that all these things are foreign, and are under the power of another? For the lord of this city shall say, " I do not wish thee to dwell in my city; go forth from this city, for thou dost not conform to my laws." Thou, therefore, who hast fields and dwellings and many other possessions, when thou art cast out by him, what wilt thou do with thy field and thy house and all the other things that thou preparedst for thyself? For the lord of this country saith to thee justly, " Either conform to my laws, or depart from my country." What then shalt thou do, who art under law in thine own city? For the sake of thy fields and the rest of thy possessions wilt thou altogether repudiate thy law, and walk according to the law of this city? Take heed, lest it be inexpedient to repudiate thy law; for if thou shouldest desire to return again to thy city, thou shalt surely not be received [because thou didst repudiate the law of thy city], and shalt be shut out from it. Take heed therefore; as dwelling in a strange land prepare nothing more for thyself but a competency which is sufficient for thee, and make ready that, whensoever the master of this city may desire to cast thee out for thine opposition to his law, thou mayest go forth from his city and depart into thine own city, and use thine own law joyfully, free from all insult. Take heed therefore, ye that serve God and have Him in your heart : work the works of God being mindful of His commandments and of the promises which He made, and believe Him that He will perform them, if His commandments be kept. Therefore, instead of fields buy ye souls that are in trouble, as each is able, and visit widows and orphans, and neglect them not; and spend your riches and all your displays, which ye received from God, on fields and houses of this kind. For to this end the Master enriched you, that ye might perform these ministrations for Him. It is much better to purchase fields [and possessions] and houses of this kind, which thou wilt find in thine own city, when thou visitest it. This lavish expenditure is beautiful and joyous, not bringing sadness or fear, but bringing joy. The expenditure of the heathen then practise not ye; for it is not convenient for you the servants of God. But practise your own expenditure, in which ye can rejoice; and do not corrupt, neither touch that which is another man's, nor lust after it; for it is wicked to lust after other men's possessions. But perform thine own task, and thou shalt be saved.'

ANOTHER PARABLE.

As I walked in the field, and noticed an elm and a vine, and was distinguishing them and their fruits, the shepherd appeareth to me and saith; 'What art thou meditating within thyself?' 'I am thinking, [Sir,]' say I, 'about the elm and the vine, that they are excellently suited the one to the other.' 'These two trees,' saith he, 'are appointed for a type to the servants of God.' 'I would fain know, [Sir,]' say I, 'the type contained in these trees, of which thou speakest.' 'Seest thou,' saith he, 'the elm and the vine?' 'I see them, Sir,' say I. 'This vine,' saith he, 'beareth fruit, but the elm is an unfruitful stock. Yet this vine, except it climb up the elm, cannot bear much fruit when it is spread on the ground; and such fruit as it beareth is rotten, because it is not suspended upon the elm. When then the vine is attached to the elm, it beareth fruit both from itself and from the elm. Thou seest then that the elm also beareth [much] fruit, not less than the vine, but rather more.' 'How more, Sir?' say I. 'Because,' saith he, 'the vine, when hanging upon the elm, bears its fruit in abundance, and in good condition; but, when spread on the ground, it beareth little fruit, and that rotten. This parable therefore is applicable to the servants of God, to poor and to rich alike.' 'How, Sir?' say I; 'instruct me.' 'Listen,' saith he; 'the rich man hath much wealth, but in the things of the Lord he is poor, being distracted about his riches, and his confession and intercession with the Lord is very scanty; and even that which he giveth is small and weak and hath not power above. When then the rich man goeth up to the poor, and assisteth him in his needs, believing that for what he doth to the poor man he shall be able to obtain a reward with God—because the poor man is rich in intercession [and confession], and his intercession hath great power with God—the rich man then supplieth all things to the poor man without wavering. But the poor man being supplied by the rich maketh intercession for him, thanking God for him that gave to him. And the other is still more zealous to assist the poor man, that he may be continuous in his life: for he knoweth that the intercession of the poor man is acceptable and rich before God. They both then accomplish their work; the poor man maketh intercession, wherein he is rich [which he received of the Lord]; this he rendereth again to the Lord Who supplieth him with it. The rich man too in like manner furnisheth to the poor man, nothing doubting, the riches which he received from the Lord. And this work is great and acceptable with God, because (the rich man) hath understanding concerning his riches, and worketh for the poor man from the bounties of the Lord, and accomplisheth the ministration of the Lord rightly. In the sight of men then the elm seemeth not to bear fruit, and they know not, neither perceive, that if there cometh a drought, the elm having water nurtureth the vine, and the vine having a constant supply of water beareth fruit twofold, both for itself and for the elm. So likewise the poor, by interceding with the Lord for the rich, establish their riches, and again the rich, supplying their needs to the poor, establish their souls.   So then both are made partners in the righteous work. He then that doeth these things shall not be abandoned of God, but shall be written in the books of the living.   Blessed are the rich, who understand also that they are enriched from the Lord.   For they that have this mind shall be able to do some good work.'

Another Parable.

He showed me many trees which had no leaves, but they seemed to me to be, as it were, withered; for they were all alike.   And he saith to me; 'Seest thou these trees?' 'I see them, Sir,' I say, 'they are all alike, and are withered.'   He answered and said to me; 'These trees that thou seest are they that dwell in this world.' 'Wherefore then, Sir,' say I, 'are they as if they were withered, and alike?' 'Because,' saith he, 'neither the righteous are distinguishable, nor the sinners in this world, but they are alike.   For this world is winter to the righteous, and they are not distinguishable, as they dwell with the sinners.   For as in the winter the trees, having shed their leaves, are alike, and are not distinguishable, which are withered, and which alive, so also in this world neither the just nor the sinners are distinguishable, but they are all alike.'

Another Parable.

He showed me many trees again, some of them sprouting, and others withered, and he saith to me; 'Seest thou,' saith he, 'these trees?' 'I see them, Sir,' say I, 'some of them sprouting, and others withered.' 'These trees,' saith he, 'that are sprouting are the righteous, who shall dwell in the world to come; for the world to come is summer to the righteous, but winter to the sinners.   When then the mercy of the Lord shall shine forth, then they that serve God shall be made manifest; yea, and all men shall be made manifest.   For as in summer the fruits of each several tree are made manifest, and are recognised of what sort they are, so also the fruits of the righteous shall be manifest, and all [even the very smallest] shall be known to be flourishing in that world.   But the Gentiles and the sinners, just as thou sawest the trees which were withered, even such shall they be found, withered and unfruitful in that world, and shall be burnt up as fuel, and shall be manifest, because their practice in their life hath been evil. For the sinners shall be burned, because they sinned and repented not; and the Gentiles shall be burned, because they knew not Him that created them. Do thou therefore bear fruit, that in that summer thy fruit may be known. But abstain from overmuch business, and thou shalt never fall into any sin. For they that busy themselves overmuch, sin much also, being distracted about their business, and in no wise serving their own Lord. How then,' saith he, 'can such a man ask anything of the Lord and receive it, seeing that he serveth not the Lord? [For] they that serve Him, these shall receive their petitions, but they that serve not the Lord, these shall receive nothing. But if any one work one single action, he is able also to serve the Lord; for his mind shall not be corrupted from (following) the Lord, but he shall serve Him, because he keepeth his mind pure. If therefore thou doest these things, thou shalt be able to bear fruit unto the world to come; yea, and whosoever shall do these things, shall bear fruit.'

ANOTHER PARABLE.

1. As I was fasting and seated on a certain mountain, and giving thanks to the Lord for all that He had done unto me, I see the shepherd seated by me and saying; 'Why hast thou come hither in the early morn?' 'Because, Sir,' say I, 'I am keeping a station.' 'What,' saith he, 'is a station?' 'I am fasting, Sir,' say I. 'And what,' saith he, 'is this fast [that ye are fasting]?' 'As I was accustomed, Sir,' say I, 'so I fast.' 'Ye know not,' saith he, 'how to fast unto the Lord, neither is this a fast, this unprofitable fast which ye make unto Him.' 'Wherefore, Sir,' say I, 'sayest thou this?' 'I tell thee,' saith he, 'that this is not a fast, wherein ye think to fast; but I will teach thee what is a complete fast and acceptable to the Lord. Listen,' saith he; 'God desireth not such a vain fast; for by so fasting unto God thou shalt do nothing for righteousness. But fast thou [unto God] such a fast as this; do no wickedness in thy life, and serve the Lord with a pure heart; observe His commandments and walk in His ordinances, and let no evil desire rise up in thy heart; but believe God. Then, if thou shalt do these things, and fear Him, and control thyself from every evil deed, thou shalt live unto God; and if thou do these things, thou shalt accomplish a great fast, and one acceptable to God.

2. 'Hear the parable which I shall tell thee relating to fasting. A certain man had an estate, and many slaves, and a portion of his estate he planted as a vineyard; and choosing out a certain slave who was trusty and well-pleasing (and) held in honour, he called him to him and saith unto him; "Take this vineyard [which I have planted], and fence it [till I come], but do nothing else to the vineyard. Now keep this my commandment, and thou shalt be free in my house." Then the master of the servant went away to travel abroad. When then he had gone away, the servant took and fenced the vineyard; and having finished the fencing of the vineyard, he noticed that the vineyard was full of weeds. So he reasoned within himself, saying, "This command of my lord I have carried out. I will next dig this vineyard, and it shall be neater when it is digged; and when it hath no weeds it will yield more fruit, because not choked by the weeds." He took and digged the vineyard, and all the weeds that were in the vineyard he plucked up. And that vineyard became very neat and flourishing, when it had no weeds to choke it. After a time the master of the servant [and of the estate] came, and he went into the vineyard. And seeing the vineyard fenced neatly, and digged as well, and [all] the weeds plucked up, and the vines flourishing, he rejoiced [exceedingly] at what his servant had done. So he called his beloved son, who was his heir, and the friends who were his advisers, and told them what he had commanded his servant, and how much he had found done. And they rejoiced with the servant at the testimony which his master had borne to him. And he saith to them; "I promised this servant his freedom, if he should keep the commandment which I commanded him; but he kept my commandment and did a good work besides to my vineyard, and pleased me greatly. For this work therefore which he has done, I desire to make him joint-heir with my son, because, when the good thought struck him, he did not neglect it, but fulfilled it." In this purpose the son of the master agreed with him, that the servant should be made joint-heir with the son. After some few days, his master made a feast, and sent to him many dainties from the feast. But when the servant received [the dainties sent to him by the master], he took what was sufficient for him, and distributed the rest to his fellow-servants. And his fellow-servants, when they received the dainties, rejoiced, and began to pray for him, that he might find greater favour with the master, because he had treated them so handsomely. All these things which had taken place his master heard, and again rejoiced greatly at his deed. So the master

called together again his friends and his son, and announced to them the deed that he had done with regard to his dainties which he had received; and they still more approved of his resolve, that his servant should be made joint-heir with his son.'

3. I say, 'Sir, I understand not these parables, neither can I apprehend them, unless thou explain them for me.' 'I will explain everything to thee,' saith he; 'and will show thee whatsoever things I shall speak with thee. Keep the commandments of the Lord, and thou shalt be well-pleasing to God, and shalt be enrolled among the number of them that keep His commandments. But if thou do any good thing outside the commandment of God, thou shalt win for thyself more exceeding glory, and shalt be more glorious in the sight of God than thou wouldest otherwise have been. If then, while thou keepest the commandments of God, thou add these services likewise, thou shalt rejoice, if thou observe them according to my commandment.' I say to him, 'Sir, whatsoever thou commandest me, I will keep it; for I know that thou art with me.' 'I will be with thee,' saith he, 'because thou hast so great zeal for doing good; yea, and I will be with all,' saith he, 'whosoever have such zeal as this. This fasting,' saith he, 'if the commandments of the Lord are kept, is very good. This then is the way, that thou shalt keep this fast [which thou art about to observe]. First of all, keep thyself from every evil word and every evil desire, and purify thy heart from all the vanities of this world. If thou keep these things, this fast shall be perfect for thee. And thus shalt thou do. Having fulfilled what is written, on that day on which thou fastest thou shalt taste nothing but bread and water; and from thy meats, which thou wouldest have eaten, thou shalt reckon up the amount of that day's expenditure, which thou wouldest have incurred, and shalt give it to a widow, or an orphan, or to one in want, and so shalt thou humble thy soul, that he that hath received from thy humiliation may satisfy his own soul, and may pray for thee to the Lord. If then thou shalt so accomplish this fast, as I have commanded thee, thy sacrifice shall be acceptable in the sight of God, and this fasting shall be recorded; and the service so performed is beautiful and joyous and acceptable to the Lord. These things thou shalt so observe, thou and thy children and thy whole household; and, observing them, thou shalt be blessed; yea, and all those, who shall hear and observe them, shall be blessed, and whatsoever things they shall ask of the Lord, they shall receive.'

4. I entreated him earnestly, that he would show me the parable

of the estate, and of the master, and of the vineyard, and of the servant
that fenced the vineyard, [and of the fence,] and of the weeds which
were plucked up out of the vineyard, and of the son, and of the friends,
the advisers. For I understood that all these things are a parable.
But he answered and said unto me; 'Thou art exceedingly importunate
in enquiries. Thou oughtest not,' [saith he,] 'to make any enquiry at all;
for if it be right that a thing be explained unto thee, it shall be explained.'
I say to him; 'Sir, whatsoever things thou showest unto me and dost
not explain, I shall have seen them in vain, and without understanding
what they are. In like manner also, if thou speak parables to me and
interpret them not, I shall have heard a thing in vain from thee.' But
he again answered, and said unto me; 'Whosoever,' saith he, 'is a
servant of God, and hath his own Lord in his heart, asketh understanding of Him, and receiveth it, and interpreteth every parable,
and the words of the Lord which are spoken in parables are made
known unto him. But as many as are sluggish and idle in intercession,
these hesitate to ask of the Lord. But the Lord is abundant in compassion, and giveth to them that ask of Him without ceasing. But
thou who hast been strengthened by the holy angel, and hast received
from him such (powers of) intercession and art not idle, wherefore
dost thou not ask understanding of the Lord, and obtain it from Him?'
I say to him, 'Sir, I that have thee with me have (but) need to ask
thee and enquire of thee; for thou showest me all things, and speakest
with me; but if I had seen or heard them apart from thee I should
have asked of the Lord, that they might be shown to me.'

5. 'I told thee just now,' saith he, 'that thou art unscrupulous and
importunate, in enquiring for the interpretations of the parables. But
since thou art so obstinate, I will interpret to thee the parable of the
estate and all the accompaniments thereof, that thou mayest make them
known unto all. Hear now,' saith he, 'and understand them. The
estate is this world, and the lord of the estate is He that created all
things, and set them in order, and endowed them with power; and the
servant is the Son of God, and the vines are this people whom He
Himself planted; and the fences are the [holy] angels of the Lord who
keep together His people; and the weeds, which are plucked up from
the vineyard, are the transgressions of the servants of God; and the
dainties which He sent to him from the feast are the commandments
which He gave to His people through His Son; and the friends
and advisers are the holy angels which were first created; and the

absence of the master is the time which remaineth over until His coming.' I say to him; 'Sir, great and marvellous are all things and all things are glorious; was it likely then,' say I, 'that I could have apprehended them?' 'Nay, nor can any other man, though he be full of understanding, apprehend them.' 'Yet again, Sir,' say I, 'explain to me what I am about to enquire of thee.' 'Say on,' he saith, 'if thou desirest anything.' 'Wherefore, [Sir,]' say I, 'is the Son of God represented in the parable in the guise of a servant?'

6. 'Listen,' said he; 'the Son of God is not represented in the guise of a servant, but is represented in great power and lordship.' 'How, Sir?' say I; 'I comprehend not.' 'Because,' saith he, 'God planted the vineyard, that is, He created the people, and delivered them over to His Son. And the Son placed the angels in charge of them, to watch over them; and the Son Himself cleansed their sins, by labouring much and enduring many toils; for no one can dig without toil or labour. Having Himself then cleansed the sins of His people, He showed them the paths of life, giving them the law which He received from His Father. Thou seest,' saith he, 'that He is Himself Lord of the people, having received all power from His Father. But how that the lord took his son and the glorious angels as advisers concerning the inheritance of the servant, listen. The Holy Pre-existent Spirit, Which created the whole creation, God made to dwell in flesh that He desired. This flesh, therefore, in which the Holy Spirit dwelt, was subject unto the Spirit, walking honourably in holiness and purity, without in any way defiling the Spirit. When then it had lived honourably in chastity, and had laboured with the Spirit, and had cooperated with it in everything, behaving itself boldly and bravely, He chose it as a partner with the Holy Spirit; for the career of this flesh pleased [the Lord], seeing that, as possessing the Holy Spirit, it was not defiled upon the earth. He therefore took the son as adviser and the glorious angels also, that this flesh too, having served the Spirit unblameably, might have some place of sojourn, and might not seem to have lost the reward for its service; for all flesh, which is found undefiled and unspotted, wherein the Holy Spirit dwelt, shall receive a reward. Now thou hast the interpretation of this parable also.'

7. 'I was right glad, Sir,' say I, 'to hear this interpretation.' 'Listen now,' saith he. 'Keep this thy flesh pure and undefiled, that the Spirit which dwelleth in it may bear witness to it, and thy flesh may be justified. See that it never enter into thine heart that this flesh of

thine is perishable, and so thou abuse it in some defilement. [For] if thou defile thy flesh, thou shalt defile the Holy Spirit also; but if thou defile †the flesh†, thou shalt not live.' 'But if, Sir,' say I, 'there has been any ignorance in times past, before these words were heard, how shall a man who has defiled his flesh be saved?' 'For the former deeds of ignorance,' saith he, 'God alone hath power to give healing; for all authority is His. [But now keep thyself, and the Lord Almighty, Who is full of compassion, will give healing for thy former deeds of ignorance,] if henceforth thou defile not thy flesh, neither the Spirit; for both share in common, and the one cannot be defiled without the other. Therefore keep both pure, and thou shalt live unto God.'

[PARABLE THE SIXTH.]

1.   As I sat in my house, and glorified the Lord for all things that I had seen, and was considering concerning the commandments, how that they were beautiful and powerful and gladsome and glorious and able to save a man's soul, I said within myself; 'Blessed shall I be, if I walk in these commandments; yea, and whosoever shall walk in them shall be blessed.' As I spake these things within myself, I see him suddenly seated by me, and saying as follows; 'Why art thou of a doubtful mind concerning the commandments, which I commanded thee? They are beautiful. Doubt not at all; but clothe thyself in the faith of the Lord, and thou shalt walk in them. For I will strengthen thee in them. These commandments are suitable for those who meditate repentance; for if they walk not in them, their repentance is in vain. Ye then that repent, cast away the evil doings of this world which crush you; and, by putting on every excellence of righteousness, ye shall be able to observe these commandments, and to add no more to your sins. If then ye add no further sin at all, ye will depart from your former sins. Walk then in these my commandments, and ye shall live unto God. These things have [all] been told you from me.' And after he had told these things to me, he saith to me, 'Let us go into the country, and I will show thee the shepherds of the sheep.' 'Let us go, Sir,' say I. And we came to a certain plain, and he showeth me a young man, a shepherd, clothed in a light cloak, of saffron colour; and he was feeding a great number of sheep, and these sheep were, as it were, well fed and very frisky, and were gladsome as they skipped about hither and thither; and the shepherd himself was all gladsome

over his flock; and the very visage of the shepherd was exceedingly gladsome; and he ran about among the sheep.

2.   And he saith to me; 'Seest thou this shepherd?'   'I see him, Sir,' I say.   'This,' saith he, 'is the angel of self-indulgence and of deceit.   He crusheth the souls of the servants of God, and perverteth them from the truth, leading them astray with evil desires, wherein they perish.   For they forget the commandments of the living God, and walk in vain deceits and acts of self-indulgence, and are destroyed by this angel, some of them unto death, and others unto corruption.'   I say to him, 'Sir, I comprehend not what means "unto death," and what "unto corruption".'   'Listen,' saith he; 'the sheep which thou sawest gladsome and skipping about, these are they who have been turned asunder from God utterly, and have delivered themselves over to the lusts of this world.   In these, therefore, there is not repentance unto life.   For the Name of God is being blasphemed through them.   The life of such persons is death.   But the sheep, which thou sawest not skipping about, but feeding in one place, these are they that have delivered themselves over to acts of self-indulgence and deceit, but have not uttered any blasphemy against the Lord.   These then have been corrupted from the truth.   In these there is hope of repentance, wherein they can live.   Corruption then hath hope of a possible renewal, but death hath eternal destruction.'   Again we went forward a little way, and he showeth me a great shepherd like a wild man in appearance, with a white goatskin thrown about him; and he had a kind of wallet on his shoulders, and a staff very hard and with knots in it, and a great whip.   And his look was very sour, so that I was afraid of him because of his look.   This shepherd then kept receiving from the young man, the shepherd, those sheep that were frisky and well-fed, but not skipping about, and putting them in a certain spot, which was precipitous and covered with thorns and briars, so that the sheep could not disentangle themselves from the thorns and briars, but [became entangled among the thorns and briars.   And so they] pastured entangled in the thorns and briars, and were in great misery with being beaten by him; and he kept driving them about to and fro, and giving them no rest, and altogether those sheep had not a happy time.

3.   When then I saw them so lashed with the whip and vexed, I was sorry for their sakes, because they were so tortured and had no rest at all.   I say to the shepherd who was speaking with me; 'Sir, who is this shepherd, who is [so] hard-hearted and severe, and has no compassion

at all for these sheep?' 'This,' saith he, 'is the angel of punishment, and he is one of the just angels, and presides over punishment. So he receiveth those who wander away from God, and walk after the lusts and deceits of this life, and punisheth them, as they deserve, with fearful and various punishments.' 'I would fain learn, Sir,' say I, 'of what sort are these various punishments.' 'Listen,' saith he; 'the various tortures and punishments are tortures belonging to the present life; for some are punished with losses, and others with want, and others with divers maladies, and others with [every kind] of unsettlement, and others with insults from unworthy persons and with suffering in many other respects. For many, being unsettled in their plans, set their hands to many things, and nothing ever goes forward with them. And then they say that they do not prosper in their doings, and it doth not enter into their hearts that they have done evil deeds, but they blame the Lord. When then they are afflicted with every kind of affliction, then they are delivered over to me for good instruction, and are strengthened in the faith of the Lord, and serve the Lord with a pure heart the remaining days of their life. But, if they repent, the evil works which they have done rise up in their hearts, and then they glorify God, saying that He is a just Judge, and that they suffered justly each according to his doings. And they serve the Lord thenceforward with a pure heart, and are prosperous in all their doings, receiving from the Lord whatsoever things they may ask; and then they glorify the Lord because they were delivered over unto me, and they no longer suffer any evil thing.'

4. I say unto him; 'Sir, declare unto me this further matter.' 'What enquirest thou yet?' saith he. 'Whether, Sir,' say I, 'they that live in self-indulgence and are deceived undergo torments during the same length of time as they live in self-indulgence and are deceived.' He saith to me, 'They undergo torments for the same length of time.' 'Then, Sir,' say I, 'they undergo very slight torments; for those who are living thus in self-indulgence and forget God ought to have been tormented sevenfold.' He saith to me, 'Thou art foolish, and comprehendest not the power of the torment.' 'True,' say I, 'for if I had comprehended it, I should not have asked thee to declare it to me.' 'Listen,' saith he, 'to the power of both, [of the self-indulgence and of the torment]. The time of the self-indulgence and deceit is one hour. But an hour of the torment hath the power of thirty days. If then one live in self-indulgence and be deceived for one day, and be tormented for one day,

the day of the torment is equivalent to a whole year. For as many days then as a man lives in self-indulgence, for so many years is he tormented. Thou seest then,' saith he, 'that the time of the self-indulgence and deceit is very short, but the time of the punishment and torment is long.'

5. 'Inasmuch, Sir,' say I, 'as I do not quite comprehend concerning the time of the deceit and self-indulgence and torment, show me more clearly.' He answered and said unto me; 'Thy stupidity cleaveth to thee; and thou wilt not cleanse thy heart and serve God. Take heed,' [saith he,] 'lest haply the time be fulfilled, and thou be found in thy foolishness. Listen then,' [saith he,] 'even as thou wishest, that thou mayest comprehend the matter. He that liveth in self-indulgence and is deceived for one day, and doeth what he wisheth, is clothed in much folly and comprehendeth not the thing which he doeth; for on the morrow he forgetteth what he did the day before. For self-indulgence and deceit have no memories, by reason of the folly, wherewith each is clothed; but when punishment and torment cling to a man for a single day, he is punished and tormented for a whole year long; for punishment and torment have long memories. So being tormented and punished for the whole year, the man remembers at length the self-indulgence and deceit, and perceiveth that it is on their account that he is suffering these ills. Every man, therefore, that liveth in self-indulgence and is deceived, is tormented in this way because, though possessing life, they have delivered themselves over unto death.' 'What kinds of self-indulgence, Sir,' say I, 'are harmful?' 'Every action,' saith he, 'is self-indulgence to a man, which he does with pleasure; for the irascible man, when he gives the reins to his passion, is self-indulgent; and the adulterer and the drunkard and the slanderer and the liar and the miser and the defrauder and he that doeth things akin to these, giveth the reins to his peculiar passion; therefore he is self-indulgent in his action. All these habits of self-indulgence are harmful to the servants of God; on account of these deceits therefore they so suffer who are punished and tormented. But there are habits of self-indulgence likewise which save men; for many are self-indulgent in doing good, being carried away by the pleasure it gives to themselves. This self-indulgence then is expedient for the servants of God, and bringeth life to a man of this disposition; but the harmful self-indulgencies aforementioned bring to men torments and punishments; and if they continue in them and repent not, they bring death upon themselves.'

[Parable the Seventh.]

After a few days I saw him on the same plain, where also I had seen the shepherds, and he saith to me, 'What seekest thou?' 'I am here, Sir,' say I, 'that thou mayest bid the shepherd that punisheth go out of my house; for he afflicteth me much.' 'It is necessary for thee,' saith he, 'to be afflicted; for so,' saith he, 'the glorious angel ordered as concerning thee, for he wisheth thee to be proved.' 'Why, what so evil thing have I done, Sir,' say I, 'that I should be delivered over to this angel?' 'Listen,' saith he. 'Thy sins are many, yet not so many that thou shouldest be delivered over to this angel; but thy house has committed great iniquities and sins, and the glorious angel was embittered at their deeds, and for this cause he bade thee be afflicted for a certain time, that they also might repent and cleanse themselves from every lust of this world. When therefore they shall repent and be cleansed, then shall the angel of punishment depart.' I say to him; 'Sir, if they perpetrated such deeds that the glorious angel is embittered, what have I done?' 'They cannot be afflicted otherwise,' saith he, 'unless thou, the head of the [whole] house, be afflicted; for if thou be afflicted, they also of necessity will be afflicted; but if thou be prosperous, they can suffer no affliction.' 'But behold, Sir,' say I, 'they have repented with their whole heart.' 'I am quite aware myself,' saith he, 'that they have repented with their whole heart; well, thinkest thou that the sins of those who repent are forgiven forthwith? Certainly not; but the person who repents must torture his own soul, and must be thoroughly humble in his every action, and be afflicted with all the divers kinds of affliction; and if he endure the afflictions which come upon him, assuredly He Who created all things and endowed them with power will be moved with compassion and will bestow some remedy. And this (will God do), if in any way He perceive the heart of the penitent pure from every evil thing. But it is expedient for thee and for thy house that thou shouldest be afflicted now. But why speak I many words to thee? Thou must be afflicted as the angel of the Lord commanded, even he that delivered thee unto me; and for this give thanks to the Lord, in that He deemed thee worthy that I should reveal unto thee beforehand the affliction, that foreknowing it thou mightest endure it with fortitude.' I say to him; 'Sir, be thou with me, and I shall be able to endure all affliction [easily].' 'I will be with thee,' saith he; 'and I will ask the angel that punisheth to afflict thee more lightly; but thou shalt be afflicted for a short time, and thou shalt be restored

again to thy house. Only continue to be humble and to minister unto
the Lord with a pure heart, thou and thy children and thy house, and
walk in my commandments which I command thee, and thus it will be
possible for thy repentance to be strong and pure. And if thou keep
these commandments with thy household, all affliction shall hold aloof
from thee; yea, and affliction,' saith he, ' shall hold aloof from all whosoever shall walk in these my commandments.'

[PARABLE THE EIGHTH.]

1. He showed me a [great] willow, overshadowing plains and
mountains, and under the shadow of the willow all have come who
are called by the name of the Lord. And by the willow there stood
an angel of the Lord, glorious and very tall, having a great sickle, and
he was lopping branches from the willow, and giving them to the people
that sheltered beneath the willow; and he gave them little rods about
a cubit long. And after all had taken the rods, the angel laid aside
the sickle, and the tree was sound, just as I had seen it. Then I
marvelled within myself, saying, ' How is the tree sound after so many
branches have been lopped off?' The shepherd saith to me, ' Marvel
not that the tree remained sound, after so many branches were lopped
off; but wait until thou seest all things, and it shall be shown to thee
what it is.' The angel who gave the rods to the people demanded
them back from them again; and according as they had received
them, so also they were summoned to him, and each of them returned
the several rods. But the angel of the Lord took them, and examined
them. From some he received the rods withered and eaten as it were
by grubs : the angel ordered those who gave up rods like these to
stand apart. And others gave them up withered, but not grub-eaten; and
these again he ordered to stand apart. And others gave them up half-
withered; these also stood apart. And others gave up their rods half-
withered and with cracks; these also stood apart. And others gave up
their rods green and with cracks ; these also stood apart. And others
gave up their rods one half withered and one half green ; these also stood
apart. And others brought their rods two parts of the rod green, and
the third part withered ; these also stood apart. And others gave them
up two parts withered, and the third part green ; these also stood apart.
And others gave up their rods nearly all green, but a very small portion
of their rods was withered, just the end; but they had cracks in them ;
these also stood apart. And in those of others there was a very small

portion green, but the rest of the rods was withered; these also stood apart. And others came bringing their rods green, as they received them from the angel; and the most part of the multitude gave up their rods in this state; and the angel rejoiced exceedingly at these; these also stood apart. And others gave up their rods green and with shoots; these also stood apart; and at these again the angel rejoiced exceedingly. And others gave up their rods green and with shoots; and their shoots had, as it were, a kind of fruit. And those men were exceeding gladsome, whose rods were found in this state. And over them the angel exulted, and the shepherd was very gladsome over them.

2. And the angel of the Lord commanded crowns to be brought. And crowns were brought, made as it were of palm-branches; and he crowned the men that had given up the rods which had the shoots and some fruit, and sent them away into the tower. And the others also he sent into the tower, even those who had given up the rods green and with shoots, but the shoots were without fruit; and he set a seal upon them. And all they that went into the tower had the same raiment, white as snow. And those that had given up their rods green as they received them, he sent away, giving them a [white] robe, and seals. After the angel had finished these things, he saith to the shepherd; 'I go away; but these thou shalt send away to (their places within) the walls, according as each deserveth to dwell; but examine their rods carefully, and so send them away. But be careful in examining them. Take heed lest any escape thee,' saith he. 'Still if any escape thee, I will test them at the altar.' When he had thus spoken to the shepherd, he departed. And, after the angel had departed, the shepherd saith to me; 'Let us take the rods of all and plant them, to see whether any of them shall be able to live.' I say unto him, 'Sir, these withered things, how can they live?' He answered and said unto me; 'This tree is a willow, and this class of trees clingeth to life. If then the rods shall be planted and get a little moisture, many of them will live. And afterwards let us try to pour some water also over them. If any of them shall be able to live, I will rejoice with it; but if it live not, I at least shall not be found neglectful.' So the shepherd bade me call them, just as each one of them was stationed. And they came row after row, and they delivered up the rods to the shepherd. And the shepherd took the rods, and planted them in rows, and after he had planted them, he poured much water over them, so that the rods could not be seen for the water. And after he had watered the rods, he saith to me; 'Let us go now, and after a

few days let us return and inspect all the rods; for He Who created this tree willeth that all those who have received rods from this tree should live. And I myself hope that these little rods, after they have got moisture and been watered, will live the greater part of them.'

3. I say to him; 'Sir, inform me what this tree is. For I am perplexed herewith, because, though so many branches were cut off, the tree is sound, and nothing appears to have been cut from it; I am therefore perplexed thereat.' 'Listen,' saith he; 'this great tree which overshadows plains and mountains and all the earth is the law of God which was given to the whole world; and this law is the Son of God preached unto the ends of the earth. But the people that are under the shadow are they that have heard the preaching, and believed on Him; but the great and glorious angel is Michael, who hath the power over this people and is their captain. For this is he that putteth the law into the hearts of the believers; therefore he himself inspecteth them to whom he gave it, to see whether they have observed it. But thou seest the rods of every one; for the rods are the law. Thou seest these many rods rendered useless, and thou shalt notice all those that have not observed the law, and shalt see the abode of each severally.' I say unto him; 'Sir, wherefore did he send away some into the tower, and leave others for thee?' 'As many,' saith he, 'as transgressed the law which they received from him, these he left under my authority for repentance; but as many as already satisfied the law and have observed it, these he has under his own authority.' 'Who then, Sir,' say I, 'are they that have been crowned and go into the tower?' ['As many,' saith he, 'as wrestled with the devil and overcame him in their wrestling, are crowned:] these are they that suffered for the law. But the others, who likewise gave up their rods green and with shoots, though not with fruit, are they that were persecuted for the law, but did not suffer nor yet deny their law. But they that gave them up green just as they received them, are sober and righteous men, who walked altogether in a pure heart and have kept the commandments of the Lord. But all else thou shalt know, when I have examined these rods that have been planted and watered.'

4. And after a few days we came to the place, and the shepherd sat down in the place of the angel, while I stood by him. And he saith to me; 'Gird thyself with a garment of raw flax, and minister to me.' So I girded myself with a clean garment of raw flax made of coarse material. And when he saw me girded and ready to minister to him,

'Call,' saith he, 'the men whose rods have been planted, according
to the rank as each presented their rods.' And I went away to the
plain, and called them all; and they stood all of them according
to their ranks.   He saith to them; 'Let each man pluck out his
own rod, and bring it to me.'   Those gave them up first, who had
had the withered and chipped rods, and they were found accordingly
withered and chipped.   He ordered them to stand apart.   Then those
gave them up, who had the withered but not chipped; and some of
them gave up the rods green, and others withered and chipped as by
grubs.   Those then that gave them up green he ordered to stand apart;
but those that gave them up withered and chipped he ordered to stand
with the first.   Then those gave them up who had had the half-withered
and with cracks; and many of them gave them up green and without
cracks; and some gave them up green and with shoots, and fruits on the
shoots, such as those had who went into the tower crowned; and some
gave them up withered and eaten, and some withered and uneaten, and
some such as they were, half-withered and with cracks.   He ordered them
to stand each one apart, some in their proper ranks, and others apart.

5.   Then those gave them up who had their rods green, but with
cracks.   These all gave them up green, and stood in their own
company.   And the shepherd rejoiced over these, because they all were
changed and had put away their cracks.   And those gave them up
likewise who had the one half green and the other half withered.   The
rods of some were found entirely green, of some half-withered, of some
withered and eaten, and of some green and with shoots.   These were
all sent away each to his company.   Then those gave them up who had
two parts green and the third withered; many of them gave them up
green, and many half-withered, and others withered and eaten.   These
all stood in their own company.   Then those gave them up who
had two parts withered and the third part green.   Many of them
gave them up half-withered, but some withered and eaten, others half-
withered and with cracks, and a few green.   These all stood in their own
company.   Then those gave them up who had had their rods green, but
a very small part [withered] and with cracks.   Of these some gave them
up green, and others green and with shoots.   These also went away to
their own company.   Then those gave them up who had a very small
part green and the other parts withered.   The rods of these were found
for the most part green and with shoots and fruit on the shoots,
and others altogether green.   At these rods the shepherd rejoiced very

[greatly], because they were found so. And these went away each to his own company.

6. After [the shepherd] had examined the rods of all, he saith to me, 'I told thee that this tree clingeth to life. Seest thou,' saith he, 'how many repented and were saved?' 'I see, Sir,' say I. 'It is,' saith he, 'that thou mayest see the abundant compassion of the Lord, how great and glorious it is, and He hath given (His) Spirit to those that are worthy of repentance.' 'Wherefore then, Sir,' say I, 'did they not all repent?' 'To those, whose heart He saw about to become pure and to serve Him with all the heart, to them He gave repentance; but those whose craftiness and wickedness He saw, who intend to repent in hypocrisy, to them He gave not repentance, lest haply they should again profane His name.' I say unto him, 'Sir, now then show me concerning those that have given up their rods, what manner of man each of them is, and their abode, that when they hear this, they that believed and have received the seal and have broken it and did not keep it sound may fully understand what they are doing, and repent, receiving from thee a seal, and may glorify the Lord, that He had compassion upon them and sent thee to renew their spirits.' 'Listen,' saith he; 'those whose rods were found withered and grub-eaten, these are the renegades and traitors to the Church, that blasphemed the Lord in their sins, and still further were ashamed of the Name of the Lord, which was invoked upon them. These then perished altogether unto God. But thou seest how not one of them repented, although they heard the words which thou spakest to them, which I commanded thee. From men of this kind life departed. But those that gave up the green and undecayed (rods), these also are near them; for they were hypocrites, and brought in strange doctrines, and perverted the servants of God, especially them that had sinned, not permitting them to repent, but persuading them with their foolish doctrines. These then have hope of repenting. But thou seest that many of them have indeed repented from the time when thou spakest to them my commandments; yea, and (others) still will repent. And as many as shall not repent, have lost their life; but as many of them as repented, became good; and their dwelling was placed within the first walls, and some of them even ascended into the tower. Thou seest then,' [saith he,] 'that repentance from sins bringeth life, but not to repent bringeth death.

7. 'But as many as gave up (the rods) half-withered, and with cracks in them, hear also concerning these. Those whose rods were half-

withered throughout are the double-minded; for they neither live nor are dead. But those that have them half-withered and cracks in them, these are both double-minded and slanderers, and are never at peace among themselves but always causing dissensions. Yet even to these,' [saith he,] 'repentance is given. Thou seest,' [saith he,] 'that some of them have repented; and there is still,' saith he, 'hope of repentance among them. And as many of them,' saith he, 'as have repented, have their abode within the tower; but as many of them as have repented tardily shall abide within the walls; and as many as repent not, but continue in their doings, shall die the death. But they that have given up their rods green and with cracks, these were found faithful and good at all times, [but] they have a certain emulation one with another about first places and about glory of some kind or other; but all these are foolish in having (emulation) one with another about first places. Yet these also, when they heard my commandments, being good, purified them- selves and repented quickly. They have their habitation, therefore, within the tower. But if any one shall again turn to dissension, he shall be cast out from the tower and shall lose his life. Life is for all those that keep the commandments of the Lord. But in the command- ments there is nothing about first places, or about glory of any kind, but about long-suffering and humility in man. In such men, therefore, is the life of the Lord, but in factious and lawless men is death.

8. 'But they that gave up their rods half green and half withered, these are they that are mixed up in business and cleave not to the saints. Therefore the one half of them liveth, but the other half is dead. Many then when they heard my commandments repented. As many then as repented, have their abode within the tower. But some of them altogether stood aloof. These then have no repentance; for by reason of their business affairs they blasphemed the Lord and denied Him. So they lost their life for the wickedness that they com- mitted. But many of them were doubtful-minded. These still have place for repentance, if they repent quickly, and their dwelling shall be within the tower; and if they repent tardily, they shall dwell within the walls; but if they repent not, they too have lost their life. But they that have given up two parts green and the third part withered, these are they that have denied with manifold denials. Many of them therefore repented, and departed to dwell inside the tower; but many utterly rebelled from God; these lost their life finally. And some of them were double-minded and caused dissensions. For these then

there is repentance, if they repent speedily and continue not in their pleasures; but if they continue in their doings, they likewise procure for themselves death.

9.   'But they that have given up their rods two thirds withered and one third green, these are men who have been believers, but grew rich and became renowned among the Gentiles.   They clothed themselves with great pride and became high-minded, and abandoned the truth and did not cleave to the righteous, but lived together after the manner of the Gentiles, and this path appeared the more pleasant unto them; yet they departed not from God, but continued in the faith, though they wrought not the works of the faith.   Many of them therefore repented, and they had their habitation within the tower.   But others at the last living with the Gentiles, and being corrupted by the vain opinions of the Gentiles, departed from God, and worked the works of the Gentiles.   These therefore were numbered with the Gentiles.   But others of them were doubtful-minded, not hoping to be saved by reason of the deeds that they had done; and others were double-minded and made divisions among themselves.   For these then that were double-minded by reason of their doings there is still repentance; but their repentance ought to be speedy, that their dwelling may be within the tower; but for those who repent not, but continue in their pleasures, death is nigh.

10.   'But they that gave up their rods green, yet with the extreme ends withered and with cracks; these were found at all times good and faithful and glorious in the sight of God, but they sinned to a very slight degree by reason of little desires and because they had somewhat against one another.   But, when they heard my words, the greater part quickly repented, and their dwelling was assigned within the tower. But some of them were double-minded, and some being double-minded made a greater dissension.   In these then there is still a hope of repentance, because they were found always good; and hardly shall one of them die.   But they that gave up their rods withered, yet with a very small part green, these are they that believed, but practised the works of lawlessness.   Still they never separated from God, but bore the Name gladly, and gladly received into their houses the servants of God.   So hearing of this repentance they repented without wavering, and they practise all excellence and righteousness.   And some of them even suffer persecution willingly, knowing the deeds that they did.   All these then shall have their dwelling within the tower.'

11.   And after he had completed the interpretations of all the rods,

he saith unto me; 'Go, and tell all men to repent, and they shall live unto God; for the Lord in His compassion sent me to give repentance to all, though some of them do not deserve it for their deeds; but being long-suffering the Lord willeth them that were called through His Son to be saved.' I say to him; 'Sir, I hope that all when they hear these words will repent; for I am persuaded that each one, when he fully knows his own deeds and fears God, will repent.' He answered and said unto me; 'As many,' [saith he,] 'as [shall repent] from their whole heart [and] shall cleanse themselves from all the evil deeds afore-mentioned, and shall add nothing further to their sins, shall receive healing from the Lord for their former sins, unless they be double-minded concerning these commandments, and they shall live unto God. [But as many,' saith he, 'as shall add to their sins and walk in the lusts of this world, shall condemn themselves to death.] But do thou walk in my commandments, and live [unto God; yea, and as many as shall walk in them and shall do rightly, shall live unto God.'] Having shown me all these things [and told me them] he saith to me; 'Now the rest will I declare (unto thee) after a few days.'

[PARABLE THE NINTH.]

1. After I had written down the commandments and parables of the shepherd, the angel of repentance, he came to me and saith to me; 'I wish to show thee all things that the Holy Spirit, Which spake with thee in the form of the Church, showed unto thee. For that Spirit is the Son of God. For when thou wast weaker in the flesh, it was not declared unto thee through an angel; but when thou wast enabled through the Spirit, and didst grow mighty in thy strength so that thou couldest even see an angel, then at length was manifested unto thee, through the Church, the building of the tower. In fair and seemly manner hast thou seen all things, (instructed) as it were by a virgin; but now thou seest (being instructed) by an angel, though by the same Spirit; yet must thou learn everything more accurately from me. For to this end also was I appointed by the glorious angel to dwell in thy house, that thou mightest see all things mightily, in nothing terrified, even as before.' And he took me away into Arcadia, to a certain rounded mountain, and set me on the top of the mountain, and showed me a great plain, and round the plain twelve mountains, the mountains having each a different appearance. The first was black as soot; the second was bare, without vegetation; the third was thorny and full of briars;

the fourth had the vegetation half-withered, the upper part of the grass green, but the part by the roots withered, and some of the grass became withered, whenever the sun had scorched it; the fifth mountain had green grass and was rugged; the sixth mountain was full with clefts throughout, some small and some great, and the clefts had vegetation, but the grass was not very luxuriant, but rather as if it had been withered; the seventh mountain had smiling vegetation, and the whole mountain was in a thriving condition, and cattle and birds of every kind did feed upon that mountain; and the more the cattle and the birds did feed, so much the more did the herbage of that mountain flourish. The eighth mountain was full of springs, and every kind of creature of the Lord did drink of the springs on that mountain. The ninth mountain had no water at all, and was entirely desert; and it had in it wild beasts and deadly reptiles, which destroy mankind. The tenth mountain had very large trees and was umbrageous throughout, and beneath the shade lay sheep resting and feeding. The eleventh mountain was thickly wooded all over, and the trees thereon were very productive, decked with divers kinds of fruits, so that one seeing them would desire to eat of their fruits. The twelfth mountain was altogether white and its aspect was cheerful; and the mountain was most beauteous in itself.

2. And in the middle of the plain he showed me a great white rock, rising up from the plain. The rock was loftier than the mountains, being four-square, so that it could contain the whole world. Now this rock was ancient, and had a gate hewn out of it; but the gate seemed to me to have been hewed out quite recently. And the gate glistened beyond the brightness of the sun, so that I marvelled at the brightness of the gate. And around the gate stood twelve virgins. The four then that stood at the corners seemed to me to be more glorious (than the rest); but the others likewise were glorious; and they stood at the four quarters of the gate, and virgins stood in pairs between them. And they were clothed in linen tunics and girt about in seemly fashion, having their right shoulders free, as if they intended to carry some burden. Thus were they prepared, for they were very cheerful and eager. After I had seen these things, I marvelled in myself at the greatness and the glory of what I was seeing. And again I was perplexed concerning the virgins, that delicate as they were they stood up like men, as if they intended to carry the whole heaven. And the shepherd saith unto me; 'Why questionest thou within thyself and art perplexed, and bringest sadness on thyself? For whatsoever things thou canst not

comprehend, attempt them not, if thou art prudent; but entreat the Lord, that thou mayest receive understanding to comprehend them. What is behind thee thou canst not see, but what is before thee thou beholdest. The things therefore which thou canst not see, let alone, and trouble not thyself (about them); but the things which thou seest, these master, and be not over curious about the rest; but I will explain unto thee all things whatsoever I shall show thee. Have an eye therefore to what remaineth.'

3. I saw six men come, tall and glorious and alike in appearance; and they summoned a multitude of men. And the others also which came were tall men and handsome and powerful. And the six men ordered them to build a tower above the gate. And there arose a great noise from those men who had come to build the tower, as they ran hither and thither round the gate. For the virgins standing round the gate told the men to hasten to build the tower. Now the virgins had spread out their hands, as if they would take something from the men. And the six men ordered stones to come up from a certain deep place, and to go to the building of the tower. And there went up ten stones square and polished, [not] hewn from a quarry. And the six men called to the virgins, and ordered them to carry all the stones which should go unto the building of the tower, and to pass through the gate and to hand them to the men that were about to build the tower. And the virgins laid the first ten stones that rose out of the deep on each other, and they carried them together, stone by stone.

4. And just as they stood together around the gate, in that order they carried them that seemed to be strong enough and had stooped under the corners of the stone, while the others stooped at the sides of the stone. And so they carried all the stones. And they carried them right through the gate, as they were ordered, and handed them to the men for the tower; and these took the stones and builded. Now the building of the tower was upon the great rock and above the gate. Those ten stones then were joined together, and they covered the whole rock. And these formed a foundation for the building of the tower. And [the rock and] the gate supported the whole tower. And, after the ten stones, other twenty-five stones came up from the deep, and these were fitted into the building of the tower, being carried by the virgins, like the former. And after these thirty-five stones came up. And these likewise were fitted into the tower. And after these came up other forty stones, and these all were put into the building of the tower. So

four rows were made in the foundations of the tower. And (the stones) ceased coming up from the deep, and the builders likewise ceased for a little. And again the six men ordered the multitude of the people to bring in stones from the mountains for the building of the tower. They were brought in accordingly from all the mountains, of various colours, shaped by the men, and were handed to the virgins; and the virgins carried them right through the gate, and handed them in for the building of the tower. And when the various stones were placed in the building, they became all alike and white, and they lost their various colours. But some stones were handed in by the men for the building, and these did not become bright; but just as they were placed, such likewise were they found; for they were not handed in by the virgins, nor had they been carried in through the gate. These stones then were unsightly in the building of the tower. Then the six men, seeing the stones that were unsightly in the building, ordered them to be removed and carried [below] into their own place whence they were brought. And they say to the men who were bringing the stones in; 'Abstain for your parts altogether from handing in stones for the building; but place them by the tower, that the virgins may carry them through the gate, and hand them in for the building. For if,' [say they,] 'they be not carried in through the gate by the hands of these virgins, they cannot change their colours. Labour not therefore,' [say they,] 'in vain.'

5. And the building was finished on that day, yet was not the tower finally completed, for it was to be carried up [still] higher; and there was a cessation in the building. And the six men ordered the builders to retire for a short time [all of them], and to rest; but the virgins they ordered not to retire from the tower. And methought the virgins were left to guard the tower. And after all had retired [and rested], I say to the shepherd; 'How is it, Sir,' say I, 'that the building of the tower was not completed?' 'The tower,' he saith, 'cannot yet be finally completed, until its master come and test this building, that if any stones be found crumbling, he may change them; for the tower is being built according to His will.' 'I would fain know, Sir,' say I, 'what is this building of this tower, and concerning the rock and gate, and the mountains, and the virgins, and the stones that came up from the deep, and were not shaped, but went just as they were into the building; and wherefore ten stones were first placed in the foundations, then twenty-five, then thirty-five, then forty, and concerning the stones that had gone to the building and were removed again and put away in their own

place—concerning all these things set my soul at rest, Sir, and explain them to me.' 'If,' saith he, 'thou be not found possessed of an idle curiosity, thou shalt know all things. For after a few days we shall come here, and thou shalt see the sequel that overtaketh this tower and shalt understand all the parables accurately.' And after a few days we came to the place where we had sat, and he saith to me, 'Let us go to the tower; for the owner of the tower cometh to inspect it.' And we came to the tower, and there was no one at all by it, save the virgins alone. And the shepherd asked the virgins whether the master of the tower had arrived. And they said that he would be there directly to inspect the building.

6. And, behold, after a little while I see an array of many men coming, and in the midst a man of such lofty stature that he overtopped the tower. And the six men who superintended the building walked with him on the right hand and on the left, and all they that worked at the building were with him, and many other glorious attendants around him. And the virgins that watched the tower ran up and kissed him, and they began to walk by his side round the tower. And that man inspected the building so carefully, that he felt each single stone; and he held a rod in his hand and struck each single stone that was built in. And when he smote, some of the stones became black as soot, others mildewed, others cracked, others broke off short, others became neither white nor black, others rough and not fitting in with the other stones, and others with many spots; these were the varied aspects of the stones which were found unsound for the building. So he ordered all these to be removed from the tower, and to be placed by the side of the tower, and other stones to be brought and put into their place. And the builders asked him from what mountain he desired stones to be brought and put into their place. And he would not have them brought from the mountains, but ordered them to be brought from a certain plain that was nigh at hand. And the plain was dug, and stones were found there bright and square, but some of them too were round. And all the stones which there were anywhere in that plain were brought every one of them, and were carried through the gate by the virgins. And the square stones were hewed, and set in the place of those which had been removed; but the round ones were not placed in the building, because they were too hard to be shaped, and to work on them was slow. So they were placed by the side of the tower, as though they were intended to be shaped and placed in the building; for they were very bright.

7. So then, having accomplished these things, the glorious man who was lord of the whole tower called the shepherd to him, and delivered unto him all the stones which lay by the side of the tower, which were cast out from the building, and saith unto him; 'Clean these stones carefully, and set them in the building of the tower, these, I mean, which can fit with the rest; but those which will not fit, throw far away from the tower.' Having given these orders to the shepherd, he departed from the tower with all those with whom he had come. And the virgins stood round the tower watching it. I say to the shepherd, ' How can these stones go again to the building of the tower, seeing that they have been disapproved?' He saith unto me in answer; 'Seest thou,' saith he, 'these stones?' 'I see them, Sir,' say I. ' I myself,' saith he, 'will shape the greater part of these stones and put them into the building, and they shall fit in with the remaining stones.' ' How, Sir,' say I, 'can they, when they are chiseled, fill the same space?' He saith unto me in answer, 'As many as shall be found small, shall be put into the middle of the building; but as many as are larger, shall be placed nearer the outside, and they will bind them together.' With these words he saith to me, ' Let us go away, and after two days let us come and clean these stones, and put them into the building; for all things round the tower must be made clean, lest haply the master come suddenly and find the circuit of the tower dirty, and he be wroth, and so these stones shall not go to the building of the tower, and I shall appear to be careless in my master's sight.'

And after two days we came to the tower, and he saith unto me; ' Let us inspect all the stones, and see those which can go to the building.' I say to him, 'Sir, let us inspect them.'

8. And so commencing first we began to inspect the black stones; and just as they were when set aside from the building, such also they were found. And the shepherd ordered them to be removed from the tower and to be put on one side. Then he inspected those that were mildewed, and he took and shaped many of them, and ordered the virgins to take them up and put them into the building. And the virgins took them up and placed them in the building of the tower in a middle position. But the rest he ordered to be placed with the black ones; for these also were found black. Then he began to inspect those that had the cracks; and of these he shaped many, and he ordered them to be carried away by the hands of the virgins for the building. And they were placed towards the outside, because they were found to be

sounder. But the rest could not be shaped owing to the number of the cracks. For this reason therefore they were cast aside from the building of the tower. Then he proceeded to inspect the stunted (stones), and many among them were found black, and some had contracted great cracks; and he ordered these also to be placed with those that had been cast aside. But those of them which remained he cleaned and shaped, and ordered to be placed in the building. So the virgins took them up, and fitted them into the middle of the building of the tower; for they were somewhat weak. Then he began to inspect those that were half white and half black, and many of them were (now) found black; and he ordered these also to be taken up with those that had been cast aside. †But all the rest were [found white, and were] taken up by the virgins; for being white they were fitted by [the virgins] them[selves] into the building.† But they were placed towards the outside, because they were found sound, so that they could hold together those that were placed in the middle; for not a single one of them was too short. Then he began to inspect the hard and rough; and a few of them were cast away, because they could not be shaped; for they were found very hard. But the rest of them were shaped [and taken up by the virgins] and fitted into the middle of the building of the tower; for they were some-what weak. Then he proceeded to inspect those that had the spots, and of these some few had turned black and were cast away among the rest; but the remainder were found bright and sound, and these were fitted by the virgins into the building; but they were placed towards the outside, owing to their strength.

9. Then he came to inspect the white and round stones, and he saith unto me; 'What shall we do with these stones?' 'How do I know, Sir?' say I. [And he saith to me,] 'Perceivest thou nothing concerning them?' 'I, Sir,' say I, 'do not possess this art, neither am I a mason, nor can I understand.' 'Seest thou not,' saith he, 'that they are very round; and if I wish to make them square, very much must needs be chiseled off from them? Yet some of them must of necessity be placed into the building.' 'If then, Sir,' say I, 'it must needs be so, why distress thyself, and why not choose out for the building those thou willest, and fit them into it?' He chose out from them the large and the bright ones, and shaped them; and the virgins took them up, and fitted them into the outer parts of the building. But the rest, which remained over, were taken up, and put aside into the plain whence they were brought; they were not however cast away, 'Because,' saith he,

'there remaineth still a little of the tower to be builded. And the master of the tower is exceedingly anxious that these stones be fitted into the building, for they are very bright.' So twelve women were called, most beautiful in form, clad in black, [girded about and having the shoulders bare,] with their hair hanging loose. And these women, methought, had a savage look. And the shepherd ordered them to take up the stones which had been cast away from the building, and to carry them off to the same mountains from which also they had been brought; and they took them up joyfully, and carried away all the stones and put them in the place whence they had been taken. And after all the stones had been taken up, and not a single stone still lay round the tower, the shepherd saith unto me; 'Let us go round the tower, and see that there is no defect in it.' And I proceeded to go round it with him. And when the shepherd saw that the tower was very comely in the building, he was exceedingly glad; for the tower was so well builded, that when I saw it I coveted the building of it; for it was builded, as it were, of one stone, having one fitting in it. And the stone-work appeared as if hewn out of the rock; for it seemed to me to be all a single stone.

10. And I, as I walked with him, was glad to see so brave a sight. And the shepherd saith to me; 'Go and bring plaster and fine clay, that I may fill up the shapes of the stones that have been taken up and put into the building; for all the circuit of the tower must be made smooth.' And I did as he bade, and brought them to him. 'Assist me,' saith he, 'and the work will speedily be accomplished.' So he filled in the shapes of the stones which had gone to the building, and ordered the circuit of the tower to be swept and made clean. And the virgins took brooms and swept, and they removed all the rubbish from the tower, and sprinkled water, and the site of the tower was made cheerful and very seemly. The shepherd saith unto me, 'All,' saith he, 'hath now been cleaned. If the lord come to inspect the tower, he hath nothing for which to blame us.' Saying this, he desired to go away. But I caught hold of his wallet, and began to adjure him by the Lord that he would explain to me [all] what he had showed me. He saith to me; 'I am busy for a little while, and then I will explain everything to thee. Await me here till I come.' I say to him; 'Sir, when I am here alone what shall I do?' 'Thou art not alone,' saith he; 'for these virgins are here with thee.' 'Commend me then to them,' say I. The shepherd calleth them to him and saith to them; 'I commend this man to you till I come,' and he departed. So I was alone

with the virgins; and they were most cheerful, and kindly disposed to me, especially the four of them that were the more glorious in appearance.

11. The virgins say to me; 'Today the shepherd cometh not here.' 'What then shall I do?' say I. 'Stay for him,' say they, 'till eventide; and if he come, he will speak with thee; but if he come not, thou shalt stay here with us till he cometh.' I say to them; 'I will await him till evening, and if he come not, I will depart home and return early in the morning.' But they answered and said unto me; 'To us thou wast entrusted; thou canst not depart from us.' 'Where then,' say I, 'shall I remain?' 'Thou shalt pass the night with us,' say they, 'as a brother, not as a husband; for thou art our brother, and henceforward we will dwell with thee; for we love thee dearly.' But I was ashamed to abide with them. And she that seemed to be the chief of them began to kiss and to embrace me; and the others seeing her embrace me, they too began to kiss me, and to lead me round the tower, and to sport with me. And I had become as it were a younger man, and I commenced myself likewise to sport with them. For some of them began to dance, [others to skip,] others to sing. But I kept silence and walked with them round the tower, and was glad with them. But when evening came I wished to go away home; but they would not let me go, but detained me. And I stayed the night with them, and I slept by the side of the tower. For the virgins spread their linen tunics on the ground, and made me lie down in the midst of them, and they did nothing else but pray; and I prayed with them without ceasing, and not less than they. And the virgins rejoiced that I so prayed. And I stayed there with the virgins until the morning till the second hour. Then came the shepherd, and saith to the virgins; 'Have ye done him any injury?' 'Ask him,' say they. I say to him, 'Sir, I was rejoiced to stay with them.' 'On what didst thou sup?' saith he. 'I supped, Sir,' say I, 'on the words of the Lord the whole night through.' 'Did they treat thee well?' saith he. 'Yes, Sir,' say I. 'Now,' saith he, 'what wouldest thou hear first?' 'In the order as thou showedst to me, Sir, from the beginning,' say I; 'I request thee, Sir, to explain to me exactly in the order that I shall enquire of thee.' 'According as thou desirest,' saith he, 'even so will I interpret to thee, and I will conceal nothing whatever from thee.'

12. 'First of all, Sir,' say I, 'explain this to me. The rock and the gate, what is it?' 'This rock,' saith he, 'and gate is the Son of God.' 'How, Sir,' say I, 'is the rock ancient, but the gate recent?'

'Listen,' saith he, 'and understand, foolish man. The Son of God is older than all His creation, so that He became the Father's adviser in His creation. Therefore also He is ancient.' 'But the gate, why is it recent, Sir?' say I. 'Because,' saith he, 'He was made manifest in the last days of the consummation; therefore the gate was made recent, that they which are to be saved may enter through it into the kingdom of God. Didst thou see,' saith he, 'that the stones which came through the gate have gone to the building of the tower, but those which came not through it were cast away again to their own place?' 'I saw, Sir,' say I. 'Thus,' saith he, 'no one shall enter into the kingdom of God, except he receive the name of His Son. For if thou wishest to enter into any city, and that city is walled all round and has one gate only, canst thou enter into that city except through the gate which it hath?' 'Why, how, Sir,' say I, 'is it possible otherwise?' 'If then thou canst not enter into the city except through the gate itself, even so,' saith he, 'a man cannot enter into the kingdom of God except by the name of His Son that is beloved by Him. Didst thou see,' saith he, 'the multitude that is building the tower?' 'I saw it, Sir,' say I. 'They,' saith he, 'are all glorious angels. With these then the Lord is walled around. But the gate is the Son of God; there is this one entrance only to the Lord. No one then shall enter in unto Him otherwise than through His Son. Didst thou see,' saith he, 'the six men, and the glorious and mighty man in the midst of them, him that walked about the tower and rejected the stones from the building?' 'I saw him, Sir,' say I. 'The glorious man,' saith he, 'is the Son of God, and those six are the glorious angels who guard Him on the right hand and on the left. Of these glorious angels not one,' saith he, 'shall enter in unto God without Him; whosoever shall not receive His name, shall not enter into the kingdom of God.'

13. 'But the tower,' say I, 'what is it?' 'The tower,' saith he, 'why, this is the Church. 'And these virgins, who are they?' 'They,' saith he, 'are holy spirits; and no man can otherwise be found in the kingdom of God, unless these shall clothe him with their garment; for if thou receive only the name, but receive not the garment from them, thou profitest nothing. For these virgins are powers of the Son of God. If [therefore] thou bear the Name, and bear not His power, thou shalt bear His Name to none effect. And the stones,' saith he, 'which thou didst see cast away, these bare the Name, but clothed not themselves with the raiment of the virgins.' 'Of what sort, Sir,' say I, 'is their raiment?' 'The names themselves,' saith he, 'are their raiment. Who-

soever beareth the Name of the Son of God, ought to bear the names
of these also; for even the Son Himself beareth the names of these
virgins.   As many stones,' saith he, 'as thou sawest enter into the
building of the tower, being given in by their hands and waiting for the
building, they have been clothed in the power of these virgins.   For
this cause thou seest the tower made a single stone with the rock.   So
also they that have believed in the Lord through His Son and clothe
themselves in these spirits, shall become one spirit and one body, and
their garments all of one colour.   But such persons as bear the
names of the virgins have their dwelling in the tower.'   'The stones
then, Sir,' say I, 'which are cast aside, wherefore were they cast aside?
For they passed through the gate and were placed in the building of
the tower by the hands of the virgins.'   'Since all these things interest
thee,' saith he, 'and thou enquirest diligently, listen as touching the
stones that have been cast aside.   These all,' [saith he,] 'received the
name of the Son of God, and received likewise the power of these
virgins.   When then they received these spirits, they were strengthened,
and were with the servants of God, and they had one spirit and one
body [and one garment]; for they had the same mind, and they
wrought righteousness.   After a certain time then they were persuaded
by the women whom thou sawest clad in black raiment, and having their
shoulders bare and their hair loose, and beautiful in form.   When they
saw them they desired them, and they clothed themselves with their
power, but they stripped off from themselves the power of the virgins.
They then were cast away from the house of God, and delivered to
these (women).   But they that were not deceived by the beauty of these
women remained in the house of God.   So thou hast,' saith he, 'the
interpretation of them that were cast aside.'

14.   'What then, Sir,' say I, 'if these men, being such as they are,
should repent and put away their desire for these women, and return
unto the virgins, and walk in their power and in their works?   Shall
they not enter into the house of God?'   'They shall enter,' saith he,
'if they shall put away the works of these women, and take again the
power of the virgins, and walk in their works.   For this is the reason
why there was also a cessation in the building, that, if these repent, they
may go into the building of the tower; but if they repent not, then
others will go, and these shall be cast away finally.'   For all these things
I gave thanks unto the Lord, because He had compassion on all that
called upon His name, and sent forth the angel of repentance to us

that had sinned against Him, and refreshed our spirit, and, when we were already ruined and had no hope of life, restored our life. ' Now, Sir,' say I, ' show me why the tower is not built upon the ground, but upon the rock and upon the gate.' 'Because thou art senseless,' saith he, 'and without understanding [thou askest the question].' ' I am obliged, Sir,' say I, ' to ask all questions of thee, because I am absolutely unable to comprehend anything at all; for all are great and glorious and difficult for men to understand.' ' Listen,' saith he. ' The name of the Son of God is great and incomprehensible, and sustaineth the whole world. If then all creation is sustained by the Son [of God], what thinkest thou of those that are called by Him, and bear the name of the Son of God, and walk according to His commandments? Seest thou then what manner of men He sustaineth? Even those that bear His name with their whole heart. He Himself then is become their foundation, and He sustaineth them gladly, because they are not ashamed to bear His name.'

15. ' Declare to me, Sir,' say I, ' the names of the virgins, and of the women that are clothed in the black garments.' ' Hear,' saith he, ' the names of the more powerful virgins, those that are stationed at the corners. The first is Faith, and the second, Continence, and the third, Power, and the fourth, Longsuffering. But the others stationed between them have these names—Simplicity, Guilelessness, Purity, Cheerfulness, Truth, Understanding, Concord, Love. He that beareth these names and the name of the Son of God shall be able to enter into the kingdom of God. Hear,' saith he, ' likewise the names of the women that wear the black garments. Of these also four are more powerful than the rest; the first is Unbelief; the second, Intemperance; the third, Disobedience; the fourth, Deceit; and their followers are called, Sadness, Wickedness, Wantonness, Irascibility, Falsehood, Folly, Slander, Hatred. The servant of God that beareth these names shall see the kingdom of God, but shall not enter into it.' ' But the stones, Sir,' say I, ' that came from the deep, and were fitted into the building, who are they?' ' The first,' saith he, ' even the ten, that were placed in the foundations, are the first generation; the twenty-five are the second generation of righteous men; the thirty-five are God's prophets and His ministers; the forty are apostles and teachers of the preaching of the Son of God.' ' Wherefore then, Sir,' say I, ' did the virgins give in these stones also for the building of the tower and carry them through the gate?' ' Because these first,' saith he, ' bore these spirits, and they

never separated the one from the other, neither the spirits from the men nor the men from the spirits, but the spirits abode with them till they fell asleep; and if they had not had these spirits with them, they would not have been found useful for the building of this tower.'

16. 'Show me still further, Sir,' say I. 'What desirest thou to know besides?' saith he. 'Wherefore, Sir,' say I, 'did the stones come up from the deep, and wherefore were they placed into the building, though they bore these spirits?' 'It was necessary for them,' saith he, 'to rise up through water, that they might be made alive; for otherwise they could not enter into the kingdom of God, except they had put aside the deadness of their [former] life. So these likewise that had fallen asleep received the seal of the Son of God and entered into the kingdom of God. For before a man,' saith he, 'has borne the name of [the Son of] God, he is dead; but when he has received the seal, he layeth aside his deadness, and resumeth life. The seal then is the water: so they go down into the water dead, and they come up alive. Thus to them also this seal was preached, and they availed themselves of it that they might enter into the kingdom of God.' 'Wherefore, Sir,' say I, 'did the forty stones also come up with them from the deep, though they had already received the seal?' 'Because,' saith he, 'these, the apostles and the teachers who preached the name of the Son of God, after they had fallen asleep in the power and faith of the Son of God, preached also to them that had fallen asleep before them, and themselves gave unto them the seal of the preaching. Therefore they went down with them into the water, and came up again. But these went down alive [and again came up alive]; whereas the others that had fallen asleep before them went down dead and came up alive. So by their means they were quickened into life, and came to the full knowledge of the name of the Son of God. For this cause also they came up with them, and were fitted with them into the building of the tower and were builded with them, without being shaped; for they fell asleep in righteousness and in great purity. Only they had not this seal. Thou hast then the interpretation of these things also.' 'I have, Sir,' say I.

17. 'Now then, Sir, explain to me concerning the mountains. Wherefore are their forms diverse the one from the other, and various?' 'Listen,' saith he. 'These twelve mountains are [twelve] tribes that inhabit the whole world. To these (tribes) then the Son of God was preached by the Apostles.' 'But explain to me, Sir, why they are various—these mountains—and each has a different appearance.' 'Listen,' saith he.

'These twelve tribes which inhabit the whole world are twelve nations; and they are various in understanding and in mind. As various, then, as thou sawest these mountains to be, such also are the varieties in the mind of these nations, and such their understanding. And I will show unto thee the conduct of each.' 'First, Sir,' say I, 'show me this, why the mountains being so various, yet, when their stones were set into the building, became bright and of one colour, just like the stones that had come up from the deep.' 'Because,' saith he, 'all the nations that dwell under heaven, when they heard and believed, were called by the one name of [the Son of] God. So having received the seal, they had one under-standing and one mind, and one faith became theirs and [one] love, and they bore the spirits of the virgins along with the Name; therefore the building of the tower became of one colour, even bright as the sun. But after they entered in together, and became one body, some of them defiled themselves, and were cast out from the society of the righteous, and became again such as they were before, or rather even worse.'

18. 'How, Sir,' say I, 'did they become worse, after they had fully known God?' 'He that knoweth not God,' saith he, 'and committeth wickedness, hath a certain punishment for his wickedness; but he that knoweth God fully ought not any longer to commit wickedness, but to do good. If then he that ought to do good committeth wickedness, does he not seem to do greater wickedness than the man that knoweth not God? Therefore they that have not known God, and commit wickedness, are condemned to death; but they that have known God and seen His mighty works, and yet commit wickedness, shall receive a double punishment, and shall die eternally. In this way therefore shall the Church of God be purified. And as thou sawest the stones removed from the tower and delivered over to the evil spirits, they too shall be cast out; and there shall be one body of them that are purified, just as the tower, after it had been purified, became made as it were of one stone. Thus shall it be with the Church of God also, after she hath been purified, and the wicked and hypocrites and blasphemers and double-minded and they that commit various kinds of wickedness have been cast out. When these have been cast out, the Church of God shall be one body, one understanding, one mind, one faith, one love. And then the Son of God shall rejoice and be glad in them, for that He hath received back His people pure.' 'Great and glorious, Sir,' say I, 'are all these things. Once more, Sir,' [say I,] 'show me the force and the doings of each one of the mountains, that every soul that

trusteth in the Lord, when it heareth, may glorify His great and marvellous and glorious name.' 'Listen,' saith he, 'to the variety of the mountains and of the twelve nations.

19. 'From the first mountain, which was black, they that have believed are such as these ; rebels and blasphemers against the Lord, and betrayers of the servants of God. For these there is no repentance, but there is death. For this cause also they are black ; for their race is lawless. And from the second mountain, the bare one, they that believed are such as these ; hypocrites and teachers of wickedness. And these then are like the former in not having the fruit of righteousness. For, even as their mountain is unfruitful, so likewise such men as these have a name indeed, but they are void of the faith, and there is no fruit of truth in them. For these then repentance is offered, if they repent quickly; but if they delay, they will have their death with the former.' 'Wherefore, Sir,' say I, 'is repentance possible for them, but not for the former? For their doings are almost the same.' 'On this account,' he saith, 'is repentance offered for them, because they blasphemed not their Lord, nor became betrayers of the servants of God ; yet from desire of gain they played the hypocrite, and taught each other [after] the desires of sinful men. But they shall pay a certain penalty ; yet repentance is ordained for them, because they are not become blasphemers or betrayers.

20. 'And from the third mountain, which had thorns and briars, they that believed are such as these; some of them are wealthy and others are entangled in many business affairs. The briars are the wealthy, and the thorns are they that are mixed up in various business affairs. These [then, that are mixed up in many and various business affairs,] cleave [not] to the servants of God, but go astray, being choked by their affairs, but the wealthy unwillingly cleave to the servants of God, fearing lest they may be asked for something by them. Such men therefore *shall hardly enter into the kingdom of God.* For as it is difficult to walk on briars with bare feet, so also *it is difficult* for such men *to enter into the kingdom of God.* But for all these repentance is possible, but it must be speedy, that in respect to what they omitted to do in the former times, they may now revert to (past) days, and do some good. If then they shall repent and do some good, they shall live unto God ; but if they continue in their doings, they shall be delivered over to those women, the which shall put them to death.

21. 'And from the fourth mountain, which had much vegetation,

the upper part of the grass green and the part towards the roots withered, and some of it dried up by the sun, they that believed are such as these ; the double-minded, and they that have the Lord on their lips, but have Him not in their heart.   Therefore their foundations are dry and without power, and their words only live, but their works are dead.   Such men are neither alive nor dead.   They are, therefore, like unto the double-minded; for the double-minded are neither green nor withered; for they are neither alive nor dead.   For as their grass was withered up when it saw the sun, so also the double-minded, when they hear of tribulation, through their cowardice worship idols and are ashamed of the name of their Lord.   Such are neither alive nor dead.   Yet these also, if they repent quickly, shall be able to live ; but if they repent not, they are delivered over already to the women who deprive them of their life.

22.   'And from the fifth mountain, which had green grass and was rugged, they that believed are such as these ; they are faithful, but slow to learn and stubborn and self-pleasers, desiring to know all things, and yet they know nothing at all.   By reason of this their stubbornness, understanding stood aloof from them, and a foolish senselessness entered into them ; and they praise themselves as having understanding, and they desire to be self-appointed teachers, senseless though they are. Owing then to this pride of heart many, while they exalted themselves, have been made empty ; for a mighty demon is stubbornness and vain confidence.   Of these then many were cast away, but some repented and believed, and submitted themselves to those that had understanding, having learnt their own senselessness.   Yea, and to the rest that belong to this class repentance is offered ; for they did not become wicked, but rather foolish and without understanding.   If these then shall repent, they shall live unto God ; but if they repent not, they shall have their abode with the women who work evil against them.

23.   'But they that believed from the sixth mountain, which had clefts great and small, and in the clefts herbage withered, are such as these ; they that have the small clefts, these are they that have aught against one another, and from their backbitings they are withered in the faith ; but many of these repented.   Yea, and the rest shall repent, when they hear my commandments ; for their backbitings are but small, and they shall quickly repent.   But they that have great clefts, these are persistent in their backbitings and bear grudges, nursing wrath against one another.   These then were thrown right away from the tower and rejected from its building.   Such persons therefore shall with difficulty

live. If God and our Lord, Who ruleth over all things and hath the authority over all His creation, beareth no grudge against them that confess their sins, but is propitiated, doth man, who is mortal and full of sins, bear a grudge against man, as though he were able to destroy or save him? I say unto you—I, the angel of repentance—unto as many as hold this heresy, put it away from you and repent, and the Lord shall heal your former sins, if ye shall purify yourselves from this demon; but if not, ye shall be delivered unto him to be put to death.

24. 'And from the seventh mountain, on which was herbage green and smiling, and the whole mountain thriving, and cattle of every kind and the fowls of heaven were feeding on the herbage on that mountain, and the green herbage, on which they fed, only grew the more luxuriant, they that believed are such as these; they were ever simple and guile- less and blessed, having nothing against one another, but rejoicing always in the servants of God, and clothed in the Holy Spirit of these virgins, and having compassion always on every man, and out of their labours they supplied every man's need without reproach and without misgiving. The Lord then seeing their simplicity and entire childliness made them to abound in the labours of their hands, and bestowed favour on them in all their doings. But I say unto you that are such— I, the angel of repentance—remain to the end such as ye are, and your seed shall never be blotted out. For the Lord hath put you to the proof, and enrolled you among our number, and your whole seed shall dwell with the Son of God; for of His Spirit did ye receive.

25. 'And from the eighth mountain, where were the many springs, and all the creatures of the Lord did drink of the springs, they that believed are such as these; apostles and teachers, who preached unto the whole world, and who taught the word of the Lord in soberness and purity, and kept back no part at all for evil desire, but walked always in righteousness and truth, even as also they received the Holy Spirit. Such therefore shall have their entrance with the angels.

26. 'And from the ninth mountain, which was desert, which had [the] reptiles and wild beasts in it which destroy mankind, they that believed are such as these; they that have the spots are deacons that exercised their office ill, and plundered the livelihood of widows and orphans, and made gain for themselves from the ministrations which they had re- ceived to perform. If then they abide in the same evil desire, they are dead and there is no hope of life for them; but if they turn again and fulfil their ministrations in purity, it shall be possible for them to live.

But they that are mildewed, these are they that denied and turned not again unto their Lord, but having become barren and desert, because they cleave not unto the servants of God but remain alone, they destroy their own souls.   For as a vine left alone in a hedge, if it meet with neglect, is destroyed and wasted by the weeds, and in time becometh wild and is no longer useful to its owner, so also men of this kind have given themselves up in despair and become useless to their Lord, by growing wild.   To these then repentance cometh, unless they be found to have denied from the heart; but if a man be found to have denied from the heart, I know not whether it is possible for him to live. And this I say not in reference to these days, that a man after denying should receive repentance; for it is impossible for him to be saved who shall now deny his Lord; but for those who denied Him long ago repentance seemeth to be possible.   If a man therefore will repent, let him do so speedily before the tower is completed; but if not, he shall be destroyed by the women and put to death.   And the stunted, these are the treacherous and backbiters; and the wild beasts which thou sawest on the mountain are these.   For as wild beasts with their venom poison and kill a man, so also do the words of such men poison and kill a man.   These then are broken off short from their faith through the conduct which they have in themselves; but some of them repented and were saved; and the rest that are of this kind can be saved, if they repent; but if they repent not, they shall meet their death from those women of whose power they are possessed.

27.   'And from the tenth mountain, where were trees sheltering certain sheep, they that believed are such as these; bishops, hospitable persons, who gladly received into their houses at all times the servants of God without hypocrisy.   [These bishops] at all times without ceasing sheltered the needy and the widows in their ministration and conducted themselves in purity at all times.   These [all] then shall be sheltered by the Lord for ever.   They therefore that have done these things are glorious in the sight of God, and their place is even now with the angels, if they shall continue unto the end serving the Lord.

28.   'And from the eleventh mountain, where were trees full of fruit, decked with divers kinds of fruits, they that believed are such as these; they that suffered for the Name [of the Son of God], who also suffered readily with their whole heart, and yielded up their lives.'   'Wherefore then, Sir,' say I, 'have all the trees fruits, but some of their fruits are more beautiful than others?'   'Listen,' saith he; 'all as many as ever suffered

for the Name's sake are glorious in the sight of God, and the sins of all these were taken away, because they suffered for the name of the Son of God. Now hear why their fruits are various, and some surpassing others. As many,' saith he, ' as were tortured and denied not, when brought before the magistracy, but suffered readily, these are the more glorious in the sight of the Lord ; their fruit is that which surpasseth. But as many as became cowards, and were lost in uncertainty, and considered in their hearts whether they should deny or confess, and yet suffered, their fruits are less, because this design entered into their heart ; for this design is evil, that a servant should deny his own lord. See to it, therefore, ye who entertain this idea, lest this design remain in your hearts, and ye die unto God. But ye that suffer for the Name's sake ought to glorify God, because God deemed you worthy that ye should bear this name, and that all your sins should be healed. Reckon yourselves blessed therefore ; yea, rather think that ye have done a great work, if any of you shall suffer for God's sake. The Lord bestoweth life upon you, and ye perceive it not ; for your sins weighed you down, and if ye had not suffered for the Name [of the Lord], ye had died unto God by reason of your sins. These things I say unto you that waver as touching denial and confession. Confess that ye have the Lord, lest denying Him ye be delivered into prison. If the Gentiles punish their slaves, if any one deny his lord, what think ye the Lord will do unto you, He Who hath the authority over all things ? Away with these designs from your hearts, that ye may live for ever unto God.

29. 'And from the twelfth mountain, which was white, they that believed are such as these ; they are as very babes, into whose heart no guile entereth, neither learnt they what wickedness is, but they remained as babes for ever. Such as these then dwell without doubt in the kingdom of God, because they defiled the commandments of God in nothing, but continued as babes all the days of their life in the same mind. As many of you therefore as shall so continue,' saith he, 'and shall be as infants not having guile, shall be more glorious [even] than all them that have been mentioned before ; for all infants are glorious in the sight of God, and stand first in His sight. Blessed then are ye, as many as have put away wickedness from you, and have clothed yourselves in guilelessness : ye shall live unto God chiefest of all.'

After he had finished the parables of the mountains, I say unto him, ' Sir, now explain to me concerning the stones that were taken from the plain and placed in the building in the room of the stones that were taken from the tower, and concerning the round (stones) which were placed in the building, and concerning those that were still round.'

30. 'Hear,' saith he, 'likewise concerning all these things. The stones which were taken from the plain and placed in the building of the tower in the room of those that were rejected, are the roots of this white mountain. When then they that believed from this mountain were all found guileless, the lord of the tower ordered these from the roots of this mountain to be put into the building of the tower. For He knew that if these stones should go to the building [of the tower], they would remain bright and not one of them would turn black. But if he had added (stones) from the other mountains, he would have been obliged to visit that tower again, and to purify it. Now all these have been found white, who have believed and who shall believe; for they are of the same kind. Blessed is this kind, for it is innocent! Hear now likewise concerning those round and bright stones. All these are from this white mountain. Now hear wherefore they have been found round. Their riches have darkened and obscured them a little from the truth, yet they never departed from God, nor did any evil word proceed from their mouth, but all equity and virtue which comes from the truth. When therefore the Lord perceived their mind, †that they could favour the truth,† and likewise remain good, He commanded their possessions to be cut from off them, yet not to be taken away altogether, so that they might be able to do some good with that which hath been left to them, and might live unto God, for that they come of a good kind. So therefore they have been cut away a little, and placed in the building of this tower.

31. 'But the other (stones), which have remained round and have not been fitted into the building, because they have not yet received the seal, have been replaced in their own position, for they were found very round. For this world and the vanities of their possessions must be cut from off them, and then they will fit into the kingdom of God. For it is necessary that they should enter into the kingdom of God; because the Lord hath blessed this innocent kind. Of this kind then not one shall perish. Yea, even though any one of them being tempted by the most wicked devil have committed any fault, he shall return speedily unto his Lord. Blessed I pronounce you all to be— I, the angel of repentance—whoever of you are guileless as infants, because your part is good and honourable in the sight of God. Moreover I bid all of you, whoever have received this seal, keep guilelessness,

and bear no grudge, and continue not in your wickedness nor in the memory of the offences of bitterness; but become of one spirit, and heal these evil clefts and take them away from among you, that the owner of the flocks may rejoice concerning them. For he will rejoice, if he find all things whole. But if he find any part of the flock scattered, woe unto the shepherds. For if the shepherds themselves shall have been found scattered, how will they answer for the flocks? Will they say that they were harassed by the flock? No credence will be given them. For it is an incredible thing that a shepherd should be injured by his flock; and he will be punished the more because of his falsehood. And I am the shepherd, and it behoveth me most strongly to render an account for you.

32.   'Amend yourselves therefore, while the tower is still in course of building. The Lord dwelleth in men that love peace; for to Him peace is dear; but from the contentious and them that are given up to wickedness He keepeth afar off. Restore therefore to Him your spirit whole as ye received it. For suppose thou hast given to a fuller a new garment whole, and desirest to receive it back again whole, but the fuller give it back to thee torn, wilt thou receive it thus? Wilt thou not at once blaze out and attack him with reproaches, saying; "The garment which I gave thee was whole; wherefore hast thou rent it and made it useless? See, by reason of the rent, which thou hast made in it, it cannot be of use." Wilt thou not then say all this to a fuller even about a rent which he has made in thy garment? If therefore thou art thus vexed in the matter of thy garment, and complainest because thou receivest it not back whole, what thinkest thou the Lord will do to thee, He, Who gave thee the spirit whole, and thou hast made it absolutely useless, so that it cannot be of any use at all to its Lord? For its use began to be useless, when it was corrupted by thee. Will not therefore the Lord of this spirit for this thy deed punish [thee with death]?' 'Certainly,' I said, 'all those, whomsoever He shall find continuing to bear malice, He will punish.' 'Trample not,' said he, 'upon His mercy, but rather glorify Him, because He is so long-suffering with your sins, and is not like unto you. Practise then repentance which is expedient for you.

33.   'All these things which are written above I, the shepherd, the angel of repentance, have declared and spoken to the servants of God. If then ye shall believe and hear my words, and walk in them, and amend your ways, ye shall be able to live. But if ye continue in wickedness and in bearing malice, no one of this kind shall live unto God.

All things which were to be spoken by me have (now) been spoken to you.' The shepherd said to me, 'Hast thou asked me all thy questions?' And I said, 'Yes, Sir.' 'Why then hast thou not enquired of me concerning the shape of the stones placed in the building, in that we filled up their shapes?' And I said, 'I forgot, Sir.' 'Listen now,' said he, 'concerning them. These are they that have heard my commandments now, and have practised repentance with their whole heart. So when the Lord saw that their repentance was good and pure, and that they could continue therein, he ordered their former sins to be blotted out. These shapes then were their former sins, and they have been chiseled away that they might not appear.'

PARABLE THE TENTH.

1. After I had written out this book completely, the angel who had delivered me to the shepherd came to the house where I was, and sat upon a couch, and the shepherd stood at his right hand. Then he called me, and spake thus unto me; 'I delivered thee,' said he, 'and thy house to this shepherd, that thou mightest be protected by him.' 'True, Sir,' I said. 'If therefore,' said he, 'thou desirest to be protected from all annoyance and all cruelty, to have also success in every good work and word, and all the power of righteousness, walk in his commandments, which I have given thee, and thou shalt be able to get the mastery over all wickedness. For if thou keep his commandments, all evil desire and the sweetness of this world shall be subject unto thee; moreover success shall attend thee in every good undertaking. Embrace his gravity and self-restraint, and tell it out unto all men that he is held in great honour and dignity with the Lord, and is a ruler of great authority, and powerful in his office. To him alone in the whole world hath authority over repentance been assigned. Seemeth he to thee to be powerful? Yet ye despise the gravity and moderation which he useth towards you.'

2. I say unto him; 'Ask him, Sir, himself, whether from the time that he hath been in my house, I have done ought out of order, whereby I have offended him.' 'I myself know,' said he, 'that thou hast done nothing out of order, nor art about to do so. And so I speak these things unto thee, that thou mayest persevere. For he hath given a good account of thee unto me. Thou therefore shalt speak these words to others, that they too who have practised or shall practise repentance may be of the same mind as thou art; and he may give a good report of

them to me, and I unto the Lord.' 'I too, Sir,' I say, 'declare to every
man the mighty works of the Lord; for I hope that all who have sinned
in the past, if they hear these things, will gladly repent and recover
life.' 'Continue therefore,' said he, 'in this ministry, and complete it
unto the end. For whosoever fulfil his commandments shall have life ;
yea such a man (shall have) great honour with the Lord. But whosoever keep not his commandments, fly from their life, and oppose him,
and follow not his commandments, but deliver themselves over to
death; and each one becometh guilty of his own blood. But I bid
thee obey these commandments, and thou shalt have a remedy for thy
sins.

3. 'Moreover, I have sent these virgins unto thee, that they may dwell
with thee; for I have seen that they are friendly towards thee. Thou
hast them therefore as helpers, that thou mayest be the better able to
keep his commandments ; for it is impossible that these commandments
be kept without the help of these virgins. I see too that they are glad
to be with thee. But I will charge them that they depart not at all from
thy house. Only do thou purify thy house; for in a clean house they will
gladly dwell. For they are clean and chaste and industrious, and all have
favour in the sight of the Lord. If, therefore, they shall find thy house
pure, they will continue with thee; but if the slightest pollution arise,
they will depart from thy house at once. For these virgins love not
pollution in any form.' I say unto him, 'I hope, Sir, that I shall please
them, so that they may gladly dwell in my house for ever ; and just as
he to whom thou didst deliver me maketh no complaint against me,
so they likewise shall make no complaint.' He saith unto the shepherd,
'I perceive,' saith he, 'that he wishes to live as the servant of God, and
that he will keep these commandments, and will place these virgins in a
clean habitation.' With these words he again delivered me over to the
shepherd, and called the virgins, and said to them ; 'Inasmuch as I see
that ye are glad to dwell in this man's house, I commend to you him
and his house, that ye depart not at all from his house.' But they heard
these words gladly.

4. He said then to me, 'Quit you like a man in this ministry;
declare to every man the mighty works of the Lord, and thou shalt have
favour in this ministry. Whosoever therefore shall walk in these commandments, shall live and be happy in his life; but whosoever shall
neglect them, shall not live, and shall be unhappy in his life. Charge
all men who are able to do right, that they cease not to practise

good works ; for it is useful for them.   I say moreover that every man ought to be rescued from misfortune ; for he that hath need, and suffereth misfortune in his daily life, is in great torment and want. Whosoever therefore rescueth from penury a life of this kind, winneth great joy for himself.   For he who is harassed by misfortune of this sort is afflicted and tortured with equal torment as one who is in chains. For many men on account of calamities of this kind, because they can bear them no longer, lay violent hands on themselves.   He then who knows the calamity of a man of this kind and rescueth him not, committeth great sin, and becometh guilty of the man's blood.   Do therefore good works, whoever of you have received (benefits) from the Lord, lest, while ye delay to do them, the building of the tower be completed.   For it is on your account that the work of the building has been interrupted.   Unless then ye hasten to do right, the tower will be completed, and ye shut out.'

When then he had finished speaking with me, he rose from the couch and departed, taking with him the shepherd and the virgins. He said however unto me, that he would send the shepherd and the virgins back again to my house.

THE EPISTLE

TO

DIOGNETUS

THE EPISTLE TO DIOGNETUS

I

WE owe the text of this work to a single MS of the thirteenth or possibly the fourteenth century, now no longer extant. This MS had originally belonged to Joann. Reuchlin († 1522), and ultimately found a home in the Strassburg Library, where it perished by fire during the Franco-German war in 1870 together with the other manuscript treasures contained therein. Two transcripts however had been made at the close of the sixteenth century, one by H. Stephens (in 1586), who first edited the Epistle to Diognetus (Paris, 1592), and another by Beurer (1587—1591), who however did not publish it. Stephens' copy is now at Leyden; that of Beurer is lost, but some of its readings are preserved by Stephens and by Sylburg (1593). Happily the portion of the Strassburg MS containing this Epistle was carefully collated by E. Cunitz in 1842 for Otto's first edition of Justin Martyr (1843), and again by E. Reuss still more accurately in 1861 for the same editor's third edition (1879).

The Strassburg MS contained several spurious or doubtful writings of Justin Martyr, at the close of which was the Epistle to Diognetus, likewise ascribed to him, τοῦ αὐτοῦ ['Ιουστίνου φιλοσόφου καὶ μάρτυρος] πρὸς Διόγνητον, besides other works following—some of them in a later hand—with which we are not concerned. Hence subsequent writers ascribed it unhesitatingly to Justin. Tillemont was the first (1691) who threw any doubt on this ascription. More recently critics, one and all, have agreed to assign it to some other author. It is not mentioned by Eusebius, or in any other ancient account of Justin's works; and its style is wholly different from that of Justin.

The most diverse opinions have been held respecting its date. Almost every epoch from the middle of the second century to the reign of Constantine in the beginning of the fourth has been assigned to it; nor indeed is any certainty possible. On the whole, however, the earlier date (c. A.D. 150) seems the more probable. Its ascription to Justin Martyr and its companionship with early writings in the MS suggest an epoch not later than the first half of the second century. The person meant by Diognetus is not improbably the tutor of Marcus Aurelius, here addressed as an enquirer after truth. The reference to the emperor commissioning his son (c. 7 ὡς βασιλεὺς πέμπων υἱὸν βασιλέα), as illustrating the great truth of Christian theology, may not improbably have been suggested by such events as the adoption of M. Aurelius by Antoninus Pius into the tribunician power (A.D. 147), or the association of his adopted son L. Aelius (A.D. 161) or of his own son Commodus (A.D. 176, 177) in the empire by M. Aurelius himself. The simplicity in the mode of stating theological truths, and the absence of all reference to the manifold heresies of later times, both point to a somewhat early date. Whenever it was written, it is one of the noblest and most impressive of early Christian apologies in style and treatment.

The dream of some very recent writers who suppose it to have been written, or rather forged, at the revival of learning in the sixteenth century may be dismissed at once as inconsistent alike with its style and contents, and with the history of the documents as given above.

2

The Epistle to Diognetus, however, does not reach beyond the tenth chapter, where it ends abruptly. The two remaining chapters belong to some different work, which has been accidentally attached to it, just as in most of the extant MSS the latter part of the Epistle of Polycarp is attached to the former part of the Epistle of Barnabas (see above, pp. 166 sq, 242), so as to form in appearance one work. Probably in this case also an archetypal MS had lost some leaves. Of this there seems to have been some indication in the Strassburg MS itself.

Who then was the author of this latter work? May we not hazard a conjecture which may be taken for what it is worth? The writer was Pantænus, the master of Clement (c. A.D. 180—210). Clearly it is Alexandrian, as its phraseology and its sentiments alike show. More especially he treats the account of the creation and the garden of Eden

(c. 12 παράδεισος τρυφῆς κ.τ.λ.) spiritually of the Church of Christ; and Pantænus is singled out with two or three other early fathers by Anastasius of Sinai in two passages as exhibiting this mode of treatment (ed. Migne, p. 860, p. 962). Nor indeed could any one more appropriately use the words (c. 11) ἀποστόλων γενόμενος μαθητὴς γίνομαι διδάσκαλος ἐθνῶν of himself than Pantænus the Apostle of the Indies. The first part of the sentence, ἀποστόλων μαθητής, wrongly understood, has given a place to the Epistle to Diognetus as a whole among the Apostolical Fathers, though (as we have shown) the last two chapters form no part of that Epistle. It is perhaps this very sentence also, or similar language of Pantænus elsewhere, which has led to the impossible statement in Photius (*Bibl.* 118) that Pantænus himself had listened to the preaching of the apostles.

THE EPISTLE TO DIOGNETUS

SINCE I see, most excellent Diognetus, that thou art exceedingly anxious to understand the religion of the Christians, and that thy enquiries respecting them are distinctly and carefully made, as to what God they trust and how they worship Him, that they all disregard the world and despise death, and take no account of those who are regarded as gods by the Greeks, neither observe the superstition of the Jews, and as to the nature of the affection which they entertain one to another, and of this new development or interest, which has entered into men's lives now and not before: I gladly welcome this zeal in thee, and I ask of God, Who supplieth both the speaking and the hearing to us, that it may be granted to myself to speak in such a way that thou mayest be made better by the hearing, and to thee that thou mayest so listen that I the speaker may not be disappointed.

2. Come then, clear thyself of all the prepossessions which occupy thy mind, and throw off the habit which leadeth thee astray, and become a new man, as it were, from the beginning, as one who would listen to a new story, even as thou thyself didst confess. See not only with thine eyes, but with thine intellect also, of what substance or of what form they chance to be whom ye call and regard as gods. Is not one of them stone, like that which we tread under foot, and another bronze, no better than the vessels which are forged for our use, and another wood, which has already become rotten, and another silver, which needs a man to guard it lest it be stolen, and another iron, which is corroded with rust, and another earthenware, not a whit more comely than that which is supplied for the most dishonourable service? Are not all these of perishable matter? Are they not forged by iron and fire? Did not the sculptor make one, and the brass-founder another, and the silversmith another, and the potter

another? Before they were moulded into this shape by the crafts of these several artificers, was it not possible for each one of them to have been changed in form and made to resemble these several utensils? Might not the vessels which are now made out of the same material, if they met with the same artificers, be made like unto such as these? Could not these things which are now worshipped by you, by human hands again be made vessels like the rest? Are not they all deaf and blind, are they not soul-less, senseless, motionless? Do they not all rot and decay? These things ye call gods, to these ye are slaves, these ye worship; and ye end by becoming altogether like unto them. Therefore ye hate the Christians, because they do not consider these to be gods. For do not ye yourselves, who now regard and worship them, much more despise them? Do ye not much rather mock and insult them, worshipping those that are of stone and earthenware unguarded, but shutting up those that are of silver and gold by night, and setting guards over them by day, to prevent their being stolen? And as for the honours which ye think to offer to them, if they are sensible of them, ye rather punish them thereby, whereas, if they are insensible, ye reproach them by propitiating them with the blood and fat of victims. Let one of yourselves undergo this treatment, let him submit to these things being done to him. Nay, not so much as a single individual will willingly submit to such punishment, for he has sensibility and reason; but a stone submits, because it is insensible. Therefore ye convict his sensibility. Well, I could say much besides concerning the Christians not being enslaved to such gods as these; but if any one should think what has been said insufficient, I hold it superfluous to say more.

3. In the next place, I fancy that thou art chiefly anxious to hear about their not practising their religion in the same way as the Jews. The Jews then, so far as they abstain from the mode of worship described above, do well in claiming to reverence one God of the universe and to regard Him as Master; but so far as they offer Him this worship in methods similar to those already mentioned, they are altogether at fault. For whereas the Greeks, by offering these things to senseless and deaf images, make an exhibition of stupidity, the Jews considering that they are presenting them to God, as if He were in need of them, ought in all reason to count it folly and not religious worship. For He that made the heaven and the earth and all things that are therein, and furnisheth

us all with what we need, cannot Himself need any of these things which He Himself supplieth to them that imagine they are giving them to Him.   But those who think to perform sacrifices to Him with blood and fat and whole burnt offerings, and to honour Him with such honours, seem to me in no way different from those who show the same respect towards deaf images; for the one class think fit to make offerings to things unable to participate in the honour, the other class to One Who is in need of nothing.

4.   But again their scruples concerning meats, and their superstition relating to the sabbath and the vanity of their circumcision and the dissimulation of their fasting and new moons, I do [not] suppose you need to learn from me, are ridiculous and unworthy of any consideration.   For of the things created by God for the use of man to receive some as created well, but to decline others as useless and superfluous, is not this impious?   And again to lie against God, as if He forbad us to do any good thing on the sabbath day, is not this profane?   Again, to vaunt the mutilation of the flesh as a token of election as though for this reason they were particularly beloved by God, is not this ridiculous?   And to watch the stars and the moon and to keep the observance of months and of days, and to distinguish the arrangements of God and the changes of the seasons according to their own impulses, making some into festivals and others into times of mourning, who would regard this as an exhibition of godliness and not much more of folly?   That the Christians are right therefore in holding aloof from the common silliness and error of the Jews and from their excessive fussiness and pride, I consider that thou hast been sufficiently instructed; but as regards the mystery of their own religion, expect not that thou canst be instructed by man.

5.   For Christians are not distinguished from the rest of mankind either in locality or in speech or in customs.   For they dwell not somewhere in cities of their own, neither do they use some different language, nor practise an extraordinary kind of life.   Nor again do they possess any invention discovered by any intelligence or study of ingenious men, nor are they masters of any human dogma as some are.   But while they dwell in cities of Greeks and barbarians as the lot of each is cast, and follow the native customs in dress and food and the other arrangements of life, yet the constitution of their own citizenship, which they set forth, is marvellous, and

confessedly contradicts expectation. They dwell in their own countries, but only as sojourners; they bear their share in all things as citizens, and they endure all hardships as strangers. Every foreign country is a fatherland to them, and every fatherland is foreign. They marry like all other men and they beget children; but they do not cast away their offspring. They have their meals in common, but not their wives. They find themselves in the flesh, and yet they live not after the flesh. Their existence is on earth, but their citizenship is in heaven. They obey the established laws, and they surpass the laws in their own lives. They love all men, and they are persecuted by all. They are ignored, and yet they are condemned. They are put to death, and yet they are endued with life. They are in beggary, and yet they make many rich. They are in want of all things, and yet they abound in all things. They are dishonoured, and yet they are glorified in their dishonour. They are evil spoken of, and yet they are vindicated. They are reviled, and they bless; they are insulted, and they respect. Doing good they are punished as evil-doers; being punished they rejoice, as if they were thereby quickened by life. War is waged against them as aliens by the Jews, and persecution is carried on against them by the Greeks, and yet those that hate them cannot tell the reason of their hostility.

6.   In a word, what the soul is in a body, this the Christians are in the world. The soul is spread through all the members of the body, and Christians through the divers cities of the world. The soul hath its abode in the body, and yet it is not of the body. So Christians have their abode in the world, and yet they are not of the world. The soul which is invisible is guarded in the body which is visible: so Christians are recognised as being in the world, and yet their religion remaineth invisible. The flesh hateth the soul and wageth war with it, though it receiveth no wrong, because it is forbidden to indulge in pleasures; so the world hateth Christians, though it receiveth no wrong from them, because they set themselves against its pleasures. The soul loveth the flesh which hateth it, and the members: so Christians love those that hate them. The soul is enclosed in the body, and yet itself holdeth the body together; so Christians are kept in the world as in a prison-house, and yet they themselves hold the world together. The soul though itself immortal dwelleth in a mortal tabernacle; so Christians sojourn amidst perishable things, while they look for the imperishability which is in the heavens. The soul when hardly treated

in the matter of meats and drinks is improved; and so Christians when punished increase more and more daily. So great is the office for which God hath appointed them, and which it is not lawful for them to decline.

7. For it is no earthly discovery, as I said, which was committed to them, neither do they care to guard so carefully any mortal invention, nor have they entrusted to them the dispensation of human mysteries. But truly the Almighty Creator of the Universe, the Invisible God Himself from heaven planted among men the truth and the holy teaching which surpasseth the wit of man, and fixed it firmly in their hearts, not as any man might imagine, by sending (to mankind) a subaltern, or angel, or ruler, or one of those that direct the affairs of earth, or one of those who have been entrusted with the dispensations in heaven, but the very Artificer and Creator of the Universe Himself, by Whom He made the heavens, by Whom He enclosed the sea in its proper bounds, Whose mysteries all the elements faithfully observe, from Whom [the sun] hath received even the measure of the courses of the day to keep them, Whom the moon obeys as He bids her shine by night, Whom the stars obey as they follow the course of the moon, by Whom all things are ordered and bounded and placed in subjection, the heavens and the things that are in the heavens, the earth and the things that are in the earth, the sea and the things that are in the sea, fire, air, abyss, the things that are in the heights, the things that are in the depths, the things that are between the two. Him He sent unto them. Was He sent, think you, as any man might suppose, to establish a sovereignty, to inspire fear and terror? Not so. But in gentleness [and] meekness has He sent Him, as a king might send his son who is a king. He sent Him, as sending God; He sent Him, as [a man] unto men; He sent Him, as Saviour, as using persuasion, not force: for force is no attribute of God. He sent Him, as summoning, not as persecuting; He sent Him, as loving, not as judging. For He will send Him in judgment, and who shall endure His presence? ...[Dost thou not see] them thrown to wild beasts that so they may deny the Lord, and yet not overcome? Dost thou not see that the more of them are punished, just so many others abound? These look not like the works of a man; they are the power of God; they are proofs of His presence.

8. For what man at all had any knowledge what God was, before He came? Or dost thou accept the empty and nonsensical statements of those pretentious philosophers: of whom some said that God was fire

(they call that God, whereunto they themselves shall go), and others water, and others some other of the elements which were created by God? And yet if any of these statements is worthy of acceptance, any one other created thing might just as well be made out to be God. Nay, all this is the quackery and deceit of the magicians; and no man has either seen or recognised Him, but He revealed Himself. And He revealed (Himself) by faith, whereby alone it is given to see God. For God, the Master and Creator of the Universe, Who made all things and arranged them in order, was found to be not only friendly to men, but also long-suffering. And such indeed He was always, and is, and will be, kindly and good and dispassionate and true, and He alone is good. And having conceived a great and unutterable scheme He communicated it to His Son alone. For so long as He kept and guarded His wise design as a mystery, He seemed to neglect us and to be careless about us. But when He revealed it through His beloved Son, and manifested the purpose which He had prepared from the beginning, He gave us all these gifts at once, participation in His benefits, and sight and understanding of (mysteries) which none of us ever would have expected.

9. Having thus planned everything already in His mind with His Son, He permitted us during the former time to be borne along by disorderly impulses as we desired, led astray by pleasures and lusts, not at all because He took delight in our sins, but because He bore with us, not because He approved of the past season of iniquity, but because He was creating the present season of righteousness, that, being convicted in the past time by our own deeds as unworthy of life, we might now be made deserving by the goodness of God, and having made clear our inability to enter into the kingdom of God of ourselves, might be enabled by the ability of God. And when our iniquity had been fully accomplished, and it had been made perfectly manifest that punishment and death were expected as its recompense, and the season came which God had ordained, when henceforth He should manifest His goodness and power (O the exceeding great kindness and love of God), He hated us not, neither rejected us, nor bore us malice, but was long-suffering and patient, and in pity for us took upon Himself our sins, and Himself parted with His own Son as a ransom for us, the holy for the lawless, the guileless for the evil, *the just for the unjust,* the incorruptible for the corruptible, the immortal for the mortal. For what else but His righteousness would have covered our sins? In whom was

it possible for us lawless and ungodly men to have been justified, save only in the Son of God? O the sweet exchange, O the inscrutable creation, O the unexpected benefits; that the iniquity of many should be concealed in One Righteous Man, and the righteousness of One should justify many that are iniquitous! Having then in the former time demonstrated the inability of our nature to obtain life, and having now revealed a Saviour able to save even creatures which have no ability, He willed that for both reasons we should believe in His goodness and should regard Him as nurse, father, teacher, counsellor, physician, mind, light, honour, glory, strength and life.

10.   This faith if thou also desirest, apprehend first full knowledge of the Father. *For God loved* men for whose sake He made the world, to whom He subjected all things that are in the earth, to whom He gave reason and mind, whom alone He permitted to look up to heaven, whom He created after His own image, to whom *He sent His only begotten Son*, to whom He promised the kingdom which is in heaven, and will give it to those that have loved Him. And when thou hast attained to this full knowledge, with what joy thinkest thou that thou wilt be filled, or how wilt thou love Him that so loved thee before? And loving Him thou wilt be an imitator of His goodness. And marvel not that a man can be an imitator of God. He can, if God willeth it. For happiness consisteth not in lordship over one's neighbours, nor in desiring to have more than weaker men, nor in possessing wealth and using force to inferiors; neither can any one imitate God in these matters; nay, these lie outside His greatness. But whosoever taketh upon himself the burden of his neighbour, whosoever desireth to benefit one that is worse off in that in which he himself is superior, whosoever by supplying to those that are in want possessions which he received from God becomes a God to those who receive them from him, he is an imitator of God. Then, though thou art placed on earth, thou shalt behold that God liveth in heaven; then shalt thou begin to declare the mysteries of God; then shalt thou both love and admire those that are punished because they will not deny God; then shalt thou condemn the deceit and error of the world; when thou shalt perceive the true life which is in heaven, when thou shalt despise the apparent death which is here on earth, when thou shalt fear the real death, which is reserved for those that shall be condemned to the eternal fire that shall punish those delivered over to it unto the end. Then shalt thou admire those who endure for righteousness' sake the

fire that is for a season, and shalt count them blessed when thou perceivest that fire...

*   *   *   *   *   *

11.   Mine are no strange discourses nor perverse questionings, but
having been a disciple of Apostles I come forward as a teacher of the
Gentiles, ministering worthily to them, as they present themselves disciples of the truth, the lessons which have been handed down.   For
who that has been rightly taught and has entered into friendship with
the Word does not seek to learn distinctly the lessons revealed openly
by the Word to the disciples; to whom the Word appeared and declared them, speaking plainly, not perceived by the unbelieving, but
relating them to disciples who being reckoned faithful by Him were
taught the mysteries of the Father?   For which cause He sent forth
the Word, that He might appear unto the world, Who being dishonoured by the people, and preached by the Apostles, was believed
in by the Gentiles.   This Word, Who was from the beginning, Who
appeared as new and yet was proved to be old, and is engendered always young in the hearts of saints, He, I say, Who is eternal, Who
to-day was accounted a Son, through Whom the Church is enriched and
grace is unfolded and multiplied among the saints, grace which confers
understanding, which reveals mysteries, which announces seasons,
which rejoices over the faithful, which is bestowed upon those who seek
her, even those by whom the pledges of faith are not broken, nor the
boundaries of the fathers overstepped.   Whereupon the fear of the law
is sung, and the grace of the prophets is recognised, and the faith of the
gospels is established, and the tradition of the apostles is preserved, and
the joy of the Church exults.   If thou grieve not this grace, thou shalt
understand the discourses which the Word holds by the mouth of those
whom He desires when He wishes.   For in all things, that by the will of
the commanding Word we were moved to utter with much pains, we
become sharers with you, through love of the things revealed unto us.

12.   Confronted with these truths and listening to them with attention, ye shall know how much God bestoweth on those that love (Him)
rightly, who become a Paradise of delight, a tree bearing all manner of
fruits and flourishing, growing up in themselves and adorned with various
fruits.   For in this garden a tree of knowledge and a tree of life hath
been planted; yet the tree of knowledge does not kill, but disobedience
kills; for the scriptures state clearly how God from the beginning planted
a tree [of knowledge and a tree] of life in the midst of Paradise, revealing

life through knowledge; and because our first parents used it not genu-
inely they were made naked by the deceit of the serpent. For neither
is there life without knowledge, nor sound knowledge without true life;
therefore the one (tree) is planted near the other. Discerning the force
of this and blaming the knowledge which is exercised apart from the
truth of the injunction which leads to life, the apostle says, *Knowledge
puffeth up, but charity edifieth.* For the man who supposes that he
knows anything without the true knowledge which is testified by the
life, is ignorant, he is deceived by the serpent, because he loved not
life; whereas he who with fear recognises and desires life plants
in hope expecting fruit. Let your heart be knowledge, and your life
true reason, duly comprehended. Whereof if thou bear the tree and
pluck the fruit, thou shalt ever gather the harvest which God looks for,
which serpent toucheth not, nor deceit infecteth, neither is Eve corrupted, but is believed on as a virgin, and salvation is set forth, and
the apostles are filled with understanding, and the passover of the Lord
goes forward, and the congregations are gathered together, and [all
things] are arranged in order, and as He teacheth the saints the Word is
gladdened, through Whom the Father is glorified, to Whom be glory
for ever and ever. Amen.

THE FRAGMENTS

OF

PAPIAS

THE following extracts contain not only the fragments of Papias' writings which survive, but also the scanty notices of his life and theological opinions which have come down to us. As therefore all the facts about him are placed before the reader herewith, it will only be necessary to add that Papias was born probably between A.D. 60—70, and published his *Exposition of Oracles of the Lord* late in life (c. A.D. 130—140). For a full account of the man, and of his evidence to the Canon of the New Testament, the reader is referred to Dr Lightfoot's *Essays on the Work entitled Supernatural Religion*, pp. 142—216 (Macmillan and Co. 1889). Reasons are there given (p. 194 sq.) for assigning to Papias the two anonymous fragments quoted by Irenæus, which appear below (pp. 548, 549) among the Reliques of the Elders (Nos. XIII, XVII).

For convenience of reference the actual quotations from Papias are given in larger type than the introductory matter and personal notices.

I.

Irenæus and others record that John the Divine and Apostle survived until the times of Trajan; after which time Papias of Hierapolis and Polycarp, bishop of Smyrna, his hearers, became well known.

EUSEBIUS *Chronicon* (Syncell. 655, 14) for Olymp. 220.

II.

At this time flourished in Asia Polycarp, a disciple of the Apostles, who had received the bishopric of the church in Smyrna at the hands of *the eye-witnesses and ministers* of the Lord. At which time Papias, who was himself also bishop of the diocese of Hierapolis, became distinguished.

EUSEBIUS *Hist. Eccl.* iii. 36. 1. 2.

III.

Five books of Papias are extant, which bear the title Expositions of Oracles of the Lord. Of these Irenæus also makes mention as the only works written by him, in the following words : 'These things Papias, who was a hearer of John and a companion of Polycarp, an ancient worthy, witnesseth in writing in the fourth of his books. For there are five books composed by him.' So far Irenæus.

Yet Papias himself, in the preface to his discourses, certainly does not declare that he himself was a hearer and eye-witness of the holy Apostles, but he shows, by the language which he uses, that he received the matters of the faith from those who were their friends :—

But I will not scruple also to give a place for you along with my interpretations to everything that I learnt carefully and remembered carefully in time past from the elders, guaranteeing its truth. For, unlike the many, I did not take pleasure in

263

those who have so very much to say, but in those who teach the truth; nor in those who relate foreign commandments, but in those (who record) such as were given from the Lord to the Faith, and are derived from the Truth itself. And again, on any occasion when a person came (in my way) who had been a follower of the Elders, I would inquire about the discourses of the elders—what was said by Andrew, or by Peter, or by Philip, or by Thomas or James, or by John or Matthew or any other of the Lord's disciples, and what Aristion and the Elder John, the disciples of the Lord, say. For I did not think that I could get so much profit from the contents of books as from the utterances of a living and abiding voice.

Here it is worth while to observe that he twice enumerates the name of John. The first he mentions in connexion with Peter and James and Matthew and the rest of the Apostles, evidently meaning the Evangelist, but the other John he mentions after an interval and classes with others outside the number of the Apostles, placing Aristion before him, and he distinctly calls him an Elder. So that he hereby makes it quite evident that their statement is true who say that there were two persons of that name in Asia, and that there are two tombs in Ephesus, each of which even now is called (the tomb) of John. And it is important to notice this; for it is probable that it was the second, if one will not admit that it was the first, who saw the Revelation which is ascribed by name to John. And Papias, of whom we are now speaking, confesses that he had received the words of the Apostles from those who had followed them, but says that he was himself a hearer of Aristion and the Elder John. At all events he mentions them frequently by name, and besides records their traditions in his writings. So much for these points which I trust have not been uselessly adduced.

It is worth while however to add to the words of Papias given above other passages from him, in which he records some other wonderful events likewise, as having come down to him by tradition. That Philip the Apostle resided in Hierapolis with his daughters has been already stated; but how Papias, their contemporary, relates that he had heard a marvellous tale from the daughters of Philip, must be noted here. For he relates that in his time a man rose from the dead, and again he gives another wonderful story about Justus who was surnamed Barsabas, how that he drank a deadly poison, and yet, by the grace of the Lord, suffered no inconvenience. Of this Justus the Book of the Acts records that after the ascension of the Saviour the holy Apostles put him forward with Matthias, and prayed for the (right) choice, in place of the traitor Judas, that should make their number complete. The passage is somewhat as follows; '*And they put forward two, Joseph, called Barsabas, who was surnamed Justus, and Matthias; and they prayed, and said.'* The same writer has recorded other notices as having come down to him from oral tradition, certain strange parables of the Saviour and teachings of His, and some other statements of a rather mythical character. Among which he says that there will be a period of some ten thousand years after the resurrection, and that the kingdom of Christ will be set up in material form on this earth. These ideas I suppose he got through a misunderstanding of the apostolic accounts, not perceiving that the things recorded there in figures were spoken by them mystically. For he evidently was a man of very mean capacity, as one may say judging from his own statements : yet it was owing to him that so many church fathers after him adopted a like opinion, urging in their own support the antiquity of the man, as for instance Irenæus and whoever else they were who declared that they held like views. Papias also gives in his own work other accounts of the words of the Lord on the authority of Aristion who has been mentioned above, and traditions of the Elder John. To these we refer the curious, and for our present purpose we will merely add to his words, which have been quoted above, a tradition, which has been set forth through these sources concerning Mark who wrote the Gospel :—

And the Elder said this also : Mark, having become the interpreter of Peter, wrote down accurately everything that he remembered, without however recording in order what was either said or done by Christ. For neither did he hear the Lord, nor did he follow Him ; but afterwards, as I said, (attended) Peter, who adapted his instructions to the needs (of his hearers) but had no design of giving a connected account of the Lord's oracles. So then Mark made no mistake, while he thus wrote down some things as he remembered them ; for he made it his one care not to omit anything that he heard, or to set down any false statement therein.

Such then is the account given by Papias concerning Mark. But concerning Matthew, the following statement is made (by him) :

So then Matthew composed the oracles in the Hebrew language, and each one interpreted them as he could.

The same writer employed testimonies from the First Epistle of John, and likewise from that of Peter. And he has related another story about a woman accused of many sins before the Lord, which the Gospel according to the Hebrews contains.

EUSEBIUS *Hist. Eccl.* iii. 39.

IV.

And they went every man unto his own house; but Jesus went unto the mount of Olives. And early in the morning He came again unto the temple, [and all the people came unto Him; and He sat down, and taught them]. And the Scribes and the Pharisees bring a woman taken in adultery; and having set her in the midst, they say unto Him, Master, this woman hath been taken in adultery, in the very act. Now in the law Moses commanded [us] to stone such: what then sayest thou? [And this they said, tempting Him, that they might have (whereof) to accuse Him.] But Jesus stooped down, and with His finger wrote on the ground. But when they continued asking [Him], He lifted up Himself, and said [unto them], He that is without sin among you, let him first cast a stone at her. And again He stooped down, and wrote on the ground. And they, when they heard it, went out one by one, beginning from the eldest: and He was left alone, and the woman, where she was, in the midst. And Jesus lifted up Himself, and said unto her, Woman, where are they? Did no man condemn thee? And she said, No man, Lord. And Jesus said, Neither do I condemn thee: go thy way; from henceforth sin no more.

PERICOPE ADULTERAE; see Westcott and Hort
The New Testament in the Original Greek
I. p. 241, II. pp. 82 sq, 91; Lightfoot *Essays
on Supernatural Religion* p. 203 sq.

V.

Papias, bishop of Hierapolis, who was a disciple of John the Divine, and a companion of Polycarp, wrote five books of Oracles of the Lord, wherein, when giving a list of the Apostles, after Peter and John, Philip and Thomas and Matthew he included among the disciples of the Lord Aristion and a second John, whom also he called 'The Elder.' [He says] that some think that this John is the author of the two short and catholic Epistles, which are published in the name of John; and he gives as the reason that the primitive (fathers) only accept the first epistle. Some too have wrongly considered the Apocalypse also to be his (i.e. the Elder John's) work. Papias too is in error about the Millennium, and from him Irenæus also. Papias in his second book says that John the Divine and James his brother were killed by the Jews. The aforesaid Papias stated on the authority of the daughters of Philip that Barsabas, who is also called Justus, when challenged by the unbelievers drank serpent's poison in the name of the Lord, and was shielded from all harm. He makes also other marvellous statements, and particularly about the mother of Manaim who was raised from the dead. As for those who were raised from the dead by Christ, (he states) that they survived till the time of Hadrian.

PHILIPPUS OF SIDE (?) *Hist. Christ.*

VI.

After Domitian Nerva reigned one year, who recalled John from the island (i.e. Patmos), and allowed him to dwell in Ephesus. He was at that time the sole survivor of the twelve Apostles, and after writing his Gospel received the honour of martyrdom. For Papias, bishop of Hierapolis, who was an eye-witness of him, in the second book of the Oracles of the Lord says that he was killed by the Jews, and thereby evidently fulfilled, together with his brother, Christ's prophecy concerning them, and their own confession and undertaking on His behalf. For when the Lord said to them ; *Are ye able to drink of the cup that I drink of?*, and they readily assented and agreed, He said ; *My cup shall ye drink, and with the baptism that I am baptized shall ye be baptized.* And reasonably so, for it is impossible for God to lie. So too the learned Origen affirms in his interpretation of S. Matthew's Gospel that John was martyred, declaring that he had learnt the fact from the successors of the Apostles. And indeed the well-informed Eusebius also in his Ecclesiastical History says ; 'Thomas received by lot Parthia, but John, Asia, where also he made his residence and died at Ephesus.'

GEORGIUS HAMARTOLUS *Chronicon.*

VII.

Papias, a hearer of John, (and) bishop of Hierapolis in Asia, wrote only five books, which he entitled An Exposition of Discourses of the Lord. Wherein, when he asserts in his preface that he is not following promiscuous statements, but has the Apostles as his authorities, he says :—

I used to inquire what had been said by Andrew, or by Peter, or by Philip, or by Thomas or James, or by John or Matthew or any other of the Lord's disciples, and what Aristion and the Elder John, the disciples of the Lord, were saying. For books to read do not profit me so much as the living voice clearly sounding up to the present day in (the persons of) their authors.

From which it is clear that in his list of names itself there is one John who is reckoned among the Apostles, and another the Elder John, whom he enumerates after Aristion. We have mentioned this fact on account of the statement made above, which we have recorded on the authority of very many, that the two later epistles of John are not (the work) of the Apostle, but of the Elder. This (Papias) is said to have promulgated the Jewish tradition of a Millennium, and he is followed by Irenæus, Apollinarius and the others, who say that after the resurrection the Lord will reign in the flesh with the saints.

JEROME *de vir. illust.* 18.

VIII.

Further a false rumour has reached me that the books of Josephus and the writings of Papias and Polycarp have been translated by me ; but I have neither leisure nor strength to render such works as these with corresponding elegance into another tongue.

JEROME *ad Lucinium* Epist. 71 (28) c. 5.

IX.

Irenæus, a disciple of Papias who was a hearer of John the Evangelist, relates.

JEROME *ad Theodoram* Epist. 75 (29) c. 3.

X.

With regard however to the inspiration of the book (i.e. the Apocalypse) we hold it superfluous to speak at length ; since the blessed Gregory (I mean, the Divine) and Cyril, and men of an older generation as well, Papias, Irenæus, Methodius and Hippolytus, bear testimony to its genuineness.

ANDREAS OF CÆSAREA *preface to the Apocalypse.*

XI.

But thus says Papias, (I quote him) word for word :—

To some of them, clearly the angels which at first were holy, He gave dominion also over the arrangement of the universe, and He commissioned them to exercise their dominion well.

And he says next :—

But it so befel that their array came to nought ; for the great dragon, the old serpent, who is also called Satan and the devil, was cast down, yea, and was cast down to the earth, he and his angels.

ANDREAS OF CÆSAREA *in Apocalypsin* c. 34 serm. 12.

XII.

Taking their start from Papias the great, of Hierapolis, the disciple of the Apostle who leaned on Christ's bosom, and Clement, Pantænus the priest of the Alexandrians and Ammonius, the great scholar, those ancient and first expositors who agree with each other in understanding all the work of the six days (as referring) to Christ and His Church.

ANASTASIUS OF SINAI *Contempl. Anagog. in Hexaëm.* i.

XIII.

So then the more ancient expositors of the churches, I mean Philo, the philosopher, and contemporary of the Apostles, and the famous Papias of Hierapolis, the disciple of John the Evangelist...and their associates, interpreted the sayings about Paradise spiritually, and referred them to the Church of Christ.

ANASTASIUS OF SINAI *Contempl. Anagog. in Hexaëm.* vii.

XIV.

The blessing thus foretold belongs undoubtedly to the times of the Kingdom, when the righteous shall rise from the dead and reign, when too creation renewed and freed from bondage shall produce a wealth of food of all kinds *from the dew of heaven and from the fatness of the earth;* as the elders, who saw John the disciple of the Lord, relate, that they had heard from him, how the Lord used to teach concerning those times, and to say,

The days will come, in which vines shall grow, each having ten thousand shoots, and on each shoot ten thousand branches, and on each branch again ten thousand twigs, and on each twig ten thousand clusters, and on each cluster ten thousand grapes, and each grape when pressed shall yield five-and-twenty measures of wine. And when any of the saints shall have taken hold of one of their clusters, another shall cry, I am a better cluster; take me, bless the Lord through me. Likewise also a grain of wheat shall produce ten thousand heads, and every head shall have ten thousand grains, and every grain ten pounds of fine flour, bright and clean, and the other fruits, seeds and the grass shall produce in similar proportions, and all the animals, using these fruits which are products of the soil, shall become in their turn peaceable and harmonious, obedient to man in all subjection. These things Papias, who was a hearer of John and a companion of Polycarp, an ancient worthy, witnesseth in writing in the fourth of his books, for there are five books composed by him. And he added, saying,

But these things are credible to them that believe. And when Judas the traitor did not believe, and asked, How shall such growths be accomplished by the Lord? he relates that the Lord said, They shall see, who shall come to these (times).

IRENÆUS *Haer.* v. 33. 3, 4.

XV.

Those who practised guilelessness towards God they used to call children, as Papias also shows in the first book of the Expositions of the Lord, and Clement of Alexandria in the Paedagogue.

MAXIMUS THE CONFESSOR *Schol. in libr. Dionys. Areopag. de eccl. hierarch.* c. 2.

XVI.

This he says, darkly indicating, I suppose, Papias of Hierapolis in Asia, who was a bishop at that time and flourished in the days of the holy Evangelist John. For this Papias in the fourth book of his Dominical Expositions mentioned viands among the sources of delights in the resurrection.... And Irenæus of Lyons says the same thing in his fifth book against heresies, and produces in support of his statements the aforesaid Papias.

MAXIMUS THE CONFESSOR *Schol. in libr. Dionys. Areopag. de eccl. hierarch.* c. 7.

XVII.

Nor again (does Stephanus follow) Papias, the bishop and martyr of Hierapolis, nor Irenæus, the holy bishop of Lyons, when they say that the kingdom of heaven will consist in enjoyment of certain material foods.

PHOTIUS *Bibliotheca* 232, on Stephanus Gobarus.

XVIII.

Apollinarius. 'Judas did not die by hanging, but lived on, having been cut down before he was suffocated. And the Acts of the Apostles show this, that *falling headlong he burst asunder in the midst, and all his bowels gushed out.* This fact is related more clearly by Papias, the disciple of John, in the fourth (book) of the Exposition of the Oracles of the Lord as follows :—

Judas walked about in this world a terrible example of impiety; his flesh swollen to such an extent that, where a waggon can pass with ease, he was not able to pass, no, not even the mass of his head merely. They say that his eyelids swelled to such an extent that he could not see the light at all, while as for his eyes they were not visible even by a physician looking through an instrument, so far had they sunk from the surface....'

Compiled from Cramer *Catena ad Acta SS. Apost.* (1838) p. 12 sq. and other sources.

XIX.

Here beginneth the argument to the Gospel according to John.

The Gospel of John was made known and given to the Churches by John, while he yet remained in the body; as (one) Papias by name, of Hierapolis, a beloved disciple of John, has related in his five exoteric (*read* exegetical) books; but he wrote down the Gospel at the dictation of John, correctly.

A Vatican MS of the ninth century.

XX.

For, last of these, John, surnamed the Son of Thunder, when he was now a very old man, as Irenæus and Eusebius and a succession of trustworthy historians have handed down to us, about the time when terrible heresies had cropped up, dictated the Gospel to his own disciple, the virtuous Papias of Hierapolis, to fill up what was lacking in those who before him had proclaimed the word to the nations throughout all the earth.

Catena *Patr. Graec. in S. Joan.* published by B. Corder.

THE RELIQUES

OF THE

ELDERS

PRESERVED IN IRENÆUS

I.

According to what was said of such cases by one better than we are :

the precious stone,
The emerald, accounted of much worth,
Is shamed by artful mimicry in glass,

whenever he is not by, who hath power to prove it, and

Detect the craft so cunningly devised.

Again, when

alloy of brass
Is mixed with silver, who that simple is
Shall easily be able to assay?

IRENÆUS *Heresies, preface to Bk.* i.

II.

As he that was better than we are affirmed of such persons, A daring and shameless thing is a soul heated with empty air.

IRENÆUS i. 13. 3.

III.

Wherefore also justly did the divine Elder and herald of the truth exclaim against thee in verse, thus saying :

Thou idol-framer, Mark, and portent-gazer,
Skill'd in the astrologer's and wizard's art,
Strengthening thereby the words of thy false lore,
Dazzling with signs whome'er thou lead'st astray,
Strange handiwork of God-defying power
Such to perform thy father Satan still
Affords thee might, by an angelic Power
Azazel :—thee, by the destroyer mark'd
Chosen forerunner of the impious craft.

Thus far that Elder, beloved of God.

IRENÆUS i. 15. 6.

IV.

But that the age of thirty years is the prime of a young man's ability, and that it reaches even to the fortieth year, every one will allow ; but after the fortieth and fiftieth year, it begins to verge towards elder age : which our Lord was of when He taught, as the Gospel and all the Elders witness, who in Asia conferred with John the Lord's disciple, to the effect that John had delivered these things unto them : for he abode with them until the times of Trajan. And some of them saw not only John, but others also of the Apostles, and had this same account from them, and witness to the aforesaid account.

IRENÆUS ii. 22. 5.

V.

As was said by one who was before us, concerning all who in any way deprave the things of God, and adulterate the truth, It is evil mingling chalk in the milk of God.

IRENÆUS iii. 17. 4.

VI.

As one of the ancients saith, God for His part transferred the curse unto the earth, that it might not continue in the man.

IRENÆUS iii. 23. 3.

VII.

For which cause they who have been before us, yea, and much better men than we, were nevertheless unable to dispute against the Valentinians, as not knowing their system : which we in our first Book have very diligently expounded unto thee.

IRENÆUS *preface to Bk. iv.*

VIII.

For God doeth all things in measure and order, and nothing with Him wants measure, since nothing is unnumbered. And well spake he who said that the Immeasurable Father Himself was measured in the Son : for the measure of the Father is the Son, since He even contains Him.

IRENÆUS iv. 4. 2.

IX.

As I have heard from a certain Elder, who had heard from those who had seen the Apostles, and from their scholars :—that it is enough for the ancients to be reproved, as they are by the Scriptures, for what they did without counsel from the Spirit. For God, being no respecter of persons, upon things not done to His pleasure brings such reproof as is suitable. [Thus in the case of David, when on the one hand he was suffering persecution from Saul for righteousness' sake, and flying from king Saul, and avenged not himself on his enemy, and was singing of Christ's Advent, and teaching the nations wisdom, and doing all by the suggestion of the Spirit, he pleased God. But when for lust he took to his own self Bathsheba Uriah's wife, the scripture hath said of him, *But the thing etc.* (2 Sam. xi. 27) : and Nathan the prophet is sent unto him, to shew him his sin, that he, passing sentence on himself, and judging himself, may find mercy and forgiveness from Christ.

And he said unto him etc. (2 Sam. xii. 1—7); and goes over the rest in order, upbraiding him, and reckoning up God's favours towards him, and how he had provoked the Lord in having done this. For that such conduct pleases not God, rather great anger is hanging over his house.

And hereupon David was pricked to the heart, and said, *I have sinned against the Lord* (2 Sam. xii. 13), and afterwards he chanted the psalm of confession, waiting for the coming of the Lord, Who washes and cleanses the man who had been bound in sin.

And so it is also concerning Solomon ; as long as he went on to judge rightly, and to declare wisdom, and was building the figure of the true Temple, and setting forth the glories of God, and announcing the peace which should come to the Gentiles, and prefiguring the Kingdom of Christ, and was speaking his three thousand parables on the coming of the Lord, and his five thousand songs, by way of hymn to God, and gathering accounts of God's wisdom in the Creation, after the manner of a natural philosopher, from every tree, and from every herb, and from all fowls and quadrupeds and fishes, and saying, *Will God indeed etc.* (1 Kings viii. 27), he both pleased God, and was admired by all, and all the kings of the Earth sought his face, to hear his wisdom which God had given him, and the Queen of the South came to him from the ends of the earth, to know the wisdom which was in him ; who also, as the Lord saith, will rise again in the judgment with the generation of those who hear His words and believe not in Him, and will pass sentence upon them : because, while she submitted herself to the wisdom declared by the servant of God, they despised that wisdom which was given by the Son of God. For Solomon was a servant; but Christ the Son of God, and the Lord of Solomon. Well then, as long as he served God without offence, and ministered to His purposes, so long he was glorified : but when he took wives of all nations, and permitted them to set up idols in Israel, the Scripture hath said of him, *And King Solomon was a lover etc.* (1 Kings xi. 1, 4, 6, 9).] The rebuke laid on him by Scripture was sufficient, as that Elder affirmed, that no flesh might glory before the Lord.

And therefore, he said, the Lord descended to the parts under the earth, announcing to them also the good news of His coming ; there being remission of sins for such as believe on Him. [And those all believed on Him, who were hoping for Him : i.e., who foretold His coming and ministered to His purposes, righteous men and prophets and patriarchs : whose sins He forgave, even as He forgave ours, neither ought we to impute the same unto them, unless we despise the grace of God. For as they did not charge us with our irregularities, which we wrought before Christ was manifested in us ; so neither is it just for us to charge the like, before the coming of Christ, on such as sinned. For *all* men *need the glory of God* (Rom. iii. 23), and are justified not of themselves, but by the coming of the Lord—those I mean who look steadily on His Light.

And their deeds, he said, were written for our admonition : to teach us, first of all, that our God and theirs is one and the same ; a God, Whom sins please not, though wrought by renowned persons : and next that we should abstain from evils. [For if those of old time who went before us in God's special graces, for whom the Son of God had not yet suffered, were visited with such disgrace, if they transgressed in some one thing, and became slaves to fleshly concupiscence ; what shall this generation suffer, as many as have despised the coming of the Lord, and turned utter slaves to their own pleasures ?

And they indeed had our Lord's death for the healing and remission of their sins : but for those who now sin Christ shall no more die, for death shall no more have dominion over Him ; but the Son shall come in the glory of the Father, exacting from His agents and stewards the money which He lent them, with usury : and to whom He gave most, of them will He require most.]

We ought not therefore, said that Elder, to be proud, nor to reproach the ancients, but ourselves to fear, lest haply, after the knowledge of Christ, if we do anything which pleases not God, we no longer have remission of our sins, but find ourselves shut out of His Kingdom. And to this he referred Paul's saying, *For if He spared not etc.* (Rom. xi. 17, 21).

In like manner again the transgressions of the people, you see, are written down, not for their sake who did then transgress, but for our rebuke, and that we might know that it is one and the same God, against Whom they sinned, and against Whom sin even now certain of those who are said to have believed. And this again, he said, the Apostle did most clearly point out, saying in the Epistle to the Corinthians, *For I would not have etc.* (1 Cor. x. 1—12).

[Whereas therefore the Apostle declares, in a way which admits not of doubt or gainsaying, that it is one and the same God, Who both judged the things which then were, and searches out those which now are, and since he tells us the purpose of their being set down : unlearned and daring and senseless withal are all those proved to be, who take occasion from the sin of them of old time, and the disobedience of the greater part of them, to affirm that their God (Who is also the Maker of the world) is a different Being from the Father taught by Christ, and is in decay, and that it is this latter who is mentally received by every one of them. Because they consider not, that as in that case God was not well pleased with the greater part of them, being sinners, so also in this case *many are called but few chosen* (S. Matt. xx. 16): as among them the unjust and idolaters and fornicators lost their life, so also among us. For both the Lord proclaims that such are sent into the eternal fire, and the Apostle saith, *Know ye not etc.* (1 Cor. vi. 9, 10).

And in proof that he said this not to those who are without, but to us, lest we be cast out of the Kingdom of God, for doing some such thing, he hath subjoined, *And these things etc.* (1 Cor. vi. 11).

And as in that case those were condemned and cast out, who did evil, and led the rest astray, so in this case also the very eye is dug out which gives offence, and the foot, and the hand, that the rest of the body perish not alike. And we have it ordained, *If any is named etc.* (1 Cor. v. 11). And again the Apostle saith, *Let no man deceive you etc.* (Eph. v. 6, 7).

And as then the condemnation of them that sinned imparted itself also to the rest, in that they were pleased with them, and they held converse together : so here also *a little leaven corrupteth the whole mass* (1 Cor. v. 6). And as there God's anger came down against the unrighteous, here also saith the Apostle in like manner, *For the wrath of God etc.* (Rom. i. 18). And as there upon the Egyptians, who were punishing Israel unjustly, vengeance from God took place, so here also ; since both the Lord saith, *And shall not God etc.* (S. Luke xviii. 7, 8), and the Apostle in the Epistle to the Thessalonians declares as follows, *Since it is a righteous thing etc.* (2 Thess. i. 6—10).]

Both here therefore and there is the same righteousness of God in maintaining God's cause. There indeed it is done typically, and for a certain time, and with comparative moderation ; but here truly, and for ever, and more severely. For the fire is eternal ; and the anger of God which shall be revealed from heaven from the countenance of our Lord brings a greater penalty on those who incur it : as David also saith, *But the countenance etc.* (Ps. xxxiv. 16). This being so, the Elders used to declare those persons to be very senseless, who from what befel God's disobedient people of old try to bring in another Father: objecting the great things which the Lord when He came had done to save those who received Him, in His pity for them ; but saying nothing of His judgment and of all that is to happen to such as have heard His words and fulfilled them not ; and how it were good for them if they had not been born : and how it shall be more tolerable for Sodom and Gomorrah in the judgment than for that city which received not the words of His disciples.

IRENÆUS iv. 27. 1—28. 1.

X.

Those again who upbraid and charge us with the circumstance, that the people by command of God, on point of departure, received of the Egyptians vessels of all sorts and apparel, and so went away, from which stores the Tabernacle also was made in the wilderness, prove themselves ignorant of God's ways of justification, and of His providences ; as that Elder likewise used to say. [Since, had not God permitted this in the typical journey, no man could at this day be saved in our real journey, i.e., in the faith wherein we are established, whereby we have been taken out of the number of the Gentiles. For we are all accompanied by some property, moderate or large, which we have gotten out of the Mammon of iniquity. For whence are the houses in which we dwell, and the garments which we put on, and the furniture which we use, and all the rest of what serves us for our daily life, but out of what in our Gentile state we gained by avarice, or what we have received from Gentile parents, or kinsmen, or friends, who acquired it by injustice ? Not to say that even now, while we are in the faith, we gain. For who sells, and desires not to gain from the buyer ? And who buys, and would not fain be dealt with by the seller to his profit ? Again, what person in business does not carry on his business, that so he may get his bread thereby ? And how is it with those believers who are in the royal court ? Have they not goods from among the things which are Cæsar's, and doth not each one of them according to his ability impart unto such as have not ? The Egyptians were debtors to the people not only for their goods but for their life also, through the former kindness of the Patriarch Joseph : but in what respect are the Gentiles debtors to us, from whom we receive both profit and the commodities of life ? Whatsoever they gain with toil, that we, being in the faith, use without toil.

Besides, the people were serving the Egyptians in the worst of servitude, as saith the Scripture, *And the Egyptians violently etc.* (Exod. i. 13, 14) ; and with much toil they built them fortified cities, adding to their stores for many years, and in every kind of servitude ; whereas the others, over and above their ingratitude toward them, were fain even to destroy them utterly.

What then was unrighteously done, if they took a little out of much, and if those who might have had much property, and gone away rich, had they not served them, went away poor, receiving for their heavy servitude very scanty wages ? So, if any free person, carried away violently by some one, and serving him many years and increasing his goods, should afterwards, upon gaining some little support, be suspected of having some small portion of his master's property (whereas in fact he goes off with a very little, out of his own many toils and of the other's great gain) and if this were charged on him by any one as a wrong ; the judge himself will rather appear unjust towards him who had been reduced to slavery by force. Now of like sort are the aforesaid, who blame the people for taking to themselves a little out of much, yet blame not themselves, who have made no due return according to the merit of their parents, but rather, reducing them into most heavy servitude, have obtained from them very great advantage. And while they charge the Jews with unjust dealings, for receiving, as we said before, in a few little vessels uncoined gold and silver ; of themselves (for the truth shall be spoken, ridiculous as it may appear to some) they say that they do justly in bearing about in their girdles stamped gold and silver and copper from others' toils, with the inscription and image of Cæsar upon it.

But if we and they are compared, which will seem to have received more honestly ? The people from the Egyptians, who were in all their debtors, or we from the Romans and other Gentiles, those even who owe us no such debt ? Rather by them the world hath peace, and we walk on the highways and sail whithersoever we will without fear. Against this sort of objector then, our Lord's saying will be applicable, *Thou hypocrite etc.* (S. Matt. vii. 5).

For, if he who lays this to thy charge, and glories in his knowledge, is cut off from the assembly of the Gentiles, and there is nothing of others' property with him ; if he be simply naked and barefoot, and haunt the mountains without a home, like some of those animals which eat grass : he will obtain pardon, as not knowing of what is needed in our manner of life. But if he take from men his share in the property of others, as it is called, while he finds fault with the type of the same, he proves himself to be most unjust, and turns back on himself the aforesaid accusation.] For he will be convicted of carrying about what is another's, and of desiring what is not his own : and with a view to this, they report, the Lord said, *Judge not that ye etc.* (S. Matt. vii. 1, 2). [Not of course that we rebuke not sinners, or consent to things done amiss, but that we judge not unfairly God's ways of ordering things, whereas He hath provided in righteousness whatsoever shall be profitable. Thus, because He knew that we would make a good use of our substance, which we should have, receiving it from another, *He that hath two coats*, saith He, *let him impart etc.* (S. Luke iii. 11). Again, *For I was an hungred etc.* (S. Matt. xxv. 35, 36). Again, *When thou doest alms etc.* (S. Matt. vi. 3) : and all other acts of bounty upon which we are justified, redeeming our own as it were by what was another's. And when I say, Another's, I do not mean that the world is alien from God, but that we receive from others and possess the aforesaid gifts, even as they from the Egyptians who knew not God ; and by these same we build up for ourselves the tabernacle of God. For with doers of good God dwelleth : as saith the Lord, *Make to yourselves friends etc.* (S. Luke xvi. 9). For whatsoever things we had acquired, when we were heathens, by unrighteousness, those same, now we have believed, we turn to the Lord's service, and so are justified.

These things were then of necessity practised in type beforehand, and out of those materials the tabernacle of God is wrought ; in which matter, as we have explained, both they received justly, and we were prophetically indicated, how that we should begin to wait on God with things not our own. For all that journey of the people, whereby God brought them out of Egypt, was the type and image of the Church's journey, which was to take place from among the Gentiles ; which journey accordingly ends also with leading her hence into her inheritance, which not indeed Moses the servant of God, but Jesus the Son of God, will give her to inherit. And if any one will look more carefully at what the Prophets say of the end, and at all that John the Lord's disciple saw in the Apocalypse, he will find the Gentiles generally enduring the same plagues, which at that time Egypt in particular endured.]

By statements of this kind touching the ancients did that Elder console us, and say that concerning those faults, which the Scriptures themselves have laid to the charge of Patriarchs and Prophets, we must not reproach them, nor be like Ham, who scoffed at the disgrace of his father, and fell into the curse ; but we must give thanks to God for them, inasmuch as their sins were forgiven them in the coming of our Lord. For that (his word it is) they give thanks and exult in our salvation.

But in respect of those things, for which the Scriptures reprove them not, but simply state the facts, we must not, he said, become accusers (for we are not more exact than God, nor can we be above our master), but look out for the typical meaning. For none of all the things, which are set down in the Scriptures without definite censure, is without its force.

IRENÆUS iv. 30. 1—31. 1.

XI.

In the same way also did that older disciple of the Apostles reason about the two Testaments : declaring that both are indeed from one and the same God ; and that there is no other God, besides Him Who made and formed us, nor any strength in their argument, who say that this world of ours was made either by Angels, or by any kind of Power, or by some other God. [For if a person once withdraw himself from the Creator of all things, and grant that the world with which we are concerned is made by some different God, or through another, such an one must needs fall into much absurdity and many contradictions ; for which he will render no reasons with either appearance or substance of truth. And therefore such as introduce other doctrines, hide from us the opinion which they themselves have concerning God ; knowing the unsoundness and futility of their own doctrine, and fearing to be overcome, and so to have their salvation endangered.]

IRENÆUS iv. 32. 1.

XII.

For the word 'son,' as a certain person also before us hath said, has two meanings : one is naturally such, as being born a son ; while another is counted for a son, because he is made such : notwithstanding the difference between the born and the made.

IRENÆUS iv. 41. 2.

XIII.

Where then was the first man placed? In paradise plainly, as it is written ; and he was cast out thence into this world, owing to his disobedience. Wherefore also the Elders, disciples of the Apostles, say that those who were translated were translated thither (for paradise was prepared for righteous and inspired men, whither also the Apostle Paul was carried and *heard words unspeakable*, to us at least in this present life), and that they who are translated remain there until the end of all things, preluding immortality.

IRENÆUS v. 5. 1.

XIV.

For since by wood we lost Him, by wood again He was made manifest unto all, shewing forth the length and height and depth and breadth in Himself ; and as one of those who have gone before said, by the divine extension of His Hands gathering the two peoples together unto one God.

IRENÆUS v. 17. 4.

XV.

Now such being the state of the case, and this number being set down in all the good and old copies, and testimony being given by the persons themselves who had seen John with their eyes, and reason teaching us that the number of the name of the Beast, according to the reckoning of the Greeks, by the letters therein, will have 600, and 60, and 6......some, I know not how, have erred, following a particular reading, and have taken liberties with the middle number of the name, subtracting the value of fifty, and choosing to have one decade instead of six.

IRENÆUS v. 30. 1.

XVI.

As the Elders, who saw John the disciple of the Lord, relate that they had heard from him, how the Lord used to teach concerning those times, and to say......

IRENÆUS v. 33. 3. See above, *Fragments of Papias*, No. XIV. p. 533.

XVII.

As the Elders say, then also shall they which have been deemed worthy of the abode in heaven go thither, while others shall enjoy *the delight of paradise*, and others again shall possess the brightness of the city ; for in every place the Saviour shall be seen, according as they shall be worthy who see Him.   They say moreover that this is the distinction between the habitation of them that bring forth a hundred-fold, and them that bring forth sixty-fold, and them that bring forth thirty-fold ; of whom the first shall be taken up into the heavens, and the second shall dwell in paradise, and the third shall inhabit the city ; and that therefore our Lord has said, *In My Father's abode are many mansions;* for all things are of God, Who giveth to all their appropriate dwelling, [according as His Word saith that allotment is made unto all by the Father, according as each man is, or shall be, worthy.   And this is the banqueting-table at which those shall recline who are called to the marriage and take part in the feast.]   The Elders, the disciples of the Apostles, say that this is the arrangement and disposal of them that are being saved, and that they advance by such steps, and ascend through the Spirit to the Son, and through the Son to the Father, the Son at length yielding His work to the Father, as it is said also by the Apostle, *For He must reign until He putteth all enemies under His feet.*

IRENÆUS v. 36. 1, 2.

INDEX OF SCRIPTURAL PASSAGES.

WHERE the reference to a patristic passage is printed in italics, the resemblance to the corresponding scriptural passage is less close than in the other instances.

The following are the abbreviations employed :—B = the Epistle of Barnabas; C = the Genuine Epistle of Clement; 2 C = the Spurious Epistle of Clement; D = the Epistle to Diognetus; Δ = the Didache; E = the Reliques of the Elders preserved in Irenæus; H = the Shepherd of Hermas; I = the Epistles of Ignatius; P = the Epistle of Polycarp; II = the Fragments of Papias; MP = the Martyrdom of Polycarp.

The Epistles of Ignatius are indicated as follows in italics :—E = Ephesians; M = Magnesians; T = Trallians; R = Romans; Ph = Philadelphians; Sm = Smyrnæans; Pol = Polycarp; the subdivisions of the Shepherd of Hermas thus :— V = Visions; M = Mandates; S = Similitudes.

The patristic references are to the chapters, except in the case of Papias and the Elders, where they refer to the number of the fragment : in the case of references to the Epistle of Barnabas and the Shepherd of Hermas the subsections also are given.